JN043877

京都府の教員採用試験過去問シリーズ ❺

2025年度版

京都府の英語科

過去問

協同教育研究会 編

協同出版

本書には，京都府の教員採用試験の過去問題を収録しています。各問題ごとに，以下のように5段階表記で，難易度，頻出度を示しています。

難　易　度

非常に難しい	☆☆☆☆☆
やや難しい	☆☆☆☆
普通の難易度	☆☆☆
やや易しい	☆☆
非常に易しい	☆

頻　出　度

◎	ほとんど出題されない
◎◎	あまり出題されない
◎◎◎	普通の頻出度
◎◎◎◎	よく出題される
◎◎◎◎◎	非常によく出題される

※本書の過去問題における資料，法令文等の取り扱いについて

本書の過去問題で使用されている資料や法令文の表記や基準は，出題された当時の内容に準拠しているため，解答・解説も当時のものを使用しています。ご了承ください。

はじめに～「過去問」シリーズ利用に際して～

教育を取り巻く環境は変化しつつあり，日本の公教育そのものも，教員免許更新制の廃止やGIGAスクール構想の実現などの改革が進められています。また，現行の学習指導要領では「主体的・対話的で深い学び」を実現するため，指導方法や指導体制の工夫改善により，「個に応じた指導」の充実を図るとともに，コンピュータや情報通信ネットワーク等の情報手段を活用するために必要な環境を整えることが示されています。

一方で，いじめや体罰，不登校，暴力行為など，教育現場の問題もあいかわらず取り沙汰されており，教員に求められるスキルは，今後さらに高いものになっていくことが予想されます。

本書の基本構成としては，出題傾向と対策，過去5年間の出題傾向分析表，過去問題，解答および解説を掲載しています。各自治体や教科によって掲載年数をはじめ，「チェックテスト」や「問題演習」を掲載するなど，内容が異なります。

また原則的には一般受験を対象としております。特別選考等については対応していない場合があります。なお，実際に配布された問題の順番や構成を，編集の都合上，変更している場合があります。あらかじめご了承ください。

最後に，この「過去問」シリーズは，「参考書」シリーズとの併用を前提に編集されております。参考書で要点整理を行い，過去問で実力試しを行う，セットでの活用をおすすめいたします。

みなさまが，この書籍を徹底的に活用し，教員採用試験の合格を勝ち取って，教壇に立っていただければ，それはわたくしたちにとって最上の喜びです。

協同教育研究会

CONTENTS

第１部

京都府の
英語科
出題傾向分析

京都府の英語科　傾向と対策

■中高共通

2017年度より共通問題として，空所補充形式の文法・語法問題が出題されている。高校英語レベルの語彙を問う問題と，時制や関係詞の用法などの文法問題で，特に難解なものではないので，時間をかけずに解答していきたいところである。どちらも過去問題を解いてみて，弱点があるようならば受験語彙集や文法問題集などで補強しておけばよい。また，2023年度に引き続き2024年度も読解問題1題が共通であった。長めではあるが，難解な文章ではない。

内容一致文，空所補充，日本語での説明問題，英文和訳，要約文の空所補充，そして整序英作文などバラエティに富んでいる。

■中学校

出題形式は2023年度と同様である。共通問題以外に，文法・語法問題1題，整序英作文1題，和文英訳問題1題，会話文問題1題，読解問題1題が出題されている。試験時間は90分である。

英作文問題は，整序英作文に加え，和文英訳と読解問題の内容に絡めた自由英作文の形式で出題されている。2023年度に引き続き，和文英訳は高校レベルの知識で対応できるものであった。過去問を解いてみて，公開解答のようにスッキリと訳せれば問題はないが，すぐにピッタリした表現が思い浮かばないような場合は，できる限り平易な英語で書くことを勧める。まずは誤訳を避けるため，原文の意味をよく嚙み砕いて理解することが第一であり，その上で語彙力や表現力が問われてくるといえるだろう。新聞の論評やエッセイなどいろいろな文体の英文を多読し，表現力を養っておきたい。おすすめの方法は『やさしく読める英語ニュース』のような2言語が提示されている記事で，和文英訳や英文和訳に取り組むことである。2024年度は長文読解の中で，どのように生徒に語彙を習得させるかについて自由英作文問題が出題された。2023年度は長文読解の中で，テストを授業にどのように活かすのかについて自由英作文問題が出題された。2022年度は長文読解の中で，英語の指導について自由英作文問題が出題された。2021年度の自由英作文の問題は，内容中心教授法に基づき日本の英語指導について100語程度で書くというものであった。2020年度は，どのように生徒のモチベーションを高めるかを100語程度で書く問題が出題されており，英語の指導に関する出題が続いている。近年，学習指導要領の内容を直接問う問題は出題されていないが，新たに設定された領域である，話すこと[やりとり]に絡めての出題や，小学校の英語教科化にあたり中学校英語との接続などについて出題される可能性もある。自分なりの考えや指導方法や指導の留意点などを，英語でも書けるようにしておくと安心である。また，中学校学習指導要領の改訂の趣旨や要点を押さえるのはもちろんであるが，小学校学習指導要領にも目を通しておくことが望ましい。他府県の出題も参考に，様々なトピックについて，いろいろな語数で簡潔で明確に表現する学習をしておきたい。

読解問題は2題であり，文量が増え900 ～ 1200語程度の長さであった。自分の読解スピードを把握し，上げる努力を，過去問題や大学入試レベルの長文問題集でしておくとよい。最近の話題が問題文のトピックとなっているものもあるので，英字新聞や雑誌などに幅広く目を通し，たくさんの語彙に触れておこう。

■高等学校

共通問題以外に，読解問題3題が出題されている。試験時間は90分である。問題の質や量などを総合的に鑑みると，中学校より難解といえる。日本語や英語での記述式解答が多い。

読解問題3題は，700語，900語，450語程度からなる。読解問題の比重が高いので，エッセイや論評などいろいろなジャンルの文章を含む問題集を使い，そこに記されている標準の時間より速く解答することを心がけるのが対策として有効である。

2024年度も2023年度と同様に自由英作文が長文問題の中で出題され，高校の英語教育に起こっている変化及び教師がどのように対応すべきかを具体例と理由を含めて150語程度の英語で述べるものであった。なお，

2023年度はペア・グループなど学習者中心の活動を成功させる方法について具体例とその理由を含めて述べるものであった。2022年度は，授業内で生徒の質問を促す方法について，2021年度は，生徒が状況に応じた適切な表現を用いてコミュニケーションができるようになるための具体的な指導方法について，2020年度は，4技能を統合させた授業展開についてと，英語を話すときの流暢さについて自分自身の考えをそれぞれ書くものであった。中学校と同じように英語の指導に関する出題が続いている。トピックを与えられてから自分の意見をまとめ，構成を考え，英文で表現するのは時間がかかるものである。あらかじめ英語教育に関することについては，自分なりの意見を英語で作成しておくことが望ましい。おおよそ何分で書きあげると150語程度になるのか，語数の感覚をつかんでおくのも有効であろう。

過去5年間の出題傾向分析

中学＝●　高校＝▲　中高共通＝◎

分類	設問形式	2020年度	2021年度	2022年度	2023年度	2024年度
リスニング	内容把握					
発音・アクセント	発音					
	アクセント					
	文強勢					
文法・語法	空所補充	◎	◎	◎	◎	◎
	正誤判断					
	一致語句		●	●	●	●
	連立完成					
	その他					
会話文	短文会話	●				
	長文会話			●	●	●
文章読解	空所補充	◎●▲	●▲	◎●▲	◎●▲	◎●▲
	内容一致文	●▲	◎●▲	◎●▲	◎●▲	◎●▲
	内容一致語句	●▲	◎●▲	◎▲	◎▲	◎▲
	内容記述	◎▲	●▲	◎▲	◎▲	◎▲
	英文和訳	◎	◎▲	▲	▲	▲
	英問英答		▲	▲	▲	▲
	その他	◎●▲	◎●▲	◎●	◎●▲	◎●▲
英作文	整序		◎●	●	●	●
	和文英訳	●	●	●	●	●
	自由英作	●▲	●▲	●▲	●▲	●▲
	その他					
学習指導要領						

第２部

京都府の
教員採用試験
実施問題

2024年度　実施問題

【中高共通】

【１】Choose the answer that best completes the sentence from the four choices.

(1) Our teacher's enthusiasm is (　　). In other words, you just can't help feeling inspired when you are with her.

A. confining　B. concise　C. contagious　D. compliant

(2) The case was (　　) candies, and Bob took some. He hoped that his mother would not notice that there were fewer candies.

A. pleased with　B. full of　C. absent from　D. based on

(3) Mary remained (　　) despite failing her driving test for the first time. She said she would definitely pass on her second attempt.

A. allied　B. misty　C. parallel　D. resolute

(4) The politician's comments were so (　　) that reporters didn't understand what he was actually going to do.

A. ambiguous　B. credulous　C. analogous　D. infectious

(5) My mother opened the mail, which (　　) that morning.

A. delivered　B. is delivered　C. had delivered

D. had been delivered

(6) Susan (　　) moving to a new house in the countryside, but in the end, she decided to keep living in the same house.

A. released　B. solved　C. considered　D. promoted

(7) (　　) at the company all day long, she was completely worn out.

A. Worked　B. Not working　C. Being working

D. Having worked

(8) Melissa studied so hard (　　) well on the test.

A. that she had not done　B. that she should not have done

C. that she must have done　D. that she had to be done

(9) Sarah wanted to keep swimming in the river. However, ( ) it was getting dark, her father told her that it was time to go home.

A. as B. unless C. though D. until

(10) When he was invited to the party, he was ( ) himself with pleasure.

A. at B. beside C. for D. over

(11) This morning, train services throughout the area were ( ) for several hours due to heavy rain overnight. Thousands of people were affected.

A. descended B. deployed C. discerned D. disrupted

(12) I have a lot of friends, many of whom ( ).

A. I was at school together B. I was at school with

C. I was at school with them D. I was together at school

(13) Although Makoto had spent a few years in Australia when he was a teenager, he still had to ( ) his English skills before applying for the job.

A. shake up B. sign off C. brush up D. knock off

(14) Computer supplies are very expensive in Japan. Just this keyboard ( ) me 20,000 yen.

A. charged B. cost C. owed D. paid

(15) Although Monica tried to ( ) a book on the top shelf, she was not tall enough to get it. She asked her brother to do it.

A. come out B. turn off C. reach for D. result in

(16) My sister and I ( ) often play tennis in the park when we were young.

A. can B. may C. should D. would

(17) The fans were ( ) into silence because their national soccer team lost the important game.

A. stunned B. dulled C. hassled D. penalized

(18) Without your ( ) advice, I would have failed in my attempt to climb the mountain.

A. valueless　　B. invaluable　　C. invalid　　D. vain

(19)　(　　) since she went over to France to study French.

A. It was three years　　B. Three years are passed

C. Three years passed　　D. Three years have passed

(20)　Mary has been reading a book about Germany for two months. She is now on the (　　) chapter of the book and has a few pages left.

A. final　　B. common　　C. foreign　　D. national

(☆☆☆☆◎◎◎)

【２】Read the following passage and answer the question below.

Earth's atmosphere can safely absorb only a limited amount of carbon dioxide. This is called the "carbon budget." Wealthy countries had already used up most of the planet's carbon budget before most poorer ones had a chance to industrialize. The reasons for this are complex, but they have to do with the legacies of colonialism and slavery. Now these lower-income countries are trying to catch up. Their people want many of ①[in / the things / granted / that / take / wealthier countries / for / people]: electricity, sanitation, and convenient transportation networks. And they have a right to them. But the trouble is ②this: if everyone in the world copies the wasteful, fossil-fuel-burning lifestyles that are common in rich nations, the planet's temperature will soar.

The idea of climate debt is a way of finding a fair solution to this dilemma. [　③　] in 2006, the relatively poor South American nation of Ecuador tried to show the world how this solution could work ― but few were willing to listen at the time.

Yasuní National Park in Ecuador is an extraordinary stretch of rain forest. Several Indigenous tribes that live in the park have rejected all contact with the outside world in order to protect their way of life. This means that they have little immunity to common diseases such as influenza and could be at great risk if forced into contact with outsiders.【　A　】

The park is also home to a vast diversity of plants and animals. As many tree species grow in just 2.5 acres (1 hectare) of the park, for example, as are native to all of North America. It is also home to many threatened animal species, like the giant otter, the white-bellied spider monkey, and the jaguar. Yasuní is the kind of place that David Attenborough makes those amazing documentaries about!

But underneath that riot of life sits oil — up to 850 million barrels of it. The oil is worth billions, and oil companies want to get at it. 【 B 】 That money could be used to fight poverty. On the down side, burning all that oil, and logging the rain forest to get it, would add 547 million tons of carbon dioxide to the atmosphere. This is a problem for everyone on Earth, [④] the people of Ecuador.

In 2006, an idea was [⑤] forth by an Ecuadorian environmental group called Acción Ecológica (Ecological Action). The government of Ecuador would agree not to allow drilling in Yasuní. In return, the other countries of the world would support that decision by paying Ecuador part of the money it would lose by leaving the oil in the ground.

⑥This arrangement would be good for everyone. It would keep planet-warming gases out of our atmosphere. It would also protect the rich biological diversity of Yasuní. 【 C 】 And it would raise money for Ecuador to invest in health, education, and clean, renewable energy.

The point of this plan was that Ecuador should not carry the whole burden of leaving its oil in the ground. The burden should be shared by the highly industrialized countries that have already put most of the excess carbon dioxide into the atmosphere — and have [⑦] wealthy doing it (with the help of slavery and colonialism, as you'll see in the next chapter). Under the plan, the money Ecuador received could be used to help the country [⑧] to a new era of green development, leapfrogging over the dirtier model that has prevailed for centuries. The Yasuní plan would be a model for paying the climate or ecological debt in other countries.

The government of Ecuador championed the Yasuní plan to the world. The people of Ecuador strongly supported it. A poll in 2011 showed that 83 percent of them wanted to leave Yasuní's oil in the ground. This was up from 41 percent just three years earlier, showing that a plan for positive change can capture people's imaginations quickly.

A goal of $3.6 billion for Ecuador was set to protect Yasuní from drilling. But contributions from developed countries were slow to arrive — or never did. After six years, only $13 million had been raised.

So, because the plan had failed to raise the hoped-for payments, in 2013 the president of Ecuador said that he was going to allow drilling. Ecuadorian supporters of the climate debt plan did not give up. 【　D　】 Citizens' groups and nonprofit organizations campaigned against drilling. Protesters [　⑨　] up to arrests and rubber bullets. Yet in spite of their efforts, drilling began in Yasuní in 2016. Three years later the government allowed drilling in a third oil field inside the park, this time in the area where tribes had lived without contact with the outside world.

Ecuador's government says that the oil extraction ⑩<u>[care / with / is / to / being / protect / done / great]</u> the environment. But even if this is so, drilling in Yasuní means more use of fossil fuels, more greenhouse gas emitted into the atmosphere, and more climate change.

Latin America, Africa, and Asia are filled with opportunities for the richer parts of the world to step up and pay their climate debts. For that to happen, the wealthy peoples, and nations of the world must acknowledge what they owe to the countries that find themselves in a crisis they did little to create.

What are the responsibilities of the rich? What are the rights of the poor, no matter where they live in the world? Until we face these questions, we will not have a worldwide approach to climate change that is big enough to solve the problem. And we will keep having more heartbreaking lost opportunities like in Yasuní.

(1)　Put the words from each of the underlined ① and ⑩ in the correct order respectively.

(2) What does the underlined ② indicate? Explain in Japanese.

(3) Choose the most appropriate word for each blank of [③], [④], [⑤], [⑦], [⑧] and [⑨] from the choices below. If necessary, make each one of them inflect appropriately and/or capitalize it. You can use each word only once.

grow	include	move	put	stand	start

(4) Choose the most appropriate place from 【 A 】 − 【 D 】 in the text, to put the sentence below.

If they did, it would bring a lot of investment to Ecuador's economy.

(5) What does the underlined ⑥ indicate? Explain in Japanese.

(6) Filling in the blanks with the designated number of words, complete the following summary of the story about Yasuní National Park.

Yasuní National Park is home to a vast diversity of plants and animals, and it is also where several Indigenous tribes lead a life without ＿A(5-6)＿.

Under Yasuní, there is oil that is worth billions. At first, the government of Ecuador didn't allow drilling. A poll in 2011 showed that many of the people in Ecuador were in ＿B(2)＿ the decision. However, Ecuador got so few payments that it couldn't help ＿C(2-3)＿ the Yasuní plan and allowed drilling.

(7) According to the text, which of the following is true?

A. Each country is allowed to emit a certain amount of carbon dioxide, and the total amount of carbon dioxide each country is allowed to emit is called the "carbon budget."

B. As soon as Ecuador tried to show the world the idea of climate debt in 2006, many people welcomed the idea and took notice.

C. Contributions to Ecuador from other countries were not enough, and it received only about one third of the money it was expected to raise.

D. In order to prevent more heartbreaking lost opportunities like in Yasuní, we should think about the duties of rich people and the rights of poor people.

(☆☆☆☆◎◎◎)

【中学校】

【１】Substitute the underlined phrase with the best alternative from the four choices.

(1) These absurd rules should have been <u>done away with</u> years ago.

A. looked up to　B. put up with　C. gotten rid of

D. dropped in on

(2) He had to <u>account for</u> his absence from the meeting.

A. explain　B. undergo　C. demand　D. inquire

(3) She thoroughly <u>went over</u> the house before deciding whether to buy it.

A. stopped　B. purchased　C. revealed　D. examined

(4) Was it an accident or did Scott do it <u>on purpose</u>?

A. occasionally　B. eventually　C. immediately

D. intentionally

(5) The writer decided to <u>leave out</u> those two lines in her book.

A. cease　B. omit　C. advocate　D. revolt

(☆☆☆◎◎◎◎)

【２】Put the words in the correct order, and answer with the numbers.

(1) この説明書を英語になおしてもらいたい。

I [① have　② manual　③ this　④ to　⑤ translated　⑥ want] into English.

(2) ボブは2，3分歩いて，博物館に着いた。

A [① Bob　② brought　③ few　④ walk　⑤ to　⑥ minutes'] the museum.

(3) 大事なのは何をするかではなく，どのようにするかである。

It is not what you do but [① counts ② do ③ how ④ it ⑤ that ⑥ you].

(4) あのドアを開けていただけませんか？

Would you [① as ② be ③ kind ④ open ⑤ so ⑥ to] that door?

(5) 兄は私にコンピュータを貸したがらないと思いますが，説得して貸してくれるか確かめましょう。

I don't think my brother is willing to lend me his computer, but I'll [① can ② him ③ I ④ if ⑤ see ⑥ talk] into it.

(☆☆☆☆◎◎◎◎)

【3】Read the following passage and choose the best sentence for each of [1]～[4] from the six choices below.

A: Hello. How are you?

B: I'm good. I heard you stayed at school to finish your assignments.

A: That's right. I had a lot of things to write yesterday, and [1].

B: OK. Can I see it?

A: Sure. Wait. Where is my file? I saved something on this computer yesterday, but [2].

B: When you turn off the school computers, all files get deleted.

A: Why?

B: The school doesn't want students to leave unwanted things on them.

A: My file was not an unwanted thing. It was my report!

B: I think [3].

A: It looks like it.

B: When is the deadline for the paper?

A: Well, [4].

A. it's gone

B. it's going very well

C. I have to submit it in two weeks

D. I saved them in a file on this computer

E. you are out of luck

F. you don't have to write your report

(☆☆☆◎◎◎)

【４】Read the following passage and answer the question below.

By listing different senses for a word, dictionaries encourage us to think that each word has several different meanings that we need to learn and store. For example, the entry for 'guilt' many have at least three senses:

1 the fact that you have done something wrong

2 the responsibility for doing something wrong

3 the feeling you have done something wrong.

It is good for dictionaries to provide detail about the different senses of words, and this information can be very helpful when encountering a word in context. However, we should not see these senses as necessarily having psychological reality; they are distinctions created by the dictionary-makers. It is no accident that the three senses are all signalled by the same word form 'guilt' , since they all share the same core meaning: 'having done wrong' . When native speakers use the language either receptively or productively, they simply [①]. To put it another way, dealing with different word senses is usually an issue not of semantics but of pragmatics. Ruhl (1989) calls this the monosemic bias — that is, the assumption that a word has one inherent meaning (semantic), with the different senses in which it is used being determined by context (pragmatic). So if two words have the same or similar forms, we should assume they have the same meaning.

There are clearly exceptions to this, namely homonyms, homographs, and homophones, which are words that have the same spoken or written form (or both) but are unrelated in meaning. 【 A 】 A commonly cited example is 'bank' (for money/by the river), but there are many other examples. Kevin Parent (2012) found that the 2,000 word families in the General Service List (1953) include 75 homonyms (words with the same spoken and written forms but unrelated meaning, for example 'bowl', 'rest' , 'yard', 'miss') and ten homographs (words with the same written forms but different pronunciation and meanings, for example 'bow', 'wind', and 'lead'). 【 B 】 Wang and Nation (2004) found that around 10% of the 570 words in the Academic Word List (Coxhead, 2000) are homonyms and homographs. There are also exceptions, where a sense of a word has deviated so far from the core meaning that it is on its way to becoming a homonym. Although most homonyms are not etymologically related, a few are; for example, 'second' (after 'first'/part of a minute). The connection between these previously related meanings became [②] to users of the language, and they effectively became different words which need to be learned separately.

The *L1 also encourages learners to see the various senses of the same word form as different words if those senses are represented by two or more different word forms in the L1. For example, in Thai and French, 'to know a person' and 'to know some facts' are expressed by two different words. 【 C 】 Similarly, the fork you eat with and a fork in the road are two different words in Indonesian and many other languages. In contrast, when an *L2 word form has a single meaning in the L1, then learners may be less likely to recognize different senses as different words.

The learning burden of word senses can be greatly reduced if both teachers and learners focus on the core meaning of words and deal with different senses largely as a matter of strategy and process rather than as a matter of learning additional meanings. 【 D 】 First, and most importantly, the guessing from context strategy needs to be applied when a word is encountered which is used in an unfamiliar sense. Look at the following sentence from a reading text:

> A couple were smoking pipes, shoving the black tobacco down into the cups with wrinkled fingers.

The use of the word 'cups' is unusual here (we would normally expect 'bowls'), but the reader should have no trouble understanding it, because it is clearly consistent with the core meaning of 'cup', which refers to a particular shape. Similarly, the use of 'cup' as a verb in 'he cupped her face in his hands' is comprehensible from the core meaning.

A second useful method of reducing the learning burden of word senses is to look at all the senses of a word given in a dictionary entry to work out the core meaning. It would be extremely helpful if dictionaries provided core meanings as well as senses, but at present this happens more by accident than by design. There is also value in learners being made consciously aware of the idea of core meanings and how a word which expresses a single core meaning in one language may express two separate meanings in another language. The goal should be to learn the core meaning of words in the L2 so that when a word is used in a strikingly new sense, it can be dealt with not as an unfamiliar word but as representing something related to what is already known about that word. Besides, seeing how different languages classify the word is part of the educational value of learning another language.

*L1 = first language　　*L2 = second language

(1) Choose the most appropriate one for [①] from the four alternatives below.

A. adapt the understanding or use of this word to the current communicative context

B. check the way of using this word in the dictionary to understand it more

C. put a lot of emphasis on the senses of words from the dictionary

D. try to find the new sense of this word by asking native speakers about it

(2) Choose the most appropriate word for [②] from the four choices below.

A. close B. deep C. difference D. lost

(3) Choose the most appropriate place, from 【 A 】～【 D 】 in the text, to put the sentence below.

There are very practical ways of doing this.

(4) According to the text, which of the following is true?

A. When you look up a word in a dictionary, you will find only a single sense of the word.

B. You can suppose that two words will have the same sense if they come from the same or similar forms.

C. It is unnecessary to think about the context when there is a word that is used in an unfamiliar sense.

D. Dictionaries provides the core meaning and sense of words intentionally.

(5) Considering what is written in the passage, write your own thoughts on how teachers should teach vocabulary to students in approximately 100 words in English.

(☆☆☆☆◎◎◎)

【5】Translate the underlined sentence into English.

(1)<u>近年では，日本への観光客の数が劇的に増えている</u>。観光客はその国の経済を助けるが，様々な問題も引き起こしている。

京都を例にあげる。公共交通機関は観光客で混み合っていて，中には大きなスーツケースを持った人もいる。その結果，住民は公共交通機関を利用できないときがある。他の問題としては，観光客のマナーがある。地元の人々は，観光客が幅の狭いショッピングストリートでお菓子を食べながら歩くのを目にする。一部の観光客は写真を撮る許可もなく，私有地へ入る。

地元の人々は，ますますいらだっている。今，(2)<u>私たちは，観光公</u>

害の問題にどう対処すべきかを考えなければならない。

(☆☆☆◎◎◎)

【高等学校】

【１】Read the following passage and answer the questions below.

Our lives are dominated by ①two great rhythms, one much slower than the other. The fast one is the daily alternation between dark and light, which repeats every 24 hours, and the slow one is the yearly alternation between winter and summer, which has a repeat time of a little over 365 days. Not surprisingly, both rhythms have spawned myths. The day-night cycle especially is rich in myth because of the dramatic way the sun seems to move from [　②　] to [　③　]. Several peoples even saw the sun as a golden chariot, driven by a god across the sky.

The aboriginal peoples of Australia were isolated on their island continent for at least 40,000 years, and they have some of the oldest myths in the world. These are mostly set in a mysterious age called the Drearmtime, when the world began and was peopled by animals and a race of giant ancestors. Different tribes of aborigines have different myths of the Dreamtime. This first one comes from a tribe who live in the Flinders Ranges of southern Australia.

During the Dreamtime, two lizards were friends. One was a goanna (the Australian name for a large monitor lizard) and the other a gecko (a delightful little lizard with suction pads on its feet, with which it climbs up vertical surfaces). The friends discovered that some other friends of theirs had been massacred by the 'sun-woman' and her pack of yellow dingo dogs.

Furious with the sun-woman, the big goanna hurled his boomerang at her and knocked her out of the sky. The sun vanished over the western horizon and the world was plunged into [　④　]. The two lizards panicked and tried desperately to knock the sun back into the sky, to restore the light. The goanna took another boomerang and hurled it westwards, to where the sun had disappeared. As you may know, boomerangs are remarkable weapons that come back to the thrower, so the lizards hoped that the boomerang would hook the sun back up into the sky. [⑤] They then tried throwing boomerangs in all directions, in a vague hope of retrieving the sun. Finally, the goanna lizard had only one boomerang left, and in desperation he threw it to the [⑥], the opposite direction from where the sun had disappeared. This time, when it returned, it brought the sun with it. Ever since then, the sun has repeated the same pattern of disappearing in the west and reappearing in the east.

Many myths and legends from all around the world have the same odd feature: a particular incident happens once, and then, for reasons never explained, the same thing goes on happening again and again for ever.

Here's another aboriginal myth, this time from southeastern Australia. Someone threw the egg of an emu (a sort of Australian ostrich) up into the sky. The sun hatched out of the egg and set fire to a pile of kindling wood which happened (for some reason) to be up there. The sky god noticed that the light was useful to men, and he told his servants to go out every night from then on, to put enough firewood in the sky to light up the next day.

The longer cycle of the seasons is also the subject of myths all around the world. Native North American myths, like many others, often have animal characters. In this one, from the Tahltan people of western Canada, there was a quarrel between Porcupine and Beaver over how long the seasons ought to be. Porcupine wanted winter to last five months, so he held up his five fingers. But Beaver wanted winter to last for more months than that — the number of grooves in his tail. Porcupine was angry and insisted on an even shorter winter. He dramatically bit off his thumb and held up the remaining four fingers. And ever since then winter has lasted four months.

I find this a rather disappointing myth, because it already assumes that there will be a winter and summer, and explains only how many months each will last. The Greek myth of Persephone is better in ⑦this respect at least.

Persephone was the daughter of the chief god Zeus. Her mother was Demeter, fertility goddess of the Earth and the harvest. Persephone was greatly loved by Demeter, whom she helped in looking after the crops. But Hades, god of the underworld, home of the dead, loved Persephone too. One day, when she was playing in a flowery meadow, a great chasm opened up and Hades appeared from below in his chariot; seizing Persephone, he carried her down and made her the queen of his dark, underground kingdom. Demeter was so grief-stricken at the loss of her beloved daughter that she stopped the plants growing, and people began to starve. Eventually Zeus sent Hermes, the gods' messenger, down to the underworld to [⑧] the land of the living and the light. Unfortunately, it turned out that Persephone had eaten six pomegranate seeds while in the underworld, and this meant (by the kind of logic we have become used to where myths are concerned) that she had to go back to the underworld for six months (one for each pomegranate seed) in every year. So Persephone lives above ground for part of the year, beginning in the spring and continuing through summer. During this time, plants flourish and all is merry. But during the winter, when she has to return to Hades because she ate those pesky pomegranate seeds, the ground is cold and [⑨] and nothing grows.

(1) What are the two great rhythms mentioned in the underlined ①? Answer both of the rhythms in Japanese respectively.

(2) Choose the best combination of words for [②], [③], and [⑥] from the four choices below.

A. ② east ③ west ⑥ east
B. ② east ③ west ⑥ west
C. ② west ③ east ⑥ east
D. ② west ③ east ⑥ west

(3) Choose the most appropriate word to put into [④] and [⑨] from the four choices below respectively.

④ A. brightness　B. colorlessness　C. darkness

D. silence

⑨ A. aesthetic B. barren C. fertile

D. immortal

(4) Choose the best sentence for [⑤] from the four choices below.

A. It did. B. It didn't. C. It was. D. It wasn't.

(5) What does the underlined ⑦ indicate? Explain in Japanese.

(6) Choose the best expression for [⑧] from the four choices below.

A. exile Demeter from B. expel Persephone from

C. take Demeter back up to D. fetch Persephone back up to

(7) Filling in the blanks with the designated number of words, complete the following summary of the myth from the Tahltan people of western Canada.

> There was a quarrel between two ___A(1-2)___, Porcupine and Beaver. Beaver wasn't satisfied with Porcupine's first suggestion that winter ___B(3-5)___. Beaver demanded a longer winter, but Porcupine didn't agree and made another suggestion. Since this quarrel, winter ended up ___C(3-4)___.

(☆☆☆☆◎◎◎)

【2】Read the following passage and answer the questions below.

Take a look at the following word, and fill in the two blank letters. Do it quickly, without thinking.

GL_ _

This is called a word-completion task. Psychologists commonly use it to test things such as memory.

I completed GL_ _ as GLUM. Remember that. The next word is:

_ _TER

I completed that as HATER. Remember that too. Here are the rest of the words:

S_ _RE	STR_ _ _	B_ _T
P_ _N	GO_ _	PO_ _ _
TOU_ _	CHE_ _	BA_ _
ATT_ _ _	_ _OR	_RA_
BO_ _	SL_ _ _	_ _ _EAT
FL_ _T	SC_ _ _	
SL_T	_ _NNER	

I started out with GLUM and HATER and ended up with SCARE, ATTACK, BORE, FLOUT SLIT, CHEAT, TRAP, and DEFEAT. That's a pretty morbid and melancholy list. But I don't think that says anything about the darkness of my soul. I'm not melancholy. I'm an optimist. I think that the first word, GLUM, popped into my head, and then I just continued in that vein.

A few years ago, ①a team of psychologists led by Emily Pronin gave a group of people that same exercise. Pronin had them fill in the blank spaces. Then she asked them the same question: What do you think your choices *say* about you? For instance, if you completed TOU_ _ as TOUCH, does that suggest that you are a different kind of person than if you completed it as TOUGH? The respondents took the same position I did. *They're just words.*

"I don't agree with these word-stem completions as a measure of my personality," one of Pronin's subjects wrote. And the others in the group agreed:

> "These word completions don't seem to reveal much about me at all.... Random completions."

"Some of the words I wrote seem to be the antithesis of how I view the world. For instance, I hope that I am not always concerned about being STRONG, the BEST, or a WINNER."

"I don't really think that my word completions reveal that much about me.... Occurred as a result of happenstance."

"Not a whole lot... They reveal vocabulary."

"I really don't think there was any relationship.... The words are just random."

"The words PAIN, ATTACK, and THREAT seem similar, but I don't know that they say anything about me."

But then things got interesting. Pronin gave the group other people's words. These were perfect strangers. She asked the same question. What do you think this stranger's choices reveal? And ②this time Pronin's panel completely changed their minds.

"He doesn't seem to read too much, since the natural (to me) completion of B_ _K would be BOOK. BEAK seems rather random, and might indicate deliberate unfocus of mind."

"I get the feeling that whoever did this is pretty vain, but basically a nice guy."

Keep in mind that these are the exact same people who just moments before had denied that the exercise had any meaning at all.

(snip)

③If the panel had seen my GLUM, HATER, SCARE, ATTACK, BORE, FLOUT, SLIT, CHEAT, TRAP and DEFEAT, they would have worried for my soul.

Pronin calls this phenomenon the "illusion of asymmetric insight." She writes:

④The conviction that we know others better than they know us — and that we may have insights about them they lack (but not vice versa) — leads us to talk when we would do well to listen and to be less patient than we ought to be when others express the conviction that they are the ones who are being misunderstood or judged unfairly.

(1) Regarding the underlined ① and ②, what did Pronin do in the experiment and what was the result? Explain in Japanese.

(2) Choose the most appropriate meaning of the underlined ③ from the four choices below.

A. The author should have let the panel see the author's answers so that they could care more about the author.

B. If the author had let the panel see the author's answers, they wouldn't have worried about the author.

C. Even though the panel didn't say it clearly, they worried for the author's soul after seeing the author's answers.

D. Although the panel didn't see the author's answers, had they had a chance to do so, they would have been anxious about the author's soul.

(3) Translate the underlined ④ into Japanese.

(☆☆☆☆◎◎◎)

【3】Read the following passage and answer the questions below.

It's sometimes assumed that the main role of a teacher is direct instruction. There's an essential place for direct instruction in teaching. Sometimes it's with a whole class, sometimes with smaller groups, and sometimes one-on-one with individual students. But expert teachers have a repertory of skills and techniques. Direct instruction is only one of ①them, and knowing how and when to use the appropriate technique is what great teaching is all about. Like all genuine professions, it takes judgment and connoisseurship to know what works best here and now.

You expect your doctor to know a lot about medicine in general as well as having some specific area of expertise. But you also expect her to apply what she knows to you in particular and to treat you as an individual with specific needs. ②Teaching is the same. Expert teachers constantly adapt their strategies to the needs and opportunities of the moment. Effective teaching is a constant process of adjustment, judgment, and responding to the energy and engagement of the students.

In her book, *Artistry Unleashed*, Hilary Austen explores great performances in work and life. In one example, she looks at the work of Eric Thomas, a former philosophy student at Berkeley, who now teaches horsemanship. The essence for the rider, he says, is to become one with the horse, a living animal with its own energy and moods. Dr. Austen describes one class where things aren't going so well for the student, who reins the horse in while Eric offers some coaching.

He tells the student that she's putting a lot of effort into trying to get the horse to turn better, but that every third or fourth turn she drops the ball and doesn't do anything. What's that about? he asks. The student says, "I'm too early and then too late, and then he reacts and I can't tell what to do." Eric pauses and then says, "You're trying to do too much. Stop thinking, and pay attention to your horse. It's about trying to feel what is happening underneath you right now. ③*You can't ride yesterday's horse*. You can't ride what might happen. Everybody who rides has the same problem: we're hoping what we learned yesterday will always apply. You often ride the problem you had a minute ago, all for the goal you want to achieve. But this is not a recipe. It changes every second, and ④you've got to change with it."

Good teachers know that however much they have learned in the past, today is a different day and you cannot ride yesterday's horse.

(1) What does the underlined ① refer to? Search the text and extract the sequential words.

(2) Regarding the underlined ②, in what aspect is teaching identical to seeing a patient? Explain it with about 50 Japanese characters.

(3)　What does the underlined ③ indicate? Explain in Japanese.

(4)　Regarding the underlined ④, what change do you think is happening in high school English education and what do teachers need to do to adapt themselves to the change you mention? Express your own idea with concrete examples and reasons, using about 150 words in English

(☆☆☆☆◎◎◎)

解答・解説

【中高共通】

【1】(1)　C　(2)　B　(3)　D　(4)　A　(5)　D　(6)　C
(7)　D　(8)　C　(9)　A　(10)　B　(11)　D　(12)　B
(13)　C　(14)　B　(15)　C　(16)　D　(17)　A　(18)　B
(19)　D　(20)　A

〈解説〉(1)　空所の後の「彼女と一緒にいると必ず触発される」より contagious「(感情・態度が)人から人へ広がりやすい」が適切。
(2)　full of～で「～でいっぱいの」の意味。　(3)　2文目「彼女は2回目の挑戦で絶対に合格すると言った」よりresolute「固く決意している」が適切。　(4)　空所の後の「レポーターは彼が実際に何をしようとしているのか理解できなかった」よりambiguous「あいまいな」が適切。
(5)　whichの先行詞がthe mailであることから受動態でなければならず，whichの前の節が過去形であるため現在形のBは不適切であり，「すでに届いていた」を表す過去完了のDが適切。　(6)　consider doingで「～することを検討する」の意味。　(7)　分詞構文Having workedを用いて「1日中働いていたので」という意味を表す。　(8)　must have doneで「～したに違いない」の意味でstudied so hardとつながる。
(9)　as it was getting dark「暗くなってきたので」とasを理由の接続詞

として用いる。　(10)　beside oneself with～で「～に我を忘れて，夢中で」の意味。　(11)　夜の大雨で電車を用いる数千人に影響があったという文なのでdisrupt「中断する，邪魔する」の受動態を用いる。
(12)　I have a lot of friends.とI was at school with many of them.の2文を関係詞でつないだ形。　(13)　brush up～「～を磨き上げる，ブラッシュアップする」が適切。　(14)　cost＋A(人)＋B(金額)で「AにBの金額をかける」の意味。　(15)　reach for～で「～を取ろうと手を伸ばす」の意味。　(16)　would often doで「よく～したものだ」と過去の習慣を表す。　(17)　be stunned into silenceで「驚きのあまり静まりかえる」の意味。　(18)　invaluableは「極めて貴重な」の意味。valuableの意味が強調された語である。　(19)　時間 have passed since～で「～から…が経った」を表す。　(20)　final chapterで「最終章」の意味。

【2】(1)　①　the things that people in wealthier countries take for granted　⑩　is being done with great care to protect　(2)　もし世界の全員が，豊かな国々でよく見られるような，無駄の多い，化石燃料の生活スタイルを真似すると，地球の気温が上昇してしまうということ。
(3)　③　Starting　④　including　⑤　put　⑦　grown　⑧　move　⑨　stood　(4)　B　(5)　石油を採掘することで得られるであろうお金の一部を，世界の他の国々が支払うという取り決め。
(6)　A　contact with the outside world　B　favor of　C　giving up on　(7)　D

〈解説〉(1)　①　関係代名詞thatの先行詞であるthe thingsは，take O for granted「Oを当然のことと思う」のO(目的語)である。　⑩　is being doneは受動態の現在進行形で「～されているところだ」の意味。この後にwith great care「とても注意を払って」という語句が入り，目的のto不定詞を用いてto protect the environmentと続く。　(2)　このthisは後ろの内容を表し，the trouble is thisは「問題は以下の通りである，こうである」という意味である。よって解答としてはif以下の文を日本語にまとめればよい。　(3)　③　Startingが入る。カンマの後にS＋Vが続くことから分詞構文を用い，目的語がないため自動詞が入ることがわかる。空所の後のin 2006につながるのはstartしかないと読み取れる。④　including「～を含む」が入る。空所の前にeveryoneがあることから「エクアドルの国民を含む全ての人」となる。　⑤　put forth～「(考え・アイデア)を出す」の受動態が入る。putは過去形・過去分詞形も語形変化せずputが適切となる。　⑦　grow wealthyで「裕福になる」。haveの後なので過去分詞grownが適切となる。　⑧　move to a new era of green development「緑化に配慮した開発の新時代へ移行する」となりmoveが適切となる。　⑨　stand up to～「～に抵抗する」を用い，時制は過去形のためstoodが入る。　(4)　主語Theyや動詞didが示しそうな単語があるのはBとDに絞られる。BとDを比較すると，多くの投資をもたらすという挿入文の内容にDはそぐわないことがわかりBが適切と判断できる。　(5)　This arrangementの内容は前文のby paying以下となる。part of the money it would lose by leaving the oil in the ground「地中に石油を残しておくことで失うであろうお金の一部」を「石油を採掘することで得られるであろうお金の一部」とわかりやすく解答例では言い換えている。　(6)　A　第3段落2文目のhave rejected all contact with the outside worldが該当し，語数指定を考慮してcontact with the outside worldとする。　B　第9段落3文目の内容から，国民の8割以上が石油の不採掘を望んだことがわかるので，in favor of～「～に賛成する」が適切。　C　第11段落の内容が該当する。「最初は石油の採掘を許さなかったが最終的には要求に屈した」という内容が入るため「～に屈する」の意味を持ち，helpの後であることを考えて動名詞にしたgiving up onを入れる。　(7)　豊かな者の義務と貧しい者の権利について疑問を投げかけた最終段落の内容がDと一致する。

【中学校】

【1】(1)　C　　(2)　A　　(3)　D　　(4)　D　　(5)　B

〈解説〉(1)　do away with～「～を廃止する」に近いのはget rid of～「～を取り除く」となる。　(2)　account for～「～を釈明する」に近いのはexplain「説明する」となる。 (3) go over～「～を詳細に調べる」に近いのはexamine「検査する」となる。 (4) on purpose「わざと，故意に」に近いのはintentionallyとなる。 (5) leave out～「～を省く」に近いのはomit「除外する」となる。

【2】(1) ⑥→④→①→③→②→⑤ (2) ③→⑥→④→②→①→⑤
(3) ③→⑥→②→④→⑤→① (4) ②→⑤→③→①→⑥→④
(5) ⑤→④→③→①→⑥→②

〈解説〉(1) want to have this manual translatedが正しい語順となる。have＋O＋過去分詞「Oを～してもらう」を用いる。 (2) few minutes' walk brought Bob toが正しい語順となる。「数分歩くことがボブを～へ連れて行った」が直訳となる表現である。 (3) how you do it that countsが正しい語順となる。「どうやるか」はhow you do itで表す。「重要である」の部分は強調構文が使われており，countは自動詞「重要である」の意味で用いられている。 (4) be so kind as to openが正しい語順となる。Would you be so kind as to～で「～してくださいますか」と物事を依頼する頻出の会話表現である。 (5) see if I can talk himが正しい語順である。see if～で「～かどうか確かめる」，talk O into～で「Oに～するよう説得する」の意味。

【3】1 D 2 A 3 E 4 C

〈解説〉1 空所の後でコンピュータに保存したファイルの話をしているためDが適切と判断できる。 2 I saved something on this computer yesterday, butの後に来るのはAのit's gone.「なくなってしまいました」が適切となる。 3 意図せずファイルが削除されてしまったAに対してBがかける言葉としてE「運が悪かったね」が適切となる。 4 レポートの期限をBから聞かれており，Aの返答としてCが適切となる。

【4】(1) A (2) D (3) D (4) B (5) In order to develop the five areas of English, teachers should try to increase students' vocabulary.

When teaching vocabulary to students, it is necessary to teach the meaning, phoneme, and form of the vocabulary to help student retain the information. It is important to have students read or listen to the vocabulary many times in communication tasks so that students will gradually become more familiar with speaking and writing the vocabulary. That will also help students understand the appropriate context or scene to use each word. (86 words)

〈解説〉(1)　空所の後でsemanticsとpragmaticsのそれぞれの意味が述べられており，異なる語の意味を扱う辞書では文脈の中で意味が決定されるpragmaticsが用いられると説明されている。これらに該当するAが空所に入ると判断できる。　(2)　空所の後で「実質的に異なる語となり別に学ぶ必要がある」とあることから，The connectionを主語とした文の空所はlost「失われた」が適切。　(3)　There are very practical ways of doing this.「これをする大変実践的な方法がある」より，その後にその実践的な方法が述べられると推測できる。この点を考慮に入れて空所A～Dを見ていくと，空所Dの後のみに具体的な方法が述べられていることよりDが正解と判断できる。　(4)　Bの内容が第2段落最終文の内容と一致する。　(5)　本文では語のcore meaningを学ぶことで単語の学習の負担が減ることが述べられている。この内容を踏まえて，解答例では英語の5領域の上達においてまず意味，音，形式といったcore meaningにあたる情報を生徒に学ばせ，リーディングやリスニングで何度もその語に触れさせることでスピーキングやライティングに役立てるだけでなくその語が用いられている文脈を理解する助けとする，という教授法が述べられている。なお，解答例では「5領域」をfive areasとしているが，現行の中学校学習指導要領(平成29年3月告示)英訳版においてはfive skill areasと訳されているので，英訳版の表記に準じることが望ましいと思われる。

【５】(1)　The number of tourists to Japan has dramatically increased in recent years.　(2)　we need to think about how to deal with the problem of overtourism.

〈解説〉(1)「～の数」はthe number of～,「近年では」はin recent yearsで表す。動詞の「増えている」は現在までのことを述べているため現在完了で表す必要がある点にも注意したい。 (2) 観光客が増えすぎて地元の人に悪影響をもたらす「観光公害」はovertourismで表す。「対処する」はdeal with～で表し,「どう対処すべきか」はhow to deal with～とする。

【高等学校】

【1】(1) 昼と夜,夏と冬 (2) A (3) ④ C ⑨ B
(4) B (5) そもそもなぜ夏と冬があるのかに言及しているという点。 (6) D (7) A animal B should last five months
C being four months

〈解説〉(1) 下線部の後で「昼と夜」,「夏と冬」の対比が述べられておりこれらが解答となる。 (2) 太陽は東から昇り西に沈むため②にはeast, ③にはwestが入る。⑥は空所の後でthe opposite direction from where the sun had disappeared「太陽が消えたのと反対の方向」に着目する。同段落4文目で太陽は西に消えたことが述べられており,その反対の方向であるeastが⑥に入る。よって正しい組み合わせはAとなる。 (3) ④ 空所の前で「太陽が西の地平線に消える」とあるのでその後に残るのはdarkness「漆黒」となる。 ⑨ 空所の前後は冬で地面が冷たくなり何も育たなくなるという内容なので空所にはBのbarren「不毛の」が入る。 (4) 空所はその前のthe boomerang would hook the sun back up into the skyを受けての文で,itがthe boomerangを指し,didn'tがdidn't hook the sun back up into the skyの省略を表すことができるBが適切。 (5) Greek myth of Persephoneは下線部の次の段落で述べられているようになぜ夏と冬ができたのかについての神話である。一方,下線部の前の段落で述べられている神話は夏と冬があるのが前提であり,夏と冬がそれぞれ何カ月続くかについての神話である。両者の差は「なぜ夏と冬ができたのかについて言及している点」であり,Greek myth of Persephoneの優れている点である。よってthis respectはこの点を記述すればよい。　(6)　Persephoneが連れ去られたことで母のDemeterが悲しみ植物が成長しなくなり人々が飢えてきたという問題を解決すべく，Persephoneを連れ戻すという内容のDが入ると読み取れる。　(7)　第7段落の内容より空所に適語を補充する。　A　解答例ではanimalとなっているが，1・2文目よりanimalsが適切と思われる。B　3文目よりshould last five monthsとする。　C　最後の2文よりfour monthsとなるが，end upの後なので動名詞が続く必要がありbeing four monthsとする。

【２】(1)　被験者たちに単語完成課題をしてもらい，その課題で答えた言葉が自分自身について言い当てているかを尋ねたところ，関係がないという意見であった。しかし，その被験者たちに，他人の単語完成課題の結果を見せ，何が分かるかと尋ねたところ，その他人が単語完成課題で答えた言葉からその他人について色々と憶測しだした。

(2)　D　　(3)　他人が私たちのことを知っている以上に私たちは他人のことを知っているという，そして，私たちには他人にはない洞察力がある(が，その逆はない)という考えによって，私たちは耳を傾けたほうがよいであろう時に話してしまったり，他の人が，誤解されているあるいは不当に判断されているという考えを表明している時に，私たちがそうであるべき程に辛抱強くなれなくなったりしてしまう。

〈解説〉(1)　下線部①の段落ではProninの単語完成課題について被験者たちは選んだ単語と自分自身についての関係性はないと述べている。それに対し，後のButで始まる段落では，被験者たちに他者の選んだ単語について聞いてみると，下線部②を含む文で示すように，今度は他者の性格についてその単語から推測し始めたことが述べられている。この2点を含めて記述すればよい。　(2)　下線部③は仮定法過去完了が用いられており，実際には審査員たちは筆者の回答を見ることができなかったことが分かる。したがってDが適切と判断できる。

(3)　The conviction「考え」が主語で2つの同格のthatが(but not vice versa)まで続き，動詞以下がleads us to do「私たちを～することに導いてしまう」という文構造である。would do well to doは「～したほうがいい」，than we ought to beの後にはpatientが省略されていることなどに留意して訳すとよい。

【3】(1) skills and techniques (2) 知っていることを個人個人に合わせて当てはめ，その一人一人を特別な手助けの必要な個々人として扱うという点。(52字) (3) 過去に学んだことは，必ずしも全てに当てはめることができるわけではないということ。 (4) Based on the current Course of Study, high school teachers are required to develop students' four skills of English in a balanced way. Teachers should not focus too much on just one of the skills or grammar alone. In order to accomplish the goal, teachers have to introduce integrated language activities into class. One integrated language activity, for example, is to have students read a text and understand the abstract and main point, and then ask them to speak to each other or in a group about what they think about the main point. To have them write what they have learned from the text is another example. In other words, through these activities, students have to use two skills in an integrated way to achieve the goal. Such integrated activities make it possible for teachers to implement what the Course of Study mentions and increase the four English language skills comprehensively. (152 words)

〈解説〉(1) 直前の複数形の語句であるskills and techniquesを指す。
(2) 下線部の前文の，医者に期待していることの内容をそのまま記述すればよい。医者に期待することと教師に期待することは同じだというのがここで述べたいことである。 (3) 下線部の後ろから最終文までの内容を検討すると，「過去の馬に乗る」というのは「過去に学んだこと」の比喩である。今日は過去とは別の日であるから，過去に学んだことは全てのことに当てはまるわけではない，ということを記述すればよい。 (4) (3)とも関連するが，下線部を含む文では，過去に学んだことがいつでも通用するわけではないため，自分自身も変化する必要がある旨が述べられている。それを踏まえて，現在の高校英語教育に起こっている変化と，その変化にどのように生徒を適応させるか150語程度で書く。従来の英語教育では「読むこと」，「書くこと」，「聞くこと」，「話すこと」などを個別に指導していた。一方，現行の高等学校学習指導要領(平成30年3月告示)外国語科では，学んだことを実際に活用・運用できる能力を身に付け，コミュニケーション能力を高めることを目的に，複数の領域を結び付けた統合的な言語活動を通して，5つの領域を総合的に扱うことと明示されている。さらに，従来一つの分野であった「話すこと」が，「話すこと[やり取り]」と「話すこと[発表]」という2つの領域に分離されたため，英語の技能は「聞くこと」，「書くこと」，「読むこと」と合わせて「5領域」(英訳版：five skill areas)に分類されることとなった。解答例では，こうした高等学校学習指導要領の改訂点を踏まえ，統合的な学習の利点とその具体的な活動例を挙げている。なお，解答例中にはfour skills of English，four English language skillsの記述があるが，高等学校学習指導要領外国語科・英語科においては，「5領域」という表現に統一されていることから，学習指導要領の表記に準じることが望ましいと思われる。

2023年度　実施問題

【中高共通】

【1】Choose the answer that best completes the sentence from the four choices.

(1) Her careless driving has (　　) her mother great anxiety.

A. changed　B. caused　C. expected　D. promoted

(2) I had left a present for him at my house, so he waited for me while I (　　) it.

A. fetched　B. neglected　C. missed　D. acclaimed

(3) We should always be (　　) for our appointments.

A. accurate　B. strict　C. precise　D. punctual

(4) She walked at such a (　　) pace that he had to run to keep up with her.

A. brisk　B. bull　C. slow　D. slack

(5) She had no (　　) of spending the rest of her life working as a doctor.

A. intervention　B. intention　C. meaning　D. mind

(6) It took Mark three years to (　　) enough savings to make the down payment on his new house.

A. accumulate　B. cultivate　C. designate　D. formulate

(7) You should believe there are still a lot of things whose worth can't be expressed (　　) money.

A. in exchange for　B. in favor of　C. in terms of

D. in consideration for

(8) New York is one of the most ethnically (　　) cities in the world because immigrants from dozens of countries arrive every year.

A. coherent　B. crucial　C. diverse　D. uniform

(9) He applied for the study abroad program to (　　) himself in an environment where only English is spoken.

A. capture　B. immerse　C. emerge　D. release

(10) It was about 6,000 kilometers to the top of the mountain, and from the bottom it looked impossible to walk up, (　　) run.

A. no less than　B. more or less　C. still more

D. much less

(11) There are many people in the group and (　　) has their own special interest.

A. all　B. every　C. each　D. no

(12) Camping alone, in complete (　　) from other people, you may feel lonely at times but have a good experience.

A. isolation　B. moderation　C. prevention

D. interruption

(13) I found she was only (　　) to read a book because her book was upside down.

A. acting　B. behaving　C. deceiving　D. pretending

(14) (　　) a fine day, I went out for a walk.

A. It was　B. It being　C. Being　D. Having been

(15) Now that he is a teacher, he thinks (　　).

A. nevertheless　B. otherwise　C. contrary　D. different

(16) The president of the company, (　　) you introduced me last Tuesday, wants to see you again.

A. to whom　B. of whom　C. of that　D. to that

(17) A: Can I borrow your computer while you are cooking, Mom?

B: Sure, but don't (　　) the papers on the desk. I don't want them to get out of order.

A. hand off　B. give up　C. mess with　D. branch out

(18) As she was so tired, she was lying on the bed with (　　).

A. her closed eyes　B. her eyes closed　C. her closing eyes

D. her eyes closing

(19) A: Tom, do you have to take American literature at your university?

B: Yes, I don't really want to, but it's (　　) for first year students.

A. biased B. compulsory C. divine D. rusty

(20) ABC bookstore's sales in the first year ( ) this company is likely to achieve its goal for the year.

A. brands B. grasps C. nourishes D. indicates

(☆☆☆☆◎◎◎◎◎)

【2】Read the following passage and answer the questions below.

David G. Smith of Eau Claire, Wisconsin, told one of our classes how he handled a delicate situation when he was asked to take charge of the refreshment booth at a charity concert.

"The night of the concert I arrived at the park and found two elderly ladies in a very bad humor standing next to the refreshment stand. Apparently each thought that she was [①] charge of this project. As I stood there [②] what to do, one of the members of the sponsoring committee appeared and handed me a cash box and thanked me for taking over the project. She introduced Rose and Jane as my helpers and then ran off.

"A great silence ensued. Realizing that the cash box was a symbol of authority (of sorts), I gave the box to Rose and explained that I might not be able to keep the money straight and that if she took care of it I would feel better. I then suggested to Jane ③[two teenagers / had been assigned / that / who / show / she] to refreshments how to operate the soda machine, and I asked her to be responsible for that part of the project.

"The evening was very enjoyable with Rose happily counting the money, Jane supervising the teenagers, and me enjoying the concert."

④You don't have to wait until you are ambassador to France or chairman of the Clambake Committee of your lodge before you use this philosophy of appreciation. You can work magic with it almost every day.

If, for example, the waitress brings us mashed potatoes when we have ordered French fried, let's say: "I'm sorry to trouble you, but I prefer French fried." She'll probably reply, "No trouble at all" and will be glad to change the potatoes, [　⑤　] we have shown respect for her.

Little phrases such as "I'm sorry to trouble you," "Would you be so kind as to ——?" "Won't you please?" "Would you mind?" "Thank you" — little courtesies like these oil the cogs of the monotonous grind of everyday life — and, incidentally, they are the hallmark of good breeding.

Let's take another illustration, Hall Caine's novels — *The Christian*, *The Deemster*, *The Manxman*, among them — were all best-sellers in the early part of *this century. Millions of people read his novels, countless millions. He was the son of a blacksmith. He never had more than eight years' schooling in his life; yet when he died he was the richest literary man of his time.

The story goes like this: Hall Caine loved sonnets and ballads; so he [　⑥　] all of Dante Gabriel Rossetti's poetry. He even wrote a lecture chanting the praises of Rossetti's artistic achievement — and sent a copy to Rossetti himself. Rossetti was delighted. "Any young man who has such an exalted opinion of my ability," Rossetti probably said to himself, "must be brilliant." So Rossetti invited this blacksmith's son to come to London and act as his secretary. ⑦<u>That</u> was the turning point in Hall Caine's life; for, in his new position, he met the literary artists of the day. Profiting by their advice and [　⑧　] by their encouragement, he launched upon a career that emblazoned his name across the sky.

His home, Greeba Castle, on the Isle of Man, ⑨<u>became a Mecca for tourists from the far corners of the world</u>, and he left a multimillion dollar estate. Yet — who knows — he might have died poor and unknown ⑩<u>[written / his admiration / not / an essay / had / expressing / he]</u> for a famous man.

Such is the power, the stupendous power, of sincere, heartfelt appreciation.

Rossetti considered himself important. That is not strange. Almost everyone considers himself important, very important.

The life of many a person could probably be changed if only someone would make him feel important. Ronald J. Rowland, who is one of the instructors of our course in California, is also a teacher of arts and crafts. He wrote to us about a student named Chris in his beginning-crafts class:

Chris was a very quiet, shy boy lacking in self-confidence, the kind of student that often does not receive the attention he deserves, I also teach an advanced class that had grown to be somewhat of a status symbol and a privilege for a student to have earned the right to be in it.

On Wednesday, Chris was diligently working at his desk. I really felt there was a hidden fire deep inside him. I asked Chris if he would like to be in the advanced class. How I wish I could express the look in Chris's face, the emotions in that shy fourteen-year-old boy, trying to hold back his tears.

"Who me, Mr. Rowland? Am I good enough?"

"Yes, Chris, you are good enough."

I had to leave at that point because tears were coming to my eyes. As Chris walked out of class that day, seemingly two inches taller, he looked at me with bright blue eyes and said in a positive voice, "Thank you, Mr. Rowland."

Chris taught me a lesson I will never forget—our deep desire to feel important. To help me never forget this rule, I made a sign which reads "YOU ARE IMPORTANT." This sign hangs in the front of the classroom for all to see and to remind me that each student I [⑪] is equally important.

The unvarnished truth is that almost all the people you meet feel themselves superior [⑫] you in some way, and a sure way to their hearts is to let them realize in some subtle way that you recognize their importance, and recognize it sincerely.

Remember what Emerson said: "Every man I meet is my superior in some way. In that, I learn of him."

*this century　This book was first published in 1936.

(1) Write the appropriate preposition for each blank of [①] and [⑫] respectively.

(2) Choose the most appropriate word for each blank of [②], [⑥],

[⑧], and [⑪] from the choices below. If necessary, make each one of them inflect appropriately. You can use each word only once.

[devour face inspire ponder]

(3) Put the words from each of the underlined ③ and ⑩ in the correct order respectively.

(4) Choose the most appropriate meaning of each of the underlined ④ and ⑨ from the four choices below respectively.

④

A. People in authority do not necessarily use the philosophy of appreciation.

B. You can make use of the philosophy of appreciation regardless of who you are.

C. The lower your status is, the more you can work magic with the philosophy of appreciation.

D. There are only a few occasions to which you can apply the philosophy of appreciation.

⑨

A. became a magnet for people throughout the world

B. became an attraction for people from a limited part of the globe

C. became a site many people wanted to visit for a religious reason

D. became a place only people who can appreciate literary works were allowed to visit

(5) Choose the most appropriate word to put into [⑤].

A. because B. before C. though D. unless

(6) What does the underlined ⑦ indicate? Explain in Japanese.

(7) Filling in the blanks with the designated number of words, complete the following summary of the story about Chris.

Chris was a very quiet, shy student and didn't feel __A(2-4)__. He didn't get the attention he deserved. Mr. Rowland, however, spotted his hidden fire and asked him whether he'd like to be in the advanced class. Chris's expression and his emotions were B(2-4). When Chris walked out of class that day, he seemed to be two inches taller because C(7-10).

(8) According to the text, which of the following is true?

A. Arriving at the park, David G. Smith found two elderly women were in a bad mood and they kept complaining about each other until Mr. Smith asked each of them a favor.

B. Without any particular intention, David G. Smith asked Rose to take care of the refreshment stand cash box, which was considered a symbol of authority.

C. Polite phrases such as "Would you mind?" not only enable us to make our daily interactions smooth, but also imply that we are a person with good manners.

D. Hall Caine was successful in the field of literature even though he didn't have much schooling, but many people think he died poor and unknown.

【中学校】

【1】Substitute the underlined phrase with the best alternative from the four choices.

(1) Although he graduated from this high school, he visits here once in a while.

A. specifically B. consequently C. occasionally
D. greatly

(2) A friend of mine told me her new novel would be published next week.

A. come out B. pull through C. drift apart D. blend in

(3) Don't put off until tomorrow what you can do today.

A. raise　B. postpone　C. occur　D. memorize

(4) Her words gave me the power to <u>carry on</u>.

A. come across　B. get over　C. continue　D. support

(5) We <u>fell out with</u> each other over trifles.

A. got back into　B. stood in for　C. delved into

D. quarreled with

(☆☆☆☆◎◎◎◎◎)

【2】Put the words in the correct order, and answer with the numbers.

(1) 彼らは，これを最後に自分たちの計画をあきらめた。

They gave up [① for　② plans　③ their　④ and　⑤ once] all.

(2) 彼女がメッセージをくれたので，そこへ行く手間が省けました。

Her [① going　② me　③ message　④ of　⑤ spared　⑥ the trouble] there.

(3) 彼は，私たちが立っていたところから約30歩以内のところにいた。

He was [① about　② of　③ paces　④ thirty　⑤ where　⑥ within] we were standing.

(4) この山を，12月に登るのは危険です。

This [① climb　② dangerous　③ in　④ is　⑤ mountain　⑥ to] December.

(5) チョコレートを食べ過ぎると虫歯になりやすい。

Teeth may [① be　② chocolate　③ eaten　④ if　⑤ is　⑥ ruined] too much.

(☆☆☆◎◎◎◎◎)

【3】Read the following passage and choose the best sentence for each of [1]～[4] from the six choices below.

A: Excuse me.

B: Good morning, sir. Can I help you?

A: [1], so I'm looking for the right flight to get there.

B: Sure. You can take Flight 310.

A: What time do I have to be at the gate for Flight 310?

B: Let's see. [2], so there is plenty of time. You have more than an hour.

A: Great. Before the flight, I think I'll have enough time to drink coffee, then.

B: [3]. You can go there and enjoy some coffee.

A: Sounds nice. Where is it?

B: [4].

A. It will leave at 11

B. You can cancel the flight

C. I'll show you the way

D. I want to go to New York today

E. You need to be in a hurry

F. We have a famous restaurant in this airport

(☆☆◎◎◎)

【4】Read the following passage and answer the questions below.

At some point in our lives, we all meet the Student Who Tests Well Without Trying. "I have no idea what happened," says she, holding up her 99 percent score. "I hardly even studied." "It's a type you can never entirely escape, even in adulthood, as parents of school-age children quickly discover. "I don't know what it is, but Daniel just scores off the charts on these standardized tests," says Mom — dumbfounded! — at school pickup. "He certainly doesn't get it from me." No matter how much we prepare, no matter how early we rise, there's always someone who does better with less, who magically comes alive at game time.

I'm not here to explain that kid. I don't know of any study that looks at test taking as a discrete, stand-alone skill, or any evidence that it is an inborn gift, like perfect pitch. I don't need research to tell me that this type exists; I've seen it too often with my own eyes. I'm also old enough to know that being jealous isn't any way to close the gap between us and them. Neither is working harder. (Trust me, I've already tried that.)

No, the only way to develop any real test taking mojo is [①]. The truth is not so self-evident, and it has more dimensions than you might guess.

The first thing to say about testing is this: Disasters happen. To everyone. Who hasn't opened a test booklet and encountered a list of questions that seem related to a different course altogether? I have a favorite story about this, a story I always go back to in the wake of any collapse. The teenage Winston Churchill spent weeks preparing for the entrance exam into Harrow, the prestigious English boys school. He wanted badly to get in. On the big day, in March of 1888, he opened the exam and found, [②] history and geography, an unexpected emphasis on Latin and Greek. His mind went blank, he wrote later, and he was unable to answer a single question. "I wrote my name at the top of the page. I wrote down the number of the question, '1.' After much reflection I put a bracket round it, thus, '(1).' But thereafter I could not think of anything connected with it that was either relevant or true. Incidentally there arrived from nowhere in particular a blot and several smudges. I gazed for two whole hours at this sad spectacle; and then merciful ushers collected up my piece of foolscap and carried it up to the Headmaster's table."

And that's *Winston Churchill.*

The next thing to say is less obvious, though it's rooted in a far more common type of blown test. We open the booklet and see familiar questions on material we've studied, stuff we've highlighted with yellow marker: names, ideas, formulas we could recite with ease only yesterday. No trick questions, no pink elephants, and still we lay an egg. Why? How? I did so myself on one of the worst possible days: a trigonometry final I needed to ace to get into an Advanced Placement course, junior year. I spent weeks preparing. Walking into the exam that day, I remember feeling pretty good. When the booklets were handed out, I scanned the questions and took an easy breath. The test had a few of the concepts I'd studied, as well as familiar kinds of questions, which I'd practiced dozens of times.

I can do this, I thought.

Yet I scored somewhere in the low 50s, in the very navel of average. (These days, a score like that would prompt many parents to call a psychiatrist.) Who did I blame? Myself. I knew the material but didn't hear the music. I was a "bad test taker," I was kicking myself—but for all the wrong reasons.

The problem wasn't that I hadn't worked hard enough, of that I lacked the test taking "gene." No, my mistake was misjudging the depth of what I knew. I was duped by what psychologists call fluency, the belief that because facts or formulas or arguments are easy to remember *right now*, they'll remain that way tomorrow or the next day. The fluency illusion is so strong that, once we feel we've nailed some topic or assignment, we assume that further study won't help. We forget that we forget. Any number of study "aids" can create fluency illusions, including (yes) highlighting, making a study guide, and even chapter outlines provided by a teacher or textbook. 【 A 】 Fluency misperceptions are automatic. They form subconsciously and make us poor judges of what we need to restudy, or practice again. "We know that if you study something twice, in spaced sessions, it's harder to process the material the second time, and so people think it's counterproductive," as Nate Kornell, a psychologist at Williams College, told me. "But the opposite is true: You learn more, even though it feels harder. Fluency is playing a trick on judgment."

So it is that we end up attributing our poor test results to "test anxiety" or —too often—stupidity.

Let's recall the Bjorks' "desirable difficulty" principle: The harder your brain has to work to dig out a memory, the greater the increase in learning (retrieval and storage strength). 【 B 】 The *easier* it is to call a fact to mind, the smaller the increase in learning. Repeating facts right after you've studied them gives you nothing, no added memory benefit.

The fluency illusion is the primary culprit in below-average test performances. 【　C　】 Not anxiety. Not stupidity. Not unfairness or bad luck. Fluency.

The best way to overcome this illusion and improve our testing skills is, conveniently, an effective study technique in its own right. The technique is not exactly a recent invention; people have been employing it since the dawn of formal education, probably longer. 【　D　】 Here's the philosopher Francis Bacon, spelling it out in 1620: "If you read a piece of text through twenty times, you will not learn it by heart so easily as if you read it ten times while attempting to recite it from time to time and consulting the text when your memory fails." And here's the irrepressible William James, in 1890, musing about the same concept: "A curious peculiarity of our memory is that things are impressed better by active than by passive repetition. I mean that in learning—by heart, for example—when we almost know the piece, it pays better to wait and recollect by an effort from within, than to look at the book again. If we recover the words in the former way, we shall probably know them the next time: if in the latter way, we shall very likely need the book once more."

The technique is testing itself. Yes, I am aware of how circular this logic appears: better testing through testing. Don't be fooled. There's more to self-examination than you know. A test is not only a measurement tool, it alters what we remember and *changes* how we subsequently organize that knowledge in our minds. And it does so in ways that greatly improve later performance.

(1) Choose the most appropriate one for [　①　] from the four choices below.

A. to know what kind of skills they are using in test taking

B. to search for the reasons why kids get high scores

C. to understand more deeply what exactly testing is

D. to make kids realize what their parents want

(2) Choose the most appropriate word for [②] from the four choices below.

A. instead of B. relying on C. on behalf of
D. depending on

(3) Choose the most appropriate place, from 【 A 】～【 D 】 in the text, to put the sentence below.

Fluency, then, is the flipside of that equation.

(4) According to the text, which of the following is true?

A. The reason why the author was a "bad test taker" was that he didn't have enough time to study for the exam.

B. The author thinks that people feel it is more difficult to process the material the second time if you study it twice.

C. The way to get over the fluency illusion and improve your testing skills is to use the latest effective study skills people have been employing.

D. Reading a piece of a text is not as effective a way to memorize something as trying to recite it from time to time and consulting it when your memory fails.

(5) Considering what is written in the passage, write your own thoughts on how teachers should use tests in approximately 100 words in English.

(☆☆☆☆☆◎◎◎◎◎)

【5】Translate the underlined sentences into English.

(1) 最近，電子マネーの普及が進んでおり，私たちの暮らしは便利になりました。現金を持っていなくても，コンビニで電子マネーを使う人の姿をしばしば見かけるようになってきた。このような変化は時代のニーズに応じたものであるが，<u>お金を消費している意識が薄れている危険性を指摘する人もいる</u>。

(2) 記録的な大雨が私たちの食卓に大きな影響を与えています。<u>大雨により，ここ数ヶ月間，日々の野菜の価格が高騰している</u>。

(☆☆☆☆◎◎◎◎◎)

【高等学校】

【１】Read the following passage and answer the questions below.

'I believe that you can be both empathetic and strong, that you can be a leader and also be kind. I always thought that the notion of "mother of the nation" also has that same implication.'

①These are the words of Prime Minister Jacinda Ardern as she comments on the fact that some New Zealanders use the terminology 'mother of the nation' to refer to her.

But the world's fascination with motherhood and Jacinda has not arisen because of such a metaphor. It is the result of her actually becoming a mother while in office, the second woman to ever do so. The first was Benazir Bhutto, the prime minister of Pakistan, back in 1990.

②The circumstances of the two pregnancies could not have been more different. Prime Minister Bhutto hid her pregnancy from her colleagues and the nation. At the same time as having her child she was at the centre of a political storm, which resulted in a no-confidence vote and the eventual dismissal of her government by the president.

In today's era, when any woman of child-bearing age in the public eye is likely to see headlines that scream 'baby bump' if she so much as eats an extra sandwich at lunch, secrecy was never going to be an option for Jacinda. On 19 January 2018, less than three months after being sworn in as prime minister, Jacinda announced she was expecting a baby with her partner, Clarke Gayford. Baby Neve was born on 21 June. ③Jacinda became the first prime minister ever to take maternity leave.

It is an extraordinary story and an ordinary one all wrapped together.

A couple in their early thirties falls in love. They decide that they want to have children but experience difficulties falling pregnant. The woman then gets an amazing promotion at work, and not long after falls pregnant. [　1　]

What is extraordinary is that Jacinda has experienced this under a white-hot global spotlight, which has thrown into stark relief all the practical and perceived issues of combining motherhood and leadership.

Male leaders who are the fathers of small children are likely to be viewed as in touch with everyday life. Specifically, a father can use his status to demonstrate he understands the pressures on voters as they struggle to make a good life for their children.

[2] As discussed in the last chapter, a woman with young children may be seen as approachable and caring. However, there is a risk that voters will worry about her ability to acquit the rigours of political life because of her caring responsibilities. For men, such questions tend not to be raised because it is assumed that wives are undertaking the principal caring role.

*Julia saw this first-hand during her political career. [3] Only her female colleagues reported being asked at community meetings about who would be minding the kids.

Our fifth hypothesis draws on these experiences and breaks down into two parts. First, that *Having children and being a leader plays out differently for women than it does for men*. We think one evidence point for this hypothesis is that, to date, the women who have made it to the top echelons of political leadership disproportionately did not have children or their children were adults at the time of their political career.

The second string to our hypothesis is that *White being childless means a woman leader has not had to face the challenges of combining work and family life, it brings other issues*. We explore this through the experiences of Theresa and Julia.

To gather information from our women leaders for this hypothesis we asked how they weighed up and made their choices about whether to marry, when to marry, whether to have children and when to have children. We also inquired whether they faced community or media questioning about their family life, including their life partner and caring for their children, that were not routinely asked of male politicians. [4] Our final question was how their families felt about the way politics impacted their lives.

To hear the answers, let us go first to the women leaders who directly combined leadership and child-raising, Jacinda and Erna.

*Julia　Julia Gillard, one of the co-authors of this book, and a former Prime Minister of Australia

(1) Translate the underlined ① into Japanese.

(2) Choose the best sentence for each blank of [　1　]−[　4　] from the four choices below. You can use each choice only once.

A. For female leaders, the perception of family is more mixed.

B. This could well be the story of your sister, your next-door neighbour, a colleague at work.

C. She served with women and men who were combining having a family with being in parliament.

D. We invited them to tell us about the practical reality of managing their multiple roles as a spouse and mother with their political career.

(3) Choose the most appropriate meaning of each of the underlined ② and ③ from the four choices below respectively.

②

A. The case of Prime Minister Ardern and that of Prime Minister Bhutto are different.

B. The case of Prime Minister Ardern and that of Prime Minister Bhutto are the same.

C. The case of Prime Minister Ardern and that of Prime Minister Bhutto are easy to compare.

D. The case of Prime Minister Ardern and that of Prime Minister Bhutto are difficult to explain.

③

A. In order not to lose her position as the prime minister, Jacinda didn't take days off for caring for her baby.

B. Before giving birth to her baby, Jacinda was determined to resign her position as the prime minister.

C. Keeping her position as the prime minister, Jacinda was allowed to be away from her work to care for her baby.

D. There was a previous example that a female prime minister took time off to care for her baby, so Jacinda did the same thing.

(4) Find a word from the passage which matches the following definition.

an idea or explanation of something that is based on a few known facts but that has not yet been proved to be true or correct

(5) Filling in the blanks with the designated number of words, complete the following summary.

When Jacinda Ardern, Prime Minister of New Zealand, fell pregnant, she faced the stereotype that women have ＿A(5-7)＿. In addition, there would be a possibility that some people would doubt whether ＿B(5-7)＿ while caring for her child. As history records, however, people in New Zealand welcomed her pregnancy.

(☆☆☆☆◎◎◎◎◎)

【2】Read the following passage and answer the questions below.

Can we say anything with confidence about the origin of language? One current theory starts from the role of grooming in the social behaviour of related species. In many other primates social groups are quite small, and, so long as they do not get too large, this is an efficient means of forming and maintaining relationships. Human societies, in contrast, are not small, and the suggestion is that over time larger groups evolved in which relationships were maintained instead through complex forms of verbal behaviour. 'Language' was a more effective way of holding such societies together.

'Language', however, must be put in inverted commas. Complex forms of vocal behaviour are not necessarily language as we know it, and, if language-like forms of communication may have had that role in the beginning, what has since evolved has many others. There is no strict analogy between language, not now in inverted commas, and anything we observe in other primates. Nor are there evident homologies. ①<u>Homologies</u> exist where similar features have a common evolutionary origin: human arms, for instance, are homologous with the front legs of quadrupeds. There are also homologies in behaviour, in the calls of primates, among others, whose lines have been separate for longer than ours and the chimpanzees'. ②<u>Analogies</u> exist where features that may have a different evolutionary origin have similar functions: a bat's wing, for example, is analogous to that of a bird. Our basic problem is that, where language is concerned, there are no similarities of either kind that we can latch on to. It is therefore difficult to rule out any plausible theory. Some have even suggested, for example, that the structure of language originally evolved in complex kinds of gestures, and that it was only later that a similar complexity developed in a spoken form.

A less speculative question is what kind of evolution we are primarily concerned with. In other species, there is little doubt that behaviour is in part [③]. For some we know that it is also, in part, [④]: one kind of evidence for this can be seen when behaviour varies from one troop of monkeys, for example, to another. Beyond that, however, behaviour is explained by genetic evolution. Individuals behaving in certain ways have had greater reproductive success; their offspring have inherited their genes and behaved similarly, and so on.

In the case of language we are insiders, and are well aware of what can only be [⑤]. If I grew up speaking English, it is because my experience as a child was of people around me who themselves spoke English. If a baby of English-speaking parents was to be adopted and taken to France by a French-speaking couple, it would as readily, with the same genes, grow up speaking French and not English. One is not genetically 'programmed', as it were, to speak English, French, or any form of speech in any particular community. Our problem then is whether that is the whole story. Particular languages are a product of 'cultural' evolution, of cumulative interactions within human societies, independent of genes. To what extent, despite that, has the structure of speech in general evolved through genetic inheritance?

There are two independent ways to approach this question, neither at all easy. One way is to ask how language is now learned by children. Can we explain its development entirely by a process of learning through experience? In the view of Noam Chomsky, in particular, we [⑥]. The crucial period in which speech develops is quite short, and in normal children it develops uniformly, with few even relative failures. What develops is remarkably complex, especially in the patterns in which units like words are combined. These vary greatly across languages, but certain kinds of pattern always seem to be excluded. The question then is whether that can be, in any strict sense, learned. The experience of language actually available to children is no more than what they hear, what is said to them, and how people react when they themselves speak. Although there is 'learning' , ⑦this does not amount to systematic 'teaching' . Yet adults know not just how words can be combined, but also that specific kinds of combination are impossible. Is the input from experience a sufficient basis for ⑧this?

The answer, according to Chomsky and many linguists who have followed him, is [⑨]. There must, in addition, be a set of abstract principles of language which are strictly not learned but genetically inherited. The development of language in a child is thus to be explained by interaction of the input from experience with the structures these principles determine.

If Chomsky is right, the basic puzzle is the evolution of these structural principles, through genetic changes. 'Language-like' behaviour could still have evolved in earlier species: perhaps as early as *H. habilis*, whose fossils are associated with stone tools. Language as we know it must, however, have evolved in *H. sapiens* alone. In one seductive view, language first appeared in a particular population that palaeontologists classify as 'anatomically modern' . ⑩This population can be dated back some 100,000 years, and with it structurally modern language would have spread across the globe, as all other *Homo* species or subspecies lost out through their failure to compete successfully. The time-scale for its evolution is so short that, in one extreme view, we are forced to posit chance genetic changes.

(1) Explain the underlined words ① with about 50 Japanese characters with the concrete example from the passage.

homologies(相同)とは，(　　)

(2) Explain the underlined words ② with about 50 Japanese characters with the concrete example from the passage.

analogies(相似)とは，(　　)

(3) Choose the best combination of phrases for [③], [④], and [⑤] from the four choices below.

A. ③ genetically inherited ④ learned through experience ⑤ learned through experience

B. ③ genetically inherited ④ learned through experience ⑤ genetically inherited

C. ③ learned through experience ④ genetically inherited ⑤ genetically inherited

D. ③ learned through experience ④ genetically inherited ⑤ learned through experience

(4) Choose the best combination of words for [⑥] and [⑨] from the four choices below.

A. ⑥ can ⑨ yes　B. ⑥ can ⑨ no

C. ⑥ cannot ⑨ yes　D. ⑥ cannot ⑨ no

(5) What does the underlined ⑦ indicate? Explain it with about 80 Japanese characters.

(6) What does the underlined ⑧ indicate? Explain it with about 50 Japanese characters.

(7) Translate the underlined ⑨ into Japanese, beginning with the words given in the answer sheet.

この集団は，(　　)

【3】Read the following passage and answer the questions below.

A crucial aspect of a successful lesson is the extent to which the teacher is able to create a positive environment for learning. Classroom management refers to ways in which both the physical and the affective dimensions of the class are arranged in order to provide an environment that promotes successful teaching and learning. In an ideal classroom, students pay attention to what the teacher is trying to achieve; they behave with respect towards the teacher and other students in the class; they participate actively in activities the teacher has assigned; and the class functions as a cohesive group that collaborates to help make the lesson a positive learning experience. When classes function in this way, the teacher is able to focus on achieving the instructional goals he or she has set for the lesson. In some classes, however, the teacher may have to work hard and use specific strategies and procedures to maintain a productive classroom learning environment. These aspects of teaching relate to issues of classroom management, which is concerned with creating an effective classroom climate, using the time and space available in the classroom efficiently and effectively, and establishing a shared understanding of appropriate norms for classroom interaction and behaviour. Classroom management is concerned with more than discipline, since it relates to how teachers and learners see their roles in the classroom and the kind of learning community that develops in the classroom. Wright (2005: 3) describes the central issues involved in classroom management as responses to three issues:

- The importance of human relations and the emotional dimensions of teaching and learning in classroom management.
- The concept of participation in classroom life, and how management practices contribute to participation patterns.

● How the ever-present factors of time and space, which define formal education, influence management practices.

Although classroom management is an aspect of the teaching of any subject, language classes present their own issues in relation to classroom management. The subject has received relatively little serious attention within applied linguistics (with the exception of Wright's exceptional book on the topic), but it is an issue that novice and experienced language teachers deal with on a daily basis. Two trends have led, in recent years, to a rethinking of the role of classroom management in language teaching. One was the emergence of communicative language teaching and learner-centred philosophies, such as the learner-autonomy movement and cooperative learning, which prompted a rethinking of traditional teacher-fronted teaching, as well as the roles of teachers and learners in the classroom. A focus on lerner-centredness in the classroom led to new learning arrangements, such as pair and group-based activities, which require different styles of participation and management from traditional teacher-directed teaching.

(1) According to the passage, what happens in an ideal classroom? Answer two concrete examples out of some examples in this passage in Japanese.

(2) What brought a focus on learner-centredness in the classroom? Answer in English.

(3) What do you think are successful pair and group-based activities and what can we do to make pair and group-based activities work well? Express your own idea with concrete examples and reasons, using about 150 words in English.

(☆☆☆☆☆◎◎◎◎◎)

解答・解説

【中高共通】

【1】(1) B (2) A (3) D (4) A (5) B (6) A
(7) C (8) C (9) B (10) D (11) C (12) A
(13) D (14) B (15) B (16) A (17) C (18) B
(19) B (20) D

〈解説〉(1) 第4文型cause A B「AにB(悪いこと)をもたらす」が適切。change A into B「AをBに変える」, expect A from B「AをBに期待する」, promote A「Aを昇進させる」はいずれも第4文型は選択しない。なお, anxiety「心配, 不安」は不可算名詞であるため冠詞がついていない。(2) 彼へのプレゼントを自分の家に置いてきてしまったため, それをfetch「～をとってくる」まで, 彼は待ってくれた。neglect A「Aを放っておく」, acclaim A「Aをほめたたえる(通常受身)」。 (3) 予約に対してpunctual [in/for] A「Aの時間を守る」でなければならない。accurate [in] A「Aに正確な」, strict [with, to/on] A「Aに厳密な」, precise [in/about] A「Aの点で慎重な」。 (4) brisk「活発な, きびきびした」はwalkと共起しやすい形容詞である。such a A that「とても～なAなので…」のthat節で述べられている内容は彼女について行くには走らなければならなかったということであるため, slowは不適切。bull「雄牛のような」, slack「ゆるい」。 (5)「彼女は残りの人生を医者として働く意図はなかった」という文意。intention of doing「～する意図, 意向, つもり」。mindも「意向, 気持ち」という意味があるが, 通例所有格の代名詞に後続する用法が多く, of doingは共起しない。(6)「Markは家の分割払いの頭金を支払うのに十分な額を貯金するのに3年かかった」の文意。accumulate A「Aを蓄積する」, cultivate A「Aを耕す」, designate A for B「AをBに指名する」, formulate A「A(計画など)を練り上げる」。 (7) in exchange for A「Aと引き換えに」, in favor of A「Aに有利になるように, Aに賛成の」, in terms of A「Aの観点から」, in consideration for[of] A「Aを考慮して, Aの返礼として」。
(8)　文意は「ニューヨークは毎年多くの国から移民がやってくるため, 世界で最も民族的に多様な都市の一つだ」である。because以下の内容を踏まえるとdiverse「多様な, 種々の」が適切。coherent「筋の通った, 一貫した」, crucial「極めて重大な」, uniform「同形の, 均一の」。
(9)　immerse oneself in A「Aに没頭する」はbe immersed in Aと置き換えることができる。英語が話されている環境にimmerse「どっぷり浸かる」ような留学プログラムに応募したことを表している。
(10)　文意は「山の頂上まで約6,000キロメートルであり, ふもとから見ると, 走るのはいわんや, 歩いて登るのは不可能に思われた」である。much less…は「(否定的語句の後で)いわんや［まして, なおさら］(…ではない)」という意味。no less than A「Aほども多くの(= as many [much] as)」, more or less「多かれ少なかれ」, still(even)＋比較級「なお一層…」。　(11)　代名詞allは複数形扱いであり, 3人称のhasに不適切。everyは形容詞としての用法のみであり, 代名詞として使えない。「誰もいない」という否定の代名詞はnoではなくnoneやneitherなどが用いられる。eachはof＋複数代名詞を伴って「おのおの, めいめい」という意味を表し, 単数扱いが原則であるが, 略式では複数扱いのこともある。　(12)　isolation from A「Aからの孤立」, moderation in A「Aの節制」, prevention against A「Aの予防」, interruption to A「Aの中断」。　(13)　文意は「本がさかさまであったため, 彼女は本を読んでいるふりをしているだけであるとわかった」である。選択肢はいずれも何かを演じることを表す語であるが,「(偽って)～のふりをする」という意味を有するのはpretendのみである。　(14)　分詞構文の主語が主節の主語と異なる際には明示されが, 天候を表す主語はitであるため, it beingが適切。It wasは接続詞がないため不適切。　(15)　文意は「今や教師であるため, 彼はそう考えていない」である。neverthelessは文修飾の副詞(主に文頭)であり「それにもかかわらず」という意味。
(16)　前置詞を伴う目的格関係代名詞の用法はwh-で始まる疑問詞のみである。introduce A to B「AをBに紹介する」。　(17)　文意は「いいわよ。でも机の上の書類をいじらないでね。乱雑にしないでほしいの」である。hand off A「Aを任せる，委託する」，give up A「Aをやめる」，mess with A「Aにちょっかいを出す，Aに干渉する」，branch out「(ビジネスの)手を広げる」。　(18)　付帯状況のwith「～のままで」の用法はwith O Cである。「目を閉じながら」は主語によって目が閉じられるため，with A's eyes closedが適切。　(19)　a compulsory subject「必修科目」はa required subjectとも呼ばれる。biased「偏った，偏見を持った」，divine「神の」，rusty「錆びついた」。　(20)　文意は「ABC書店の初年度の売上は，この会社が今期の目標を達成する可能性が高いことを示している」である。brand A as B「AをBだと烙印を押す」，grasp A「Aを握る，Aを理解する」，nourish A「Aに栄養を与える」，indicate that「～であることを示す」。

【2】(1)　①　in　⑫　to　(2)　②　pondering　⑥　devoured　⑧　inspired　⑪　face　(3)　③　that she show two teenagers who had been assigned　⑩　had he not written an essay expressing his admiration　(4)　④　B　⑨　A　(5)　A　(6)　ロセッティがこの鍛冶屋の息子をロンドンに招き，彼の秘書として務めるように招いたこと。　(7)　A　confident in himself　B　beyond description　C　he found that Mr. Rowland recognized his importance　(8)　C

〈解説〉(1)　①　A is in charge of B「AはBに責任を負う」はB is in the charge of Aという関係性にある。　⑫　superiorはthanではなくtoを用いることに注意。類似する表現としてはinferior，minor，prior，preferなどがある。　(2)　devour A「Aをむさぼる，Aの虜になる」，face A「Aに直面する，出会う」，inspire A「Aを奮起させる」，ponder A「Aを熟考する」。　②　チャリティコンサートの責任者になったSmithが何をするべきかを考えていた時に権力のシンボルである手提げ金庫をスタッフが渡してくれた。　⑥　Hall Caineがソネット(14行詩)とバラッド(民間伝承の物語詩)が好きであることが述べられており，Dante Gabriel Rossettiの詩の虜になったと推測できる。　⑧　blacksmith(鍛冶屋)の息子であるHall CaineがRossettiの秘書としてロンドンに招待されて以来，文学作家と会うようになった。この作家たちのアドバイスと励ましを受けて自分の名前を世間に轟かせるようになった。このことから，inspiredが適切。　⑪　教室で出会う生徒の一人ひとりが世界にとって重要であることを思い出させるように“YOU ARE IMPORTANT”と書かれた掲示を教室に飾っていることが述べられている。　(3)　③　動詞suggest to A that「Aに～と提案する，～を勧める」の目的語となるthat節では，動詞が原形となる。assign A to B「AをBに割り当てる」。　⑩　express A's admiration for B「Bに対するAの賞賛を示す」。助動詞hadを主語の前に出すことで(倒置)，withoutと同じ意味を表している。　(4)　④　下線部の内容はフランスの大使や集会の議長になる前に，philosophy of appreciationを使うことができることを表している。つまり権力を持たない人であったとしてもphilosophy of appreciationが使えるということであるため，Bが適切。⑨　世界中から観光客(tourists)が訪れるメッカ(聖地)になることを意味している。Bはa limited partの部分がfrom the far corners of the worldと矛盾する。Cはa religious reasonの部分がtouristsと矛盾する。Dはonly people who can appreciate literary workの部分がtouristsと矛盾する。
(5)　フライドポテトを注文したのに，店員がマッシュポテトを出したとき，「ご迷惑をかけて申し訳ないけれど，フライドポテトの方が好きなの」と言うことで，「全然かまいませんよ」と返してくれることが述べられている。これは店員に対して敬意を払ったためであると考えられることから，因果関係を示すbecauseが適切。　(6)　下線⑦の直前の内容をまとめればよい。なお，blacksmith's sonは前の段落で登場しているHall Caineのことである。　(7)　本文中に述べられているある生徒についての要約文を空所補充する。Chrisは，美術工芸に関して自信のない(lacking in self-confidence)14歳の内気な生徒だが，Chrisの内なる情熱を見抜いたMr. Rowlandは上級のクラスにChrisを招待する。B　本文中のI had to leave at that point because tears were coming to my eyes.から「言い表せない感情」であったと言える。　C　本文中のour

deep desire to feel importantや "Every man I meet is my superior in some way. In that, I learn of him." などから，他人から大切な存在であると思われることが示されている。 (8) A David G. Smithが依頼したのはRoseのみであるため2人の両方に依頼していない。 B without any particular intentionの部分が不適切。実際には雰囲気の悪かった2人の雰囲気をよくする意図があった。 D Hall Caineがベストセラーを発売しているためbut many people think he died poor and unknownの部分が不適切。

【中学校】

【1】(1) C (2) A (3) B (4) C (5) D

〈解説〉(1) once in a while「ときどき」に最も意味が近いのはoccasionally「ときどき」である。なお，occasionallyはsometimesより頻度が低く，日常会話ではonce in a whileがよく使われる。specifically「明確に」，consequently「その結果，したがって」。 (2) publish A「Aを出版する」が受動態で用いられているため，選択肢は自動詞である必要がある。come outには，「(本などが)出版される」以外にも「(花が)咲く」，「(ニュースなどが)知られる，広まる」などの意味もある。 (3) put off Aには，「Aを～まで延期する」，「Aを不快にする」，「A(電灯やラジオなど)を消す」などの意味がある。今回はuntil節が後続していたため，postpone A「Aを延期する」が適切。 (4) ここでのcarry onは自動詞として使われており，「続ける」という意味を表す。come across A「Aに偶然出くわす」，get over A「Aを乗り越える，Aを克服する」。 (5) fall out with A「Aと喧嘩する，仲違いする」。get back into A「Aに復帰する」，stand in for A「Aの代理を務める」，delve into A「A(資料・情報など)を求めて掘り下げる，徹底的に調べる，手を突っ込む」，quarrel with A「Aと口論する」。

【2】(1)　③→②→⑤→④→①　　(2)　③→⑤→②→⑥→④→①
(3)　⑥→①→④→③→②→⑤　　(4)　⑤→④→②→⑥→①→③
(5)　①→⑥→④→②→⑤→③

〈解説〉(1)　整序後の英文はThey gave up their plans once and for all.である。give up A「A (考えなど) を諦める」, once and for all「この一回限りで, これを最後にキッパリと」。　(2)　整序後の英文はHer message spared me the trouble of going there.である。spare A the trouble「Aに面倒をかけない」。　(3)　整序後の英文はHe was within about thirty paces of where we were standing.である。paceは可算名詞で「1歩」という意味を表す。「私たちが立っていたところから」を表現する際には前置詞fromが選択肢の候補にないため, ofが用いられている。このofの用法は出所や根源を表すofである。　(4)　整序後の英文はThis mountain is dangerous to climb in December.である。この構文はtough構文とも呼ばれ, 難易や安全・危険, 快・不快を表す形容詞を使う際に目的語が主語になるという特徴がある。　(5)　整序後の英文はTeeth may be ruined if chocolate is eaten too much.である。主節とif節の両方で受動態が用いられておりbe動詞と過去分詞が2つあるが, 助動詞mayに後続するのは原形であるためbeが最初に用いられる。ruin A「Aをだめにする」。

【3】1　D　　2　A　　3　F　　4　C

〈解説〉1　航空会社の職員に問い合わせをする旅行客の発話である。thereに該当する地名を述べているDが適切。　2　310便に搭乗するにはゲートにいつまでに行けばいいかという質問に対する返答。飛行機の出発時刻が11時であることを述べたAが適切。空所直後に十分に時間があることが述べられているため, Eは不適切。　3　空所の直後では, そこでコーヒーを飲めると言っているので, 有名レストランが空港にあると述べているFが適切。　4　レストランはどこかを尋ねられたため, 道順を教えることを申し出ているCが適切。

【4】(1) C (2) A (3) B (4) D (5) Although tests are often used as some assessment of whether a student is studying hard enough, teachers should use tests as a reflection of themselves in some sense. They can see how well their students understand what they have learnt. Through the tests, teachers can check their students' ability and see what students can understand or not. Teachers can think about how to improve the weak points of their students in theirs classes. They also have a chance to look back on their lessons using the results and think about how they will change their classes in the future. (99 words)

〈解説〉(1) 空所①では「勉強をしなくともテストでいい点を取ることができる生徒の謎」に取り組む方法について述べている。前の段落ではテスト受験に関するスキルが絶対音感のように生得的な能力であり，このような能力に関する研究やこの能力を有する人と普通の人と比べることは不要であることが示されている。そのためAやBは不適切。親が子どもに求めていることは述べられていないため，Dも不適切。テスト受験者やテスト受験の方略に関する研究よりも，テストそのものに関する研究が重要であることが示されているCが適切。

(2) イギリスの名門男子校であるハーロウ校に入学しようと思って何週間も準備していたウィンストン・チャーチルは，受験日当日にテスト冊子を開くとラテン語とギリシア語のテストであった。1問も解答できないチャーチルは全ての解答に1と記入をした。このことから，何週間もかけて勉強した歴史と地理の代わりにラテン語とギリシア語が出題されていたと分かる。instead of A「Aの代わりに」，relying on A「Aを頼りにする」，on behalf of A「Aを代表して」，depending on A「Aに応じて」。 (3) Fluency, then, is the flipside of that equation.「そうしたら，fluencyはその方程式のマイナス面である」が入る適切な位置をA～Dの中で選ぶ。 A fluencyの特徴を説明している途中であり，flipsideはまだ説明されていないので，不適切。 B 前後ではBjorkの「望ましい困難さ」について述べている。「望ましい困難さ」は記憶を思い出す際に一定の困難を伴う方が学習に効果的であることを指しており，fluencyが高くなることは思い出しやすくなるため学習が逆に効果的でなくなることを意味している。よって，fluencyのflipsideについて述べているため，適切。　C　一生懸命に勉強してfluencyが高い状態で，テストの平均点以下の得点しか取れなかった原因はテストへの不安や自分自身の愚かさ，不公平，運のなさではなく，fluency illusionであることが述べられているのみであるため，不適切。　D　初期の研究者の引用などを紹介しているセクションであり，fluencyのflipsideについてはほとんど言及されていないため，不適切。　(4)　A　インストラクションを聞かずにテストを解いていたことが理由であるため不適切。　B　fluencyが上がることから，2回目にはdifficultではなくeasyであるため不適切。また，そのように著者が考えていることは述べられていない。　C　冒頭でテスト受験の方略を研究することは必要ないことが述べられているため不適切。　D　空所Aのセクションで述べられていることと一致するので，正しい。　(5)　本文で述べられていることに基づいて，教師としてテストをどのように使うべきかを100語程度で作文させる問題。解答例ではテスト評価論に基づき，テストのフィードバックについて述べている。テストを実施するだけでなく，生徒は自分の能力を測定でき，教師は自分自身の授業改善もできる。

【5】(1)　some people point out that we may be at the risk of losing the sense that we are spending money.　(2)　The heavy rain caused the prices of vegetables to rise daily for a few months.

〈解説〉(1)　point out that「～と指摘する」，at the risk of A「Aをかけて，Aの危険を冒して」，lose A「Aを失う」，the sense that「～という感覚」，spend money「お金を使う」。　(2)　heavy rain「大雨」，cause A to do「Aに～させる」，rise「(価格が)上がる，(商品が)値上がりする」。無生物主語を用いて「大雨によって」という原因を表現している。価格の増加にはincreaseを使わないことに注意が必要である。

【高等学校】

【1】(1)　これらは，彼女について言及するために「国家の母」という用語を用いるニュージーランド人がいるという事実について彼女が意見を言うときの，ジャシンダ・アーダーン首相の言葉である。

(2)　1　B　　2　A　　3　C　　4　D　　(3)　②　A　　③　C

(4)　hypothesis　　(5)　A　a larger responsibility for child rearing

B　she could lead the country

〈解説〉(1)　Prime Minister「首相」，as「～のときに」，comment on A「Aについて意見を述べる」，the fact that「～という事実」，terminology「用語」，nation「国家」，refer to A「Aについて言及する」。

(2)　1　空所直前に，なかなか子どもを授からなかった30代夫婦で，妻が素晴らしい昇進を遂げてまもなく妊婦になったことが述べられている。このような話は，読者の身近にもあると述べているBが適切である。　2　空所前の段落では小さい子どものいる男性の政治家について述べられ，空所のある段落では子育てをする女性の政治家について述べているので，政治活動と家庭のことを述べているAが適切。

3　空所前に，元オーストラリア首相ジュリア・ギラードのキャリアについて触れていることから，空所にはジュリア・ギラードに関する内容が入ると推察できる。代名詞sheが使われており，家庭を持つ男女が議員として両立できるように献身してきたという内容のCが適切。

4　空所の前後では，仮説を検証するために女性指導者から情報を得ようとしていることが述べられている。よって，政治的な側面と母親としての側面を併せ持つ女性政治家の現実について話してくれる人々を招いたとするDが適切。　(3)　②　下線部は「2人の妊婦の状況は全く異なる」という意味。not be moreは「この上なく～，最高に～」という意味であり，ネガティブな表現にもポジティブな表現にも使うことができる。この2人の妊婦とはニュージーランド首相ジャシンダ・アーダーンと元パキスタン首相ベナジル・ブットのことを指している。　③　下線部は「ジャシンダは首相として史上初となる産休をとった」という意味。　A　didn'tの部分が不適切。　B　resign A「Aを辞職する，辞任する」が不適切。　D　下線部のthe first prime minister everと矛盾する。　(4)　定義は「いくつかの既知の事実に基づいてはいるが，真実であったり正しかったりすることがまだ証明されていない考えや説明のこと」。よって，文中から「仮説」を意味する語を抜き出せばよい。　(5)　本文の内容の一部を要約した文を空所補充する。A　ジャシンダ・アーダーンは首相として初めて産休をとった女性であり，女性は育児をするべきであるというステレオタイプに立ち向かった。ステレオタイプの内容を5～7語でまとめる。　B　世間では首相が子どもの面倒を見ながら国を率いることができるのかどうか，疑問に思う人もいる。本文ではthere is a risk that voters will worry about her ability to acquit the rigours of political life because of her caring roleと述べられている。

【2】(1)　(homologies〔相同〕とは,)例えば人間の腕と四足動物の前足のように，ある共通の進化上の起源をもつ似たような特徴のことを指す。(48字)　(2)　(analogies〔相似〕とは,)例えばコウモリの翼と鳥の翼のように，進化上の起源は異なるかもしれないが，同じような機能をもつ特徴のことを指す。(55字)　(3)　A　(4)　D　(5)　子どもが実際に触れることのできる言語の体験は，彼らが耳にしたことや，彼らに向けて言われたこと，人々が話をするときに彼ら自身がどのように反応するかに過ぎないということ。(83字)　(6)　大人は，どのように語が結びつくのかだけでなく，特定の組み合わせは不可能であるということも理解しているということ。(57字)　(7)　(この集団は，)およそ10万年前にさかのぼることができ，他の全てのホモ属やその亜種が生存競争に失敗して消えゆく一方で，その集団とともに，現代の言語は世界中に広がっていったのだろう。

〈解説〉(1)・(2)　ともに，下線部の直後を50字程度にまとめればよい。(3)　第3段落・第4段落では，生き物の行為には③「(種によって)遺伝的に受け継がれる」ものと，④「経験を踏まえて学ばれる」ものとがあることが述べられている。人間が言語を話せることは，他の生き物と類似しておらず，相同関係も相似関係も見られない。また，同じ遺伝子であるにもかかわらず，英語が話されている環境で生まれ育ったのであれば英語を話し，フランス語が話されている環境で生まれ育ったのであればフランス語を話す。このことから，言語は⑤「経験を踏まえて学ばれる」ものと考えられる。　(4)　空所⑥の前には，「言語の習得はすべて経験を踏まえて学ぶ過程で説明できるのだろうか」と疑問が呈されており，第5段落・第6段落では，言語の習得に遺伝子がどの程度影響しているのかを明らかにする方法について述べられている。方法には2つあり，その1つは言語習得の経験について子どもに尋ねるというもの。しかし，アメリカの言語学者チョムスキーによると臨界期は非常に短く，通常に子どもは均一に言語を習得できる一方で言い間違いをする傾向にある。さらに，子どもはこれまでに聞いたことのないような文を話すことができる。このことから，チョムスキーは「できない」と考えている。さらに，多くの言語学者が述べることとして，子どもの言語発達は経験によるインプットと抽象的な原理の相互作用によるというものがあることから，子どもに言語習得の方法を尋ねることは不可能であると言える。よって，空所⑥・⑨のいずれにも否定的な語が入る。　(5)　下線部を含む文の直前の文The experience of language…に述べられている内容をまとめればよい。no more than「～に過ぎない」，they themselves「彼ら自身が」。　(6)　下線部を含む文の直前の文Yet adults know…に述べられている内容をまとめればよい。not just A, but also B「(＝not only A, but also B)AだけでなくBも」，combination「組み合わせ」。　(7)　population「集団」，date back「さかのぼる」，modern language「現代の言語」，spread across the globe「世界中に広がる」，as「(＝while)一方で」，subspecies「亜種」，lose out A「A(競争など)に負ける」，failure to do「～することの失敗」，compete successfully「競争して優勢になる」。

【3】(1)　・生徒たちが，教師が成し遂げようとしていることに注意を払う　・生徒たちが，クラスの中で教師や他の生徒に対して敬意をもってふるまう　・生徒たちが，教師が指示した活動に積極的に参加する　・授業が有益な言語体験となるのを助けるために協力するようなまとまりのある集団としてクラスが機能する　から2つ

(2)　The emergence of communicative language teaching and leaner-centered philosophies did.　(3)　We can consider the activities successful if students learn a lot through pair and group-based activities. In order for students to learn a lot through the activities, it is important that they have time for self-reflection after the activities. Then, students can find out what they've done well and what they haven't. Such awareness will make students not only realize what to improve but also keep them motivated for the next activity. One concrete way for them to look back is to use a self-assessment sheet. It will help them understand their own achievement level. Also, if students are informed beforehand about self-assessment, they may pay more attention to what they should do in the activities, and try harder to get involved in them. That will lead to more meaningful pair and group-based activities. So, carrying out self-assessment and informing students about it beforehand can make the activities successful and effective. (151 words)

〈解説〉(1)　望ましい教室環境については，第1パラグラフの3文目In an ideal classroom,…以下に具体例が述べられているので，そのうち2つを日本語で述べればよい。　(2)　学習者中心の教室環境をもたらしたものは，第2パラグラフ4文目前半に述べられている。　(3)　ペア・グループなどの学習者中心の活動を成功させるにはどうすればよいかを具体例と理由を含めて150語程度の英語で述べる。解答例では自己評価を挙げ，学習者が自己評価することによって改善すべき点が見えてくるだけでなく，次の活動へのモチベーションを保つことができるとしている。

2022年度　実施問題

【中高共通】

【1】Choose the answer that best completes the sentence from the four choices.

(1) All of the city's train lines were (　　) due to the heavy, unexpected snowfall.

A. halted　B. displaced　C. formulated　D. resembled

(2) The snack company (　　) their new line of low-calorie chocolate cake at last month's Natural Food Convention.

A. simulated　B. conserved　C. unveiled　D. retained

(3) Modern healthcare has (　　) people's average lifespan. People live much longer than they did only a few hundred years ago.

A. prolonged　B. informed　C. harvested　D. curbed

(4) A: Could I see the full report by Friday, Ken? And please don't (　　) any details.

B: Yes, of course. I'll be sure to include everything we know so far.

A. omit　B. berate　C. thrust　D. entwine

(5) Ten minutes earlier, (　　) we could have caught the last train.

A. so　B. and　C. therefore　D. unless

(6) A: You always fail because you act without thinking.

B: Right. I've always (　　). I take your advice to heart.

A. coped with things　B. gone over everything

C. ruled out risks　D. played my hunches

(7) We should avoid driving through downtown if you want to get there quickly. There is a lot of traffic (　　) at this time of day.

A. transcription　B. congestion　C. isolation

D. connection

(8) A: Do you have any (　　)?

B: Yes, I have two brothers and two sisters. I'm the oldest member of the family.

A. guardians　　B. tenants　　C. siblings　　D. spouses

(9) Taro's favorite thing about his new job was that there was no dress code. He'd always hated wearing business (　　).

A. ordeal　　B. stalwart　　C. attire　　D. perseverance

(10) It's an awful (　　) your son couldn't come. I was looking forward to seeing him.

A. shocking　　B. wrong　　C. shame　　D. deplore

(11) With a mighty (　　), the movers were just barely able to lift the refrigerator onto the back of the truck.

A. entourage　　B. upshot　　C. heave　　D. austerity

(12) Ryoko keeps (　　) records of her finances, so she knows exactly how much money she is spending each month.

A. meticulous　　B. blissful　　C. notarized　　D. odious

(13) The lion was within about thirty paces of (　　) we had been sitting.

A. which　　B. the place of　　C. what　　D. where

(14) The silent beach near my house was my favorite, but today the children running there had it all (　　).

A. in themselves　　B. to themselves　　C. by themselves

D. with themselves

(15) A: I think Mina is a (　　) accountant.

B: I agree, but she still needs a lot more experience before she can be called an expert.

A. parallel　　B. chaotic　　C. competent　　D. fictitious

(16) They invited him to stay for dinner, but he couldn't (　　) because he had a plan later that evening.

A. pull through　　B. play up　　C. take off　　D. stick around

(17) When Jessica's train (　　) at five o'clock, her mother was waiting on the platform to greet her.

A. waved on　　B. picked through　　C. pulled in

D. made over

(18) Steve attempted to ( ) his depression by devoting himself entirely to his work. As long as he kept busy, he didn't have time to feel sad.

A. whip up B. fend off C. churn out D. cater to

(19) With the release of their new gaming system, G-mart has ( ) the competition. It has better graphics and better processing speed, and even a lower price.

A. worn through B. blown away C. parted with

D. fixed on

(20) When Bob's boss demanded to see the written contract, he ( ) his file cabinet, praying that he hadn't thrown it away by mistake.

A. snuffed out B. firmed up C. rifled through

D. threw in

(☆☆☆☆◎◎◎◎)

【2】Read the following passage and answer the questions below.

The art of persuasion is one of the most crucial business skills. Without the ability to persuade others to support your ideas, you won't be able to attract the support you need to turn those ideas [①] realities. And though most people are unaware [②] it, the ways you seek to persuade others and the kinds of arguments you find persuasive are deeply rooted [③] your culture's philosophical, religious, and educational assumptions and attitudes. Far [④] being universal, then, the art of persuasion is one that is profoundly culture-based.

That was the hard lesson learned by Kara Williams, an American engineer newly working [⑤] a research manager for a German firm in the automotive industry. As one of the leading experts in her field Williams had extensive experience presenting recommendations and influencing her American colleagues to follow her ideas. But when Williams began working in a German environment she didn't realize that being persuasive would require ❶a different approach. "When I think back to my first presentation to my new German bosses, I wish I had understood the difference and hadn't ❷let their feedback get under my skin. If I had held my cool I might have been able to salvage the situation."

Williams has faced many challenges in her career. Before taking the job with the German firm, she worked for an Australian company from her home office in Boston, traveling frequently to the Sydney headquarters to give presentations and offer advice. "A lot of my job relies on my ability to sell my ideas and influence my internal clients to take the best path," she explains. "I'm good [⑥] what I do, but I hate constant long-distance travel. When offered a similar position working for a German auto supplier, ❸I jumped at the opportunity for shorter travel distances."

Williams's first project was providing technical advice on how to reduce carbon emissions from one of the group's "green" car models. After visiting several automotive plants, observing the systems and processes there, and meeting with dozens of experts and end users, Williams developed a set of recommendations that she felt would meet the company's strategic and budgetary goals. She traveled to Munich to give a one-hour presentation to the decision makers—a group of German directors.

"❹It was my first internal presentation, and its success would be important for my reputation," Williams recalls. In presentation for the meeting Williams thought carefully about how to give the most persuasive presentation, practicing her arguments, anticipating questions that might arise, and preparing responses to those questions.

Williams delivered her presentation in a small auditorium with the directors seated in rows of upholstered chairs. She began by getting right to the point, explaining the strategies she would recommend based on her findings. But before she had finished with the first slide, one of the directors raised his hand and protested, "How did you get to these conclusions? You are giving us your recommendations, but I don't understand how you got here. How many people did you interview? What questions did you ask?"

Then another director jumped in: "Please explain what methodology you used for analyzing your data and how ❺that led you to come to these findings."

"I was taken aback," Williams remembers. "I assured them that the methodology behind my recommendations was ❻sound, but the questions and challenges continued. The more they questioned me, the more I got the feeling that they were attacking my credibility, which puzzled and annoyed me. I have a Ph.D. in engineering and expertise that is widely acknowledged. Their effort to test my conclusions, I felt, showed a real lack of respect. What arrogance ❼[than / they / judge / better able to / I / would be / to think that / am]!"

Williams reacted defensively, and the presentation went downhill from there. "I kick myself now for having allowed their approach to derail my point," she says. "Needless to say, they did not approve my recommendations, and three months of research time went down the drain."

The stone wall Williams ran into illustrates the hard truth that our ability to persuade others depends not simply on the strength of our message but on how we build our arguments and the persuasive techniques we employ.

Jens Hupert is a German director at the company Williams worked for. Having lived in the United States for many years, he had experienced similar failures at persuading others, though the cultural disconnect ran in the opposite direction. Hupert recalled the problems he'd had the first few times he tried to make a persuasive argument before a group of his American colleagues. He'd carefully launched his presentation by laying the foundation for his conclusions, setting the parameters, outlining his data and his methodology, and explaining the premise of his argument. He was taken back when his American boss told him, "In your next presentation, get right to the point. You lost their attention before you even got to the important part."

Hupert was unsure. "These are intelligent people," he thought. "Why would they swallow my argument if I haven't built it carefully for them from the ground up?"

The opposing reactions that Williams and Hupert received reflect the cultural differences between German and American styles of persuasion. The approach taken by the Germans is based on a specific style of reasoning that is deeply ingrained in the cultural psyche. Hupert explains:

> In Germany, we try to understand the theoretical concept before adapting it to the practical situation. To understand something, we first want to analyze all of the conceptual data before coming to a conclusion. When colleagues from cultures like the U.S. or the U.K. make presentations to us, we don't realize that they were taught to think differently from us. So when they begin by presenting conclusions and recommendations without setting up the parameters and how they got to those conclusions, it can actually shock us. We may feel insulted. Do they think we are stupid—that we will just swallow anything? Or we may question whether their decision was well thought out. This reaction is based on our deep-seated belief that you cannot come to a conclusion without first defining the parameters.

Hupert's time in the United States taught him that Americans have a very different approach. They focus on practicalities rather than theory, so they are much more likely to begin with their recommendations. Unfortunately, this reasoning method can backfire when making presentations to an audience whose method of thinking is the opposite—as Kara Williams discovered.

(1) Write the appropriate preposition for each blank of [①]-[⑥].

(2) According to the text, what does the underlined ❶ indicate? Choose the most appropriate explanation from the four choices below.

A. a way of presenting Williams's ideas and advice to her colleagues which is strongly related to her cultural background

B. a way of presenting Williams's ideas and advice to her colleagues which is firmly based on her ability to influence and persuade them

C. a German way of persuasion in which they try to have listeners understand the theoretical concept before adapting it to the practical situation

D. a German way of persuasion in which they try to give conclusion and recommendation first without setting up the parameters and how they got to those conclusions

(3) Choose the most appropriate meaning of the underlined ❷ from the four choices below.

A. blow my cool because of their feedback

B. keep my cool in spite of their feedback

C. make them angry after their feedback

D. let them be offended at the feedback

(4) Choose the reason for why Williams "jumped up at the opportunity" (the underlined ❸) from the four choices below.

A. Because she was proud of her ability to persuade her internal clients and very confident if she had enough time for preparing for that.

B. Because she wanted to present her ideas and influence her internal clients without taking a lot of time for her business trips.

C. Because she didn't want to travel long-distance to the German firm to give her presentation without any help offered by her internal clients.

D. Because she didn't think it was the best path to choose to work for a German auto supplier even if it didn't require long-distance travel.

(5) Complete the following explanation about what the underlined ❹ indicates, filling in the blanks with the designated number of words.

> It indicates Williams's first presentation for the new position she got. For that one-hour presentation, in which she would give ___A(6)___ from the target car model, she did research for several months and got some findings in the automotive field, so that she would ___B(7-8)___ a set of recommendations and she wanted to be ___C(1)___ in that presentation for her future career.

(6) Write what the underlined ❺ refers to with eight words.

(7) Choose the alternative word to the underlined ❻.

A. healthy　B. safe　C. sure　D. difficult

(8) Put the words from the underlined ❼ in the correct order.

(9) According to the text, which of the following is true?

A. Hupert believed that people to whom he presented were not able to understand the point even if it came after carefully defining the parameters, because they felt insulted.

B. Hupert successfully got through his persuading experience in the United States even in the first year because he had lived there for a long time and understood much about the difference between the ways of persuasion which is related to cultural background.

C. When Williams delivered her presentation for a German auto supplier, she had trouble with a lot of unpredicted questions, but her recommendations were finally adopted.

D. When Williams delivered her presentation for a German auto supplier, she was embarrassed and irritated because the questions the directors asked made her feel that she was attacked.

(☆☆☆☆◎◎◎)

【中学校】

【1】Substitute the underlined phrase with the best alternative from the four choices.

(1) I cannot <u>do without</u> this dictionary even for a single day.

A. dispense with　B. go with　C. inquire into

D. lead into

(2) She <u>had words with</u> her friend and then struck him.

A. made an arrangement　B. quarreled with　C. stood up for

D. cut in

(3) Being a graduate of this university, she visits here <u>from time to time</u>.

A. in advance B. by turns C. once in a while

D. in the nick of time

(4) I agree with you <u>to some extent</u>.

A. to the minutes B. by nature C. to a certain degree

D. at any moment

(5) Today we are going to discuss this problem <u>from the standpoint of</u> morality.

A. in terms of B. in place of C. by way of

D. by and large

(☆☆☆☆◎◎◎◎)

【2】Put the words in the correct order, and answer with the numbers.

(1) 私には海の美しさを言葉で表すことはできない。

[① to ② fail ③ describe ④ words ⑤ me] the beauty of the sea.

(2) 好きな歌手が引退したらしい。それが本当であろうとなかろうと，私は依然として彼のファンです。

They say my favorite singer has bowed out of show business. [① not ② it ③ be ④ true ⑤ or], I will still be his fan.

(3) 彼の計画が成功するかどうかまだ分からない。

It [① to ② seen ③ yet ④ is ⑤ be ⑥ whether] his plan will succeed.

(4) 彼女は病気になり，会社の経営を息子に託さざるをえなかった。

When she got sick, she had [① but ② give ③ no ④ to ⑤ over ⑥ choice] control of the company to her son.

(5) 安くて使いやすければ，どんな歯ブラシでも良い。

[① will ② long ③ toothbrush ④ as ⑤ do ⑥ any] as it is cheap and easy to use.

(☆☆☆☆◎◎◎◎)

【3】Read the following passage and choose the best sentence for each of [1]～[4] from the six choices below.

A: Hello. This is Wakaba Warehouse.

B: Hi. May I ask you a question?

A: Sure.

B: [1]. Do you have many left?

A: We just have the display model left in our store. [2], which we can easily have sent over.

B: OK. Thank you. I'll come in today.

A: What time will you come? [3].

B: Really? The website says that your store is open until eight.

A: Right. [4], but we're upgrading our computer system today.

B: I'll come in tomorrow then.

A. We will be closing at five today
B. We can't accept credit cards
C. Our normal business hours are ten to eight
D. I'd like to take a look at the chair that is on sale now
E. I will wait for you
F. There are still several in our warehouse nearby

(☆☆☆◎◎◎)

【4】Read the following passage and answer the questions below.

In order to improve HOW and WHAT we do, we constantly look to what others are doing. We attend conferences, read books, talk to friends and colleagues to get their input and advice, and sometimes we are also the dispensers of advice. We ①<u>are in pursuit of</u> understanding the best practices of others to help guide us.【 A 】But it is a flawed assumption that what works for one organization will work for another. Even if the industries, sizes and market conditions are the same, the notion that "if it's good for them, it's good for us" is simply not true.

I know of a company with an amazing culture. When asked, the employees say they love that all the conference rooms have ping-pong tables in them. Does that mean that if you were to put ping-pong tables in all your conference rooms your culture would improve? Of course not. But this is an example of "best practices." The idea that copying WHAT or HOW things are done at high-performing organizations will inherently work for you is just not true. 【 B 】 Like the Ferrari and the Honda, what is good for one company is not necessarily good for another. Put simply, best practices are not always best.

It is not just WHAT or HOW you do things that matters; what matters more is that WHAT and HOW you do things is consistent with your WHY. 【 C 】 There is nothing inherently wrong with looking to others to learn what they do, the challenge is knowing what practices or advice to follow. Fortunately, there is a simple test you can apply to find out exactly WHAT and HOW is right for you. It's a simple metaphor called the Celery Test.

Imagine you go to a dinner party and somebody comes up to you and says, "You know what you need in your organization? M&M's. If you're not using M&M's in your business, you're leaving money on the table."

Somebody else comes up to you and says, "You know what you need? Rice milk. The data shows that all the people are buying rice milk these days. You should be selling rice milk in this economy."

While you're standing over the punch bowl, yet another person offers some sage advice. "Oreo cookies," he says. "We made millions from implementing Oreo cookies in our organization. You've got to do it."

Still somebody else comes up to you and says, "Celery. You've got to get into celery."

You get all this great advice from all these highly accomplished people. Some of them are in the same industry. Some of them are more successful than you. Some of them have offered similar advice to others with great success. 【 D 】 Now, what do you do?

You go to the supermarket and you buy celery, rice milk, Oreos and M&M's. You spend a lot of time at the supermarket walking the aisles. You spend a lot of money because you buy everything. But you may or may not get any value from some or all of these products; there are no guarantees. Worse, if you're budget-constrained, you had to whittle down your choices again. And then which do you choose?

But one thing's for sure: when you're standing in line at the supermarket with all of these items in your arms, your celery, rice milk, Oreos and M&M's, nobody can see what you believe. What you do is supposed serve as the tangible proof of what you believe, and you bought everything.

But what if you knew your WHY before you went to the supermarket? What if your WHY is to do only things that are healthy? To always do the things that are good for your body? You'll get all the same good advice from all the same people, the only difference is, the next time you go to the supermarket, you'll buy only rice milk and celery. Those are the only products that make sense. It's not that the other advice isn't good advice, it's just not good for you. The advice doesn't fit.

②[　　], you spend less time at the supermarket and you spend less money so there's an efficiency advantage also. You're guaranteed to get value out of all the products you bought. And, most importantly, when you're standing in line with your products in your arms, everybody can see what you believe. With only celery and rice milk it's obvious to people walking by what you believe. "I can *see* that you believe in looking after your health," they may say to you. "I feel the same way. I have a question for you." Congratulations. You just attracted a customer, an employee, a partner or a referral simply by making the right decisions. Simply ensuring that WHAT you do proves what you believe makes it easy for those who believe what you believe to find you. You have successfully communicated your WHY based on WHAT you do.

This is an idealistic concept and in the real world that level of discipline is not always possible. I understand that sometimes we have to make short-term decisions to pay bills or get some short-term advantage. That's fine. The Celery Test still applies. If you want a piece of chocolate cake, go right ahead. The difference is, when you start with WHY, you know full well that the chocolate cake is a short-term decision that doesn't fit with your beliefs. You're under no illusions. You know you are only doing it for the short-term sugar rush and you'll have to work a little harder to get it out of your system. It's astounding the number of businesses I see that view an opportunity as the one that's going to set them on a path to glory, only to have it blow up or slowly deflate over time. They see the chocolate cake and can't resist. Starting with WHY not only helps you know which is the right advice for you to follow, but also to know which decisions will put you out of balance. You can certainly make those decisions if you need to, but don't make too many of them, otherwise over time, no one will know what you believe.

But here's the best part. As soon as I told you the WHY, you knew that we were going to buy only celery and rice milk even before you read it. As soon as I gave you the filter, as soon as I said the WHY, you knew exactly what decisions to make before I said so.

That's called scale.

With a WHY clearly stated in an organization, anyone within the organization can make a decision as clearly and as accurately as the founder. A WHY provides the clear filter for decision-making. Any decisions—hiring, partnerships, strategies and tactics—should all pass the Celery Test.

(1) Choose the most appropriate meaning of the underlined ① from the four choices below.

A. accept　B. argue　C. remove　D. seek

(2) Choose the most appropriate place, from 【 A 】～【 D 】 in the text, to put the sentence below.

Only then will your practices indeed be best.

(3) Choose the most appropriate one for ②[　　] from the four alternatives below.

A. Thinking about WHAT and HOW before filtering your reason

B. Filtering your decisions through your WHY

C. Executing the best practices of others

D. Knowing the best belief for copying

(4) According to the text, which of the following is true?

A. Thinking about what to do next helps you to know a short-term decision that doesn't fit with the beliefs.

B. The Celery Test is not suitable for making short-term decisions to get some short-term advantage.

C. Getting the advice of others is the most effective way to think about HOW and WHAT we do.

D. Thinking about WHY you do so is the effective filter for making the right decisions.

(5) Considering what is written in the passage, write your own thoughts on how thinking about "Why?" is related to learning in approximately 100 words in English.

(☆☆☆☆◎◎◎)

【５】Translate the underlined sentences into English.

(1) 2020年12月21日，木星と土星が大接近した。木星と土星の接近は20年に一度程度発生する。しかし，今回ほどの大接近は2080年まで起こらない，非常に貴重な現象だった。

(2) 科学者らはその病気の原因を見つけ出すため，熱心に取り組んでいる。それが分かれば治療法が分かる。

(☆☆☆◎◎◎)

【高等学校】

【１】Read the following passage and answer the questions below.

From near mount Kangrinboqe in Tibet rise four major rivers, which stretch east and west across the Himalaya and down to the sea like the limbs of a venerable water goddess. Where these rivers flow, they define civilizations and nations: Tibet, Pakistan, northern India, Nepal, Bangladesh. How their water is spent has long depended on the people living downstream. How the rivers are replenished depends on two things: monsoon rains and glacial ice melt. Both phenomena, for millennia the preserve of the gods, are now in the hands of humans too.

Rivers emerging from the eastern Himalaya, like the Brahmaputra, are mostly ❶fed by the summer monsoon; their flow may well increase as a warming climate puts more moisture in the atmosphere. But most water in the Indus, which flows west from Mount Kangrinboqe, comes from the snows and glaciers of the Himalaya, the Karakoram, and the Hindu Kush. Glaciers especially are "water towers": They store winter snowfall as ice, high in the mountains, and they surrender ❷it as meltwater in spring and summer. In this way, they provide a steady flow that nourishes humans and ecosystems. Downstream, in the plains of Pakistan and northern India, the world's most extensive system of irrigated agriculture depends on the Indus. The glaciers that feed it are lifeline for ❸some 270 million people.

Most of those glaciers are now shrinking. At first, that will increase the flow in the Indus. But if temperatures rise as predicted, and the glaciers continue to melt back, the Indus will reach "peak water" by 2050. After that, the flow will decline.

Humans already use 95 percent of the Indus, and the population of the basin is growing fast. Writing recently in the journal *Nature*, an international group of scientists (supported by the National Geographic Society) analyzed glacial water towers worldwide. The Indus is the most critical, they said: Given the region's "high baseline water stress and limited government effectiveness," it is "unlikely that the Indus...can sustain this pressure." Pakistan will suffer most.

From 2003 to 2006, I traveled the 2,000-mile river, from the Arabian Sea to its source in Tibet, researching my book *Empires of the Indus*. Already it was clear that it was under strain. The Indus had changed out of all recognition from the mighty river described by British colonial officials. It had been diminished by the demands of irrigation, industry, and daily life. Because of dams and barrages, it no longer reached the sea, and its mangrove-forested delta was dying. Its lakes were polluted with effluents and sewage.

I was struck by how the Indus, celebrated from ancient times in sacred Sanskrit hymns, was treated as a resource but no longer as an object of reverence. Everyone I met, from peasants to politicians, thought the river was being mismanaged. They spoke of corrupt or inefficient engineering projects, inequitable water sharing, and ecosystems destroyed in the name of profit.

At the time, not many people were talking about the effect of global warming on the Indus. ❹<u>It wasn't until 2010 that the scale of the problem became clear</u>—through dramatic floods rather than a shortage. The future of total rainfall in the Himalayan region is uncertain, but there has been a clear increase in extreme rains. In August 2010, when the Indus was already full of summer meltwater, it was hit by a freak monsoon. The torrential rain—in some places, a year's worth in a few hours—caused the river to breach its banks throughout its southern course. More than 1,600 people died; damages reached $10 billion.

"Flooding on that scale was unheard of," said Usman Qazi, an Islamabad-based disaster-relief expert with the United Nations Development Programme. "But ❺<u>it</u> will become more common," he added. "Climate change-related floods are one of the biggest hazards in this country."

(1) Which one of the following includes the same meaning of "feed" as that of the underlined ❶?

A. They have a large family to feed.

B. Feed the plants once a week.

C. Gossip and speculation are constantly fed to us by the media.

D. Power is fed into the electricity line through an underground cable.

(2) What does the underlined ❷ refer to? Search the text and extract two sequential words.

(3) Choose the alternative word to the underlined ❸.

A. approximately B. considerable C. partial D. several

(4) Rewrite the underlined ❹ into a sentence which has exactly the same meaning as the original, beginning with "Not" .

(5) According to the text, what does the underlined ❺ indicate? Choose the most appropriate explanation from the four choices below.

A. one of the big hazards which the United Nations previously warned to 1,600 people

B. climate change-related floods which are bigger than any other similar disaster in other countries

C. the freak monsoon people in India have never heard of since 2010

D. the flooding whose amount of damage was $10 billion

(6) According to the text, which of the following is true?

A. The water flow of each of the four major rivers from near mount Kangrinboqe in Tibet depends only on rains and as the warming climate releases more moisture into the air, their flow could increase.

B. The Indus is the source of a large irrigation system in the plains of Pakistan and northern India and a group of scientists reported that the Indus would continue to meet the water demand of its basin.

C. When the author traveled from the Arabian Sea to its source in Tibet, she noticed signs of the Indus being damaged by humans and was shocked to find that the Indus was no longer treated with respect.

D. The terrible flood in August 2010 in India was caused by an unusual amount of melting water rather than by extreme rains which caused some places' annual amount of rainfall in a few hours.

(☆☆☆◎◎◎)

【２】Choose the most appropriate word for each blank of [①]−[⑥] from the choices below. Also, make each one of them inflect appropriately if necessary. You can use each word only one time. Note that the choices include an unnecessary word.

Studies of language's effect on colour categorisation have [①] interesting insight into the linguistic relativity hypothesis. One of the key studies was Berlin and Kay (1969). In this study, the researchers first [②] colour terms from native speakers of twenty different languages and then asked the informants to map each colour term in their native languages with all the possible colours on a colour board, as well as identifying one prototypical colour. In the second phase of the research, the researchers [③] a pool of ninety-eight languages using the colour categories derived in the first phase. The study [④] that there were a limited number of 'basic colour terms' such as white, brown and red in world languages, and these colour terms appeared to [⑤] an evolutionary sequence in world languages. Despite some strong criticism of its research design, particularly its inclusion of bilingual speakers as informants, Berlin and Kay's proposal of colour term universals and commonality in human cognition was generally [⑥] as a substantial counter-argument against linguistic determinism.

[analyse　conclude　elicit　follow　object　produce　regard]

(☆☆☆☆◎◎◎)

【３】Read the following passage and answer the questions below.

If you could peer inside the mind of a questioning child, you'd get a hint as to why kids seem to enjoy asking "Why?". Neurological research shows that merely wondering about an interesting question activates regions of the brain linked to reward-processing. Curiosity—the act of wondering—feels good in and of itself, and thus, questions beget more questions. Think of curiosity as a condition— "like an itch," says the neuroscientist Charan Ranganath. And that condition often leads to the action known as questioning, which is how we scratch the itch.

The four-year-old child scratches away—until, at some point, she is told to stop. But for a time, during her peak questioning years, she has no reluctance to ask about anything and everything—including the most fundamental questions, those basic "Why?" queries that many of us are loathe to ask for fear of looking stupid. The questioning child isn't weighed down by accumulated knowledge, biases, or assumptions about how the world works and why things are the way they are. Her mind is both open and expansive—an ideal condition for wondering, inquiring, and growing.

❶This seems to begin changing somewhere around age five or six. The asking of questions (at least the ones that are verbalized by young students in school) tends to subside steadily, year by year, according to research from the nonprofit Right Question Institute, which studies questioning and devises question-formulation exercises for schools. What was once a hundred-per-day questioning habit among four-year-olds dwindles down to a few questions—or none—among teenagers.

It is convenient to blame ❷this on our education system, which, for the most part, is test-driven and answers-based. And ❸our schools could be doing much more to encourage questioning by students. But clearly, a number of additional forces and pressures work against questioning.

Foremost among what I think of as the "five enemies of questioning" is *fear*. Though many young children start out as fearless questioners, they gradually get the message—from teachers, parents, other kids—that asking a question carries risks, including the risk of revealing what they don't know and perhaps ought to know. It is a near-paralyzing problem for young students and seems to get worse as they move into the peer-pressure-cooker environments of junior high and high school. ❹Students fear they'll ask the "wrong" question—one that could be seen as off-topic or obvious—or that by

<u>asking *any* question, they'll potentially be seen as uncool.</u> As children become teenagers, coolness is generally associated with being in-the-know already—or acting as if you don't care. To ask a question is an admission that 1) you don't know, and 2) you do care—doubly uncool.

As we move into adulthood, the fear of revealing that we "don't know" is still there and in some ways may be even [①]. Kids at least have the excuse of being [②], but adults have no excuse for not knowing something [③]. Fear of asking questions can be particularly strong in the workplace, as employees worry: ***Will asking questions make it seem as if I don't know how to do my job? Will it annoy my colleagues and supervisors? Or worse, will it threaten them in some way?*** These concerns are [④]—questions can, indeed, sometimes be irritating or [⑤]. There are ways to address those problems, as we'll see later, but most people don't know them—because we don't teach "questioning" in school (or in college or in most employee training programs.)

The reluctance to question extends beyond the classroom or workplace to the privacy of our homes. Many of our closest personal relationships could benefit from more questions, particularly the kinds of queries that show genuine interest and a desire to understand. Yet we are far more inclined to offer opinions and dispense advice—to do more telling than asking.

Even in the privacy of our own minds—when we're mentally grappling with problems or trying to work through difficult decisions—we're apt to worry, stew, or gripe about something (or avoid thinking about it altogether). What we should be doing is asking ourselves questions that can help break down the problem or get to the crux of it. But we may be unsure of how to formulate those questions. And we may fear not having the answers to ❺<u>them</u>.

If fear is the first enemy of questioning, running a close second is [⑥]. The more you know, the less you feel the need to ask. But the problem here is twofold. First, we can easily fall into the "trap of expertise," wherein knowledgeable people begin to rely too much on what they already know and fail to keep expanding upon and updating that knowledge. This is particularly perilous in times of rapid change. And there's another problem with depending too much on our existing knowledge: To put it bluntly, we don't know as much as we think we do.

This brings up the third and fourth enemies of questioning, which are related to each other: *bias* and *hubris*. In terms of biases, some of them are hardwired in us; others may be based on our own limited experiences. But in either case, if we are predisposed to think something, we may be less open to considering questions that challenge that view. The book's second section, on decision-making, looks at some of the ways we can use self-questioning to better understand and challenge our own biases and assumptions.

But to do that, we also must contend with hubris—which can lead us to believe our biases are correct or are not biases at all.("*Everyone else* is biased!") The relationship between humility and questioning is interesting—❻<u>if you lack the former, you'll probably do less of the latter</u>. You may be more inclined to think and say things like: "If I don't know it already, it can't be that important," or "I just go with my gut instincts—they're usually right," or "I don't have to sit through intelligence briefings because I'm a really smart guy."

The last enemy of questioning is *time* (or the supposed lack of it). We just don't seem to make time for questioning—starting in school. Ask any teacher about this; there is so much material to "download" that little time remains for student questions. And time is an even bigger source of pressure on adult questioning. To make this point at companies I visit, I often share a quote attributed to the late comedian George Carlin: "Some people see things that are and ask, 'Why?' Some people dream of things that never were and ask, 'Why not?' Some people have to go to work and don't have time for all that."

Carlin's joke did not reflect his own view (he was a passionate believer in the importance of questioning *everything*), but it does capture ❼<u>an attitude</u>

<u>that is quite common in business and in everyday life</u>—perhaps more today than ever before. As our lives move faster and have become more complicated little time is allotted for inquiry, contemplation, or critical thinking. We're under pressure to make quick decisions and render snap judgments, and to *do, do, do*—without necessarily asking ***why*** we're doing what we're doing or whether we should be doing it at all.

The paradox is that in the rush to do more with our limited time, we may end up using that time *less* efficiently—because rushed decisions and actions can send us down the wrong path. This was understood by some of the most successful—and busiest—people today and in recent times.

Case in point: The late founder of Apple, Steve Jobs, was one of the busiest people on the planet, yet he made a conscious effort to regularly ask fundamental "Why?" questions while making the rounds of his company's various departments. At each stop, whether in the marketing area or accounting, "I always asked why we're doing things the way we're doing them, "jobs said. As Jobs took on the role of the inquisitive four-year-old wandering the company, it had a powerful effect on him and those around him —forcing everyone to reexamine assumptions.

In my research, I found a similar questioning habit among many of the highly productive business leaders or creative professionals I studied. In the midst of hectic schedules, they seem to be able to find the time to ask thoughtful questions of themselves and others, particularly when confronting a new challenge, starting out on an endeavor, or forming a new relationship. ❽<u>The ability and inclination to maintain that fearless, open-minded approach of a young questioner is part of what makes them successful.</u>

(1) According to the text, what does the underlined ❶ indicate? Explain it with about 100 Japanese characters.

(2) According to the text, what does the underlined ❷ indicate? Explain it with about 50-60 Japanese characters.

(3) Choose the most appropriate meaning of the underlined ❸ from the four

choices below.

A. We were able to encourage students to answer the questions in classes when they were there.

B. We are able to encourage students to answer the questions in classes, but we don't.

C. We should try to have students ask more questions at school, but we don't do that enough.

D. We should have tried to let students ask any questions to teachers anytime they wanted to.

(4) Translate the underlined ❹ into Japanese.

(5) Choose the most appropriate word for each blank of [①]-[⑤] from the choices below. You can use each word only one time.

A. confrontational B. important C. legitimate

D. stronger E. young

(6) According to the text, what does the underlined ❺ indicate? Explain it with about 60-70 Japanese characters.

(7) Choose the most appropriate word for [⑥] from the choices below.

A. *belief* B. *flexibility* C. *knowledge* D. *pride*

E. *resilience*

(8) Translate the underlined ❻ into Japanese, making what "the former" and "the latter" refer to clear.

(9) According to the text, what does the underlined ❼ mean? Explain it with about 100 Japanese characters.

(10) In order to foster the students' ability or inclination as mentioned in the underlined ❽, what do you think teachers can do in English classes? Express your own idea with concrete examples and reasons, using about 150 words in English.

(☆☆☆☆◎◎◎)

解答・解説

【中高共通】

【1】(1)　A　(2)　C　(3)　A　(4)　A　(5)　B　(6)　D
(7)　B　(8)　C　(9)　C　(10)　C　(11)　C　(12)　A
(13)　D　(14)　B　(15)　C　(16)　D　(17)　C　(18)　B
(19)　B　(20)　C

〈解説〉(1)　haltは自動詞・他動詞の両方で用いられ「停止する，停止させる」の意。ここでは他動詞で受動態の形。　(2)　unveilは「明らかにする，公表する」。　(3)　prolongは「長くする，引き伸ばす」。(4)　Bの発話「これまで我々が知っていることすべてを必ず含めます」よりomit「省略する」が適切。　(5)　名詞＋andで仮定法を表現できる。「10分早ければ最終電車に乗ることができたのに」の意。
(6)　play one's hunchで「勘に頼る」の意。　(7)　traffic congestionで「交通渋滞」の意。　(8)　siblingは「兄弟，姉妹」の意。
(9)　business attireで「ビジネススーツ，ビジネス用の服装」の意。
(10)　It's a shame (that)～で「～であるのは残念だ」の意。
(11)　heaveは「(重い物の)持ち上げ」の意。with a mighty heaveで「力いっぱい持ち上げて」となる。　(12)　meticulousは「極めて注意深い」の意。　(13)　ここでのpaceは「歩幅」を表し，…paces of～で「～から…歩」の意。ofの後は名詞が来るため，関係副詞whereを用いて「私たちが座っていた場所」とする。　(14)　to oneselfで「独占して」の意。　(15)　competentは「有能な」の意。　(16)　stick aroundで「近くにいる，ブラブラしている」の意。　(17)　pull inで「(列車が駅に)入ってくる，到着する」の意。　(18)　fend offで「払いのける」の意。(19)　blow awayで「完全に負かす，圧勝する」の意。　(20)　rifle through「くまなく探る，引っかきまわして探す」の意。

【2】(1)　①　into　②　of　③　in　④　from　⑤　as
⑥　at　(2)　C　(3)　A　(4)　B　(5)　A　some ideas for

reducing carbon emissions (6words)　B　satisfy the decision makers of the company with (8words)　C　successful (1words)

(6)　the methodology Williams used for analyzing her data　(7)　C

(8)　(What arrogance) to think that they would be better able to judge than I am(!)　(9)　D

〈解説〉(1)　①　turn A into Bで「AをBに変える」の意。　②　be unaware of～で「～に気づかない，自覚がない」の意。　③　root in～は「～に根ざす」の意。　④　far from～で「～からかけ離れていて，～どころではない」の意。　⑤　work as～で「～として働く」の意。　⑥　be good at～で「～が得意である」の意。　(2)　ドイツ人の説得の特徴は最後から2番目の段落のHupert explains: の項に述べられている。　(3)　let O get under one's skinは「Oをひどく怒らせる」といった意味。最も近いのはAで，blow one's coolは「冷静さを失う，怒りを爆発させる」である。　(4)　下線部❸の段落では，Williamsはオーストラリアの会社までの長距離出張がとても嫌だったと述べられている。それを考慮すると，その直後のfor shorter travel distancesは出張の時間が少ない機会に飛びついたという内容になりBが適切。　(5)　Williamsのプレゼンテーションの内容は下線部❹の前の段落で述べられている。A　technical advice on how to reduce carbon emissionsを言い換える内容が来る。reduce carbon emissionsはそのまま用いるしかなく，6語という語数制限を考えると前半部分をsome ideas forとし，reduceをreducingと動名詞にすることで対応できる。　B　that she felt would meet the company's strategic and budgetary goalsの部分が該当する。7，8語という語数制限を考えるとmeet the company's strategic and budgetary goalsをsatisfy the decision makers of the company「会社の意思決定者を満足させる」と大きく書き換え，a set of recommendationsに続くwithを補う。C　下線部❹の段落で「成功が自分のキャリアに重要」と述べられていることからsuccessfulが適切。　(6)　このthatは後ろに動詞があることから代名詞のthatだと判断できる。thatが指しているのは直前のwhat methodology you used for analyzing your dataであるが，会話文での表現のため，代名詞thatにあてはまるようthe methodology Williams used for analyzing her dataとする。　(7)　ここでのsoundは「理にかなった，正当な」である。　(8)　What arroganceは感嘆文で，to不定詞を続けることができるためWhat arrogance to think thatで「～と考えることはなんと傲慢なことだろうか」となる。that以下はbetterやthanがあることから比較級を用いることがわかる。主語は前文の内容からIではなくtheyが来てthey would be better able to judgeとする。残ったthan I amのあとにはable to judgeが省略されている適切な文となる。

(9)　第8段落の内容がDと一致する。

【中学校】

【1】(1)　A　(2)　B　(3)　C　(4)　C　(5)　A

〈解説〉(1)　do without～で「～なしですます」の意。　(2)　have words with～で「～と口論する」の意。　(3)　from time to timeで「時々」の意。　(4)　to some extentで「ある程度」の意。　(5)　from the standpoint of～で「～の観点から」の意。

【2】(1)　④→②→⑤→①→③　(2)　③→②→④→⑤→①

(3)　④→③→①→⑤→②→⑥　(4)　③→⑥→①→④→②→⑤

(5)　⑥→③→①→⑤→④→②

〈解説〉(1)　Words fail me to describeが適切な語順。S fail O to doで「Sによって0は～することができない」の意。　(2)　Be it true or notが適切な語順。Whether it is true or notと書き換えられる。　(3)　is yet to be seen whetherが適切な語順。it is yet to be 過去分詞で「まだ～することはできない」の意。　(4)　no choice but to give overが適切な語順。have no choice but to doで「～せざるを得ない，～する以外の選択肢はない」の意。give over～は「～を託す，譲る」の意。　(5)　Any toothbrush will do as longが適切な語順。S will doで「Sで問題ない」の意。as long as～は「～である限り」という条件を表す。

【3】1　D　2　F　3　A　4　C

〈解説〉1　空所の次のAの発話「店内の展示モデルのみ残っています」より，空所に当てはまるのはD「現在販売中の椅子を見たいのですが」が適切。　2　which we can easily have sent overより，空所にはsent overに続く目的語が入ることがわかり，適切なものはF「近くの倉庫にはまだ何点かあります」のみである。　3　直後のBの発話で「そうなんですか？ウェブサイトでは8時まで営業だとあったのですが」と意外な気持ちを表していることから空所はAの「今日は5時で閉店です」が適切。　4　Bの発話「ウェブサイトでは8時まで営業だとあったのですが」にAがRight.と肯定していることからCが適切。

【4】(1)　D　(2)　C　(3)　B　(4)　D　(5)　I think that as teacher we need to think about why we do things in our classes. We think about the skill that we want our students to acquire. We spend a lot of time focusing on what to teach and how to teach and sometimes depend on activities and methods to make students enjoy classes. Students may be happy during classes but they may not get any skills that we want our students to acquire. Teachers need to set a goal about what kind of abilities we want students to acquire and think about what kind of materials to use and how to teach effectively. (106 words)

〈解説〉(1)　be in pursuit of～で「～を追跡して」の意。　(2)「その時初めてあなたの実践が最善のものとなるだろう」という一文が入るのはCとなる。それ以外の選択肢はOnly thenが指すものが存在しない。　(3)　空所の後の文「スーパーでより少ない時間を費やし使うお金もより少なくなる」に結びつくのはBとなる。　(4)　第12段落の内容がDと一致する。　(5)　本文の内容を踏まえて，「なぜ」を考えることがどのように学習に関連するか，自分の考えを100語程度で記述する。解答では，最初に，教師としてなぜ授業をするのか考える必要があると述べた上で，教師が教室内で生徒に英語を教える際の目標やそれを達成する手段について言及している。

【5】(1)　A conjunction of the two planets takes place about once every 20 years.　(2)　Scientists are working hard to track down the cause of the disease.

〈解説〉(1)　地球から見て2つの天体が重なって見える現象を天文学で「合」や「会合」(conjunction)という。2020年12月21日に起こった木星と土星の大接近は，The Great Conjunctionとしてニュースでも大きく取り上げられた。「発生する」はtake place,「20年に一度」はonce every 20 yearsで表現できる。　(2)　track downは,「(多くの労力や時間をかけて)物・人を探し出す，見つけ出す」という意味になる。

【高等学校】

【1】(1)　D　(2)　winter snowfall　(3)　A　(4)　Not until 2010 did the scale of the problem become clear.　(5)　D　(6)　C

〈解説〉(1)　この文のfeed(過去分詞fed)は「供給する」の意味で用いられている。　(2)　itを含む文の意味は「氷河は高山地帯に冬季の降雪を氷として蓄え，春夏にはそれを融雪水として放出する」なので，itは「冬季の降雪」をさす。　(3)　someは数字の前でabout, approximatelyの意味を持つ。　(4)　Notを冒頭に持ってくる文で書き換えるという問題文の指示より，Not until 2010「2010年になって初めて」と書き始め，否定語が文頭に来ている場合には倒置が起こることからdid the scale of the problem become clearとなる。　(5)　itは下線部の前の段落の内容，すなわち「洪水で100億ドルの被害を出したこと」であるためDが適切。(6)　第6段落参照。インダス川が人の手によって破壊され，もはや尊敬の対象ではないことに衝撃を受けたと著者が述べており，Cと一致する。

【2】①　produced　②　elicited　③　analysed　④　concluded　⑤　follow　⑥　regarded

〈解説〉①　目的語interesting insightに結びつくのはproducedとなる。
②「母語話者から色という用語を[　②　]」という文であり，②には

elicited「引き出した」が入る。 ③ 空所を含む文は研究の第2段階であり，第1段階の色分類を用いて行うのは分析であると判断できる。 ④ concludeは後ろにthat節を取り，「～という結論に達する，～と結論づける」の意となる。 ⑤ 空所を含む文は，「基本の色の用語があり，それらが進化の過程をたどる」とするのが適切。 ⑥ asがあることからregard A as Bの受動態だと判断できる。

【3】(1) 4歳の子どもが，積み上げられた知識や偏見，世の中に関する思い込みのない開放的な心で，多くの人が愚かに見えることを恐れて躊躇するような最も基本的な問いも含め，何事に対しても抵抗なく問いかけること。(97字) (2) 4歳の頃には1日に100個も質問していたのが，5，6歳頃から減り始め，10代では数個しか，あるいは全く質問しなくなること。(59字) (3) C (4) 生徒たちは，的外れだったり，明らかに答えがわかるような「間違った」質問をしてしまうことや，何か質問することで，自分がもしかするとかっこ悪く見えるかもしれないことを恐れている。 (5) ① D ② E ③ B ④ C ⑤ A (6) 心の中で何かの問題に取り組んだり，難しい決断を乗り越えるときに，その問題を解決する，あるいはその核心に迫るのに役立つような問い。(64字) (7) C (8) もし謙遜する気持ちが十分でなければ，おそらく質問もさらに少ないだろう。 (9) 仕事が忙しいほど質問，熟考，批判的思考の時間がなく，自分が今やっていることを，なぜやらなければならないのか，そもそも必要なのかということを考えもせずに素早く判断することを常に迫られている心の状態。(99字) (10) I think English class can be a good place for students to practice questioning. They usually need critical thinking when trying to understand some written materials, and critical thinking will require good questions which can get to the point of an issue.

In order to have them ask questions without fear, I should use scaffolding. Although some students are not good at questioning, they can easily make yes/no question sentences from the text. So, they can begin with asking such an easy kind of question in pairs. After a lot of practice of closed questioning, they probably come up with other kinds of questions, to which they really want to know the answer. Those questions might include the one which has no exact answer in the text, and it is the chance for them to enjoy thinking deeply and discuss with others. Once they find it enjoyable, it can be expected that they become willing to ask more questions. (159 words)

〈解説〉(1)　段落冒頭のThisであり，前段落の内容を指していると判断できるため前段落の内容を語数以内に適切にまとめる。　(2)　(1)と同様，前段落の内容を指しているので，子どもは大きくなるにつれ質問しなくなるという内容をまとめる。　(3)　このcouldは「～できるのに(実際はしていない)」という仮定法過去の用法のためCが適切な内容となる。　(4)　代名詞oneは直前のthe “wrong” questionを指すことと，後ろのthatは動詞fearの目的語となるthat節であることに注意して訳す。(5)　①「恐れが『より強くなる』」となりstrongerが入る。　②「子供は『若い』という口実がある」となりyoungが入る。　③「大人は『重要な』ことを知らないという口実を持たない」となりimportantが入る。　④「これらの懸念は『筋が通っている』」となりlegitimateが入る。　⑤　直前のirritatingに近い意味の語であるconfrontationalが入る。(6)　同段落の最初の2文の内容をまとめる。answer toに続く名詞として文末はquestions「問い」とする。　(7)　直後の文のThe more you knowの言い換えである*knowledge*が適切である。　(8)　formerがhumility，latterがquestioningを指すことを把握する必要がある。(9)　下線部の次の文As our lives～から同段落の最終文までをまとめる。　(10)　生徒が恐れずに質問をできるようになる英語の授業について，具体例と根拠を示しながら自分の考えを150語程度で述べる。解答では授業の進め方や質問の内容まで詳細に説明している。

2021年度　実施問題

【中高共通】

【1】Choose the answer that best completes the sentence from the four choices.

(1) I expected that he (　　) the bar examination and he did.

A. gets through　B. will get through　C. would get through
D. has got through

(2) We started business only a year ago, so it is still (　　) to open a branch office in Tokyo.

A. preliminary　B. prime　C. premature　D. incompetent

(3) I could not help (　　) at his joke.

A. but laugh　B. laugh　C. in laughing　D. to laugh

(4) She (　　) at the park yesterday, but I didn't see her.

A. might be　B. might have been　C. should be
D. must have to be

(5) (　　) I a little younger, I would go abroad.

A. If　B. Did　C. Should　D. Were

(6) How careless (　　) you to injure his leg.

A. for　B. of　C. with　D. to

(7) A: Ryan had an idea to sell our products at the event the other day. Is that going well?

B: Well, his idea was (　　). That's why our floor manager rejected his proposal.

A. impassable　B. immaculate　C. impractical
D. immediate

(8) I was seen (　　) a piece of cake at the restaurant.

A. eat　B. ate　C. eaten　D. eating

(9) (　　) sports all day long, she was completely tired out.

A. Having played　B. Not playing　C. Played
D. Being playing

(10) Please sign your name here to ( ) that your address and phone number on this form are correct.

A. adjust　B. modify　C. reclaim　D. certify

(11) These rules ( ) many ways.

A. write　B. read　C. understand　D. interpret

(12) He ( ) a man from captivity.

A. rescued　B. supported　C. assisted　D. contributed

(13) Computerization has ( ) in the gradual disappearance of many manual jobs.

A. got　B. followed　C. finished　D. resulted

(14) I couldn't ( ) why my mother told me to come back early, but then I found out that she had arranged a surprise party for me.

A. figure in　B. make out　C. draw in　D. act out

(15) He will call me as soon as he ( ) his work.

A. will finish　B. will have finished　C. would finish
D. has finished

(16) Since she is a born ( ), she tends to look at the best side of things.

A. gambler　B. liar　C. optimist　D. pessimist

(17) A: Can I borrow your computer tomorrow?
B: Of course. I have two, ( ) will be used tomorrow, so you can use either one of them.

A. both of which　B. all of which　C. one of which
D. neither of which

(18) My mother will go out on urgent business, so she can't go to your house. I will come to your house ( ) her.

A. by way of　B. in place of　C. in position to
D. in spite of

(19) A: How ( ) will the new factory be operational?

B: In a few months.

A. soon B. fast C. hastily D. rapidly

(20) ( ) you are right, but others don't agree.

A. No doubtfully B. No doubt C. Not doubt
D. Not any doubt

(☆☆☆◎◎◎◎◎)

【2】Read the following passage and answer the questions below.

A recent survey concluded that the average British person will say *sorry* more than 1.9 million times in his lifetime. This may strike some as a conservative estimate. From this, one could deduce that the British are especially polite. This might be true if *sorry* were always, or even usually, a straightforward apology. It isn't. The reason they stay on the sorry-go-round is that the word, in their English, is so very ①<u>versatile</u>. A. A, Gill, writing for the benefit of visitors to the London Olympics, bragged, "Londoners are just permanently petulant, irritated. I think we wake up taking offense. All those English teacup manners, the exaggerated please and thank yous, are really the muzzle we put on our short tempers. There are, for instance, a dozen inflections of the word sorry. Only one of them means 'I'm sorry.'"

Here are just a few of the many moods and meanings these two syllables can ②<u>convey</u>:

"Sorry!" (I stepped on your foot.)

"Sorry." (You stepped on my foot.)

"Sorr?" (I didn't catch what you just said.)

"SOrry." (You are an idiot.)

"SORRY." (Get out of my way.)

"SorRY." (The nerve of some people!)

"I'm sorry but..." (Actually I'm not at all.)

"Sorry..." (I can't help you,)

It's all in the tone, of course, ③<u>[permanently lost / this is / translation / *sorry* /</u>

in / and / where / becomes]. An American friend will never forget when she finally figured out that *sorry* can be a tool of passive aggression in Britain's hierarchical social system—a form of dismissal. When she was a college kid in England and people gave her an apology that was not sincere, but meant to put her in her place, she would respond earnestly, "Oh, no, it's OK! Don't worry!" ④Why wouldn't she? There are times when luck favors the ignorant.

⑤The British have a reputation for being passive-aggressive because they seem not to be saying what they mean— at least, not with words. In British culture, an anodyne word like *sorry* takes on shades of meaning that someone from outside will not be able to discern with any degree of sophistication, especially if he is from a culture that is more comfortable with confrontation, or one that condones a wider range of small talk among strangers. The British use *sorry* to protest, to ask you to repeat yourself, to soothe, and to smooth over social awkwardness as much as—if not more than—they use it to apologize. But most of the time, their object is politeness of a particularly British kind, to wit: politeness as refusal.

British courtesy often takes the form of what sociolinguists Penelope Brown and Stephen C. Levinson have called "negative politeness" —which depends on keeping a respectful distance from others and not imposing on them. Its opposite, positive politeness, is inclusive and assumes others' desire for our approval.

Only the Japanese—masters of negative politeness—have anything even approaching the British *sorry* reflex. No wonder visiting Americans are so often caught off guard, and so often feel they've been the objects of passive aggression or dismissal instead of politeness. Their misunderstanding of what constitutes politeness in Britain is not surprising, since Americans epitomize positive politeness.

When Americans say *sorry*, they mostly mean it. But, at least to British ears, they don't necessarily mean anything else they say. Americans repeat seemingly empty phrases like "Have a nice day!" They also give and receive compliments easily, even among strangers. The British find this behavior highly suspect. Hence, ⑥the American reputation for insincerity.

The English novelist Patricia Finney has said that she loves Americans because "it doesn't matter whether people actually respect me or not, so long as they treat me with courtesy and respect...I really don't mind if nice American check-out guys tell me to have a nice day and are really thinking, 'hope you have a terrible day, you snotty Brit,' so long as I don't know about it. I think sincerity is overrated in any case." ⑦Americans don't. Americans prize sincerity above most qualities. An American friend of Finney's accordingly defended the practice, saying Americans "... do respect people. It's not faked."

It could be that Americans have stopped hearing themselves. Just like the British with their *sorry*, they have certainly stopped expecting a response. Imagine the shock of a salesman who said, "Have a nice day!" to the grandfather of a friend, who answered, "Thank you, but I have other plans."

Americans are sociable and approval-seeking. They look for common ground with others and genuinely want to connect. This often takes the form of compliments—especially to complete strangers. ("I really like your wapdoodle!" "What a great snockticker!") This is because American society's fluidity can lead to insecurity. Your place in the hierarchy is based not on who you *are*, but what you *do* (and how much you *make*). Therefore, Americans incessantly seek reassurance that they are doing all right. But the marvelous thing is that they also seek to give reassurance. That may be the quality that Finney was responding to.

In British culture, you're assumed to be secure in your place, to know where you stand. But in real life, who does? ⑧Practically no one. *Sorry* and American compliments serve similar social purposes. When there's nothing to say, we can avoid social awkwardness and either deflect (UK) or connect (USA)—all in the name of politeness. *Sorry* simultaneously avoids confrontation and, when used sincerely, allows people to show how lovely they are, *really*, despite their minor transgressions. American compliments allow for a little connection, and reinforce your belonging on a level that's comfortable—at least if you're American.

(1) Choose the most appropriate meaning of the underlined ① from the four choices below.

A. having so many different uses

B. being the only one of its kind

C. being used instead of something else

D. being agreed or approved of by most people in a society

(2) Choose the most appropriate meaning of the underlined ② from the four choices below.

A. to have a conversation with somebody

B. to make ideas, feelings, etc. known to somebody

C. to make somebody or yourself believe that something is true

D. to change or make something change from one form, purpose, system, etc. to another

(3) Put the words from the underlined ③ in the correct order.

(4) Choose the most appropriate meaning of the underlined ④ from the four choices below.

A. She had no choice but to say "It's OK." without recognizing the real reason why people say *sorry* in British culture.

B. When people would say *sorry*, she didn't want to accept it and say "It's OK." but she did because she worried about her relationship to them.

C. She took it for granted that she accepted an apology in British culture, and she knew it was lucky for her to experience this way of communication.

D. She knew that people would apologize sincerely in British culture, so she really understood that she didn't have to ignore their feeling.

(5) Translate the underlined ⑤ into Japanese.

(6) Choose the most appropriate meaning of the underlined ⑥ from the four

choices below.

A. To British people, Americans seem to only mean apology when they say *sorry*, so everyone believes that American people speak sincerely.

B. Generally speaking, Americans often say something good for others and try being friendly, so British people think Americans behave sincerely.

C. Americans are famous for their dishonesty because they always say empty phrases to British people.

D. Americans easily say something which praises or admires someone, but British people don't believe in such an attitude, so they think Americans lack sincerity.

(7) What does the sentence underlined ⑦ mean? Complete the following answer to this question, filling in the blanks with the designated number of words.

> According to the English novelist Patricia Finney, she doesn't care about whether American people speak ___A(1-3)___. She thinks it is OK as long as ___B(4-6)___. She thinks sincerity should not ___C(3-4)___. However, the author shows some disagreements to this, mentioning ___D(8-12)___.

(8) Choose the most appropriate meaning of the underlined ⑧ from the four choices below.

A. People never say *sorry* stubbornly in British culture.

B. Everyone feels that they are doing right with assurance.

C. Nobody recognizes his/her precise position in their society.

D. It can be assumed that both British people and American people behave similarly.

(9) According to the text, which of the following is NOT true?

A. In American society, people have nothing in common such as a social system like the hierarchy in British culture, so they tend to seek something different from others in order to be confident of doing something right.

B. British people and Americans basically have different social systems, so it is natural for them to react differently when they meet strangers— one says "sorry" , the other gives compliments.

C. Even if Americans and British people use different ways of expression, both of them try to be polite to others in their own way, although a kind of misunderstanding in communication will sometimes happen.

D. Even when people meet strangers, they often take different ways of communication in American culture and British culture, but both of them are afraid of being clumsy in communication, so they try to avoid it.

(☆☆☆☆◎◎◎◎◎)

【中学校】

【１】Substitute the underlined phrase with the best alternative from the four choices.

(1) Mike will surely recognize Ken because he <u>stands out</u>.

A. is prominent B. is on fire C. is all ears

D. is under way

(2) I might briefly <u>have another look at</u> my notes again tonight.

A. come at B. catch at C. go over D. build over

(3) Somebody <u>removed</u> the trophy I left on the desk.

A. made bold with B. made away with C. take the chill off

D. played the bear with

(4) Meg gave up her attempt <u>once and for all</u>.

A. precisely B. gradually C. leisurely D. definitely

(5) Keiko adopted stern measures against it but <u>to no avail</u>.

A. at heart B. in vain C. up in the air D. in the way

(☆☆☆◎◎◎◎◎)

【２】Put the words in the correct order, and answer with the numbers.

(1) その先生は話を始める前に講堂内の騒がしさが静まるまでじっと待っていた。

The teacher waited patiently [① for ② die ③ the noise ④ to ⑤ down] in the auditorium before starting his speech.

(2) マリは大変腹を立てたので，自制心を失った。

Such [① Mari's anger ② she ③ lost ④ that ⑤ was] control of herself.

(3) 少女時代の経験で彼女は幸福がどういうものかを知った。

Her childhood experiences taught her [① to ② what ③ be ④ like ⑤ was ⑥ it] happy.

(4) 空港に着いて初めてパスポートを家に置き忘れてきたことに気づき，ケンはとても落胆した。

Much [① , ② his dismay ③ to ④ Ken ⑤ upon ⑥ realized] arriving at the airport that he had left his passport at home.

(5) 私は2，3分歩いたら動物園に出た。

[① me ② to ③ a few minutes'walk ④ the zoo ⑤ brought].

(☆☆☆◎◎◎◎◎)

【３】Read the following passage and answer the questions below.

Content-based language teaching (CBLT) is an instructional approach in which nonlinguistic content such as geography, history, or science is taught to students through the medium of a language that they are learning as an additional language. A major focus of CBLT is the development of literacy and academic ability with language. CBLT is a more effective and motivating way to develop such abilities than more traditional grammar-based approaches. [①] traditional methods isolate the target language from content other than the language itself, CBLT enriches classroom discourse through substantive content in a way that provides both a cognitive basis for language learning and a motivational basis for purposeful communication. Based on the premise that the best way to learn a second or foreign language (L2) is by using it rather than studying about it, CBLT provides learners with many opportunities for meaningful and purposeful language use. CBLT, however, does not preclude language instruction. Instead, CBLT promotes its integration through a counterbalanced approach that entails a dynamic interplay between language and content.

CBLT comes in many different shapes and sizes and in fact is called by other names and acronyms, including content-based instruction (CBI) and content and language integrated learning (CLIL).

At the core of CBLT is teacher scaffolding. 【　A　】 Scaffolding refers to the assistance that a teacher provides to students so that they can understand language and accomplish tasks in ways that they would be unable to do on their own without such support. Thus, while one type of scaffolding assists students in understanding content presented through their L2, another type supports them in productively using the L2 to engage with the content. Such scaffolding is essential to successful CBLT.

Teachers have at their disposal a wide range of scaffolding strategies that facilitate students' comprehension of curricular content taught through the target language. 【　B　】 In tandem with their verbal input, teachers can use props, graphs, and other graphic organizers, as well as visual and multimedia resources. To further facilitate comprehension, teachers can rely on body language, including gestures, facial expressions, and a range of other such paralinguistic elements. This type of teacher scaffolding helps to answer the burning question of how students can understand increasingly complex subject matter presented through their L2. Students can draw on the contextual clues provided in the scaffolding, while also drawing on their own prior knowledge about the topic, in order to engage with content in a language they know only partially.

Scaffolding the interaction to facilitate comprehension, however, needs to be seen as a temporary support, similar to the role of scaffolding in the construction industry. 【 C 】 That is, students need to develop increasingly more advanced comprehension strategies that enable them to process the target language autonomously without the scaffolding. Instructional techniques that rely too much on linguistic redundancy, gestures, and other visual and nonlinguistic support are unlikely over time to make the kinds of increasing demands on the learners' language system that are necessary for continued L2 learning. This means that [②], on one hand, just the right amount of support to make the target language comprehensible, while being demanding enough, on the other hand, to ensure that learners engage in higher-order cognitive skills. In other words, teachers need to avoid simplifying the curricular content and, instead, need to challenge students to interact with increasingly complex academic content. Teachers have been observed doing so by structuring their lessons as cyclical rather than linear to ensure an exploration of the content from multiple perspectives instead of as a list of facts.

Teachers need to draw on students' prior knowledge while helping them to engage in deeper levels of processing. In this way, students develop technical academic knowledge and move beyond the realm of only common-sense everyday knowledge.

Teachers need also to provide support for their students to use the target language productively. 【 D 】 First, in their own interaction with students, teachers need to give students appropriate wait time to interpret questions and formulate responses. Second, they need to create many opportunities for students to use the target language, including role plays, debates, and presentations, while also using a variety of interactive groupings in order to promote learning from and with peers (e.g., peer editing, peer tutoring, peer correction). Oral interaction between teacher and students as well as among peers is considered an important catalyst for L2 development in CBLT.

(1) Choose the most appropriate word for [①] from the four choices

below.

A.　Since　　B.　Whereas　　C.　Unless　　D.　In case

(2)　Choose the most appropriate place, from 【　A　】～【　D　】 in the text, to put the sentence below.

For example, teachers can build redundancy into their speech to convey similar meanings in various ways by using self-repetition and paraphrase, as well as multiple examples, definitions, and synonyms.

(3)　Choose the most appropriate one for [　②　] from the four choices below.

A.　learners have to accept teacher scaffolding

B.　learners should learn without instructional techniques

C.　teachers need to engage in a delicate balancing act of providing

D.　teachers need to allow students to have a say so of what they need

(4)　According to the text, which of the following is true?

A.　CBLT is a way of language education to learn L2 using a language other than the L2.

B.　Paralinguistic elements help students understand the question about complex subject matter through L2.

C.　It is important for teachers to create scaffolding to provide L2 learning opportunities that students can learn alone for CBLT.

D.　Verbal interaction between teachers and students or among peers develop students'common practice.

(5)　Considering what is written in the passage, what do you think English education in Japan should be? Write your answer with concrete reasons in approximately 100 words in English.

【4】Read the following passage and summarize this passage within 150 Japanese letters.

Why do we feel fear? It's a natural emotion that helps us and animals survive. When we think there is danger, the brain makes special hormones that send messages to the rest of the body. The heart beats faster and blood moves around the body more quickly. We also make a kind of sugar called glucose. These changes make the body stronger and make us pay more attention to the things around us. Then we are ready to find the best way to survive: fight, hide, or run away.

So, are we born with fear or do we learn it? In the early 20th century, the American scientist John Watson did a very famous experiment with an 11-month-old baby named Albert. A white rat was put near Albert many times and, each time, Watson made a very loud, frightening noise. This made the baby cry. Eventually, the baby learned to cry every time he saw the rat, even when there was no noise. Watson believed that Baby Albert had learned to fear rats.

Fortunately, experiments have gotten better and less cruel since then. By studying animals, scientists have shown that the fear hormone is made in a part of the brain called the amygdala.

Recently, Dr. Dean Mobbs from Cambridge University has shown that the emotion of fear is experienced in two ways. Twenty people were asked to put their foot in a special box with six different parts. Then, a tarantula was put in a different part of the box from the person's foot. The people watched on video as the different parts of the box were opened, allowing the tarantula to move closer to their foot.

Mobbs found that when the spider was farther away from a person's foot, there was more activity in the part of the brain that controls emotion and worry. When the spider got nearer, the part of the brain connected with panic was more active. So, we act in different ways depending on how near danger is.

But sometimes the amygdala doesn't work in the right way. This often happens when people have had a terrible experience, for example, during a war. In this case, they think danger is always present, and they feel afraid all the time. It can cause serious health problems. Life can become a nightmare.

Fear can be a good thing. People can sometimes do amazing things when they're afraid. In 2006, for example, American Tom Boyle saw a car hit an 18-year-old boy. Tom saw that he was caught under the wheels of the car. He ran over and lifted the car up, saving the young man's life!

There are also times when we feel no fear. A mother might enter a burning house to save her child, for example. Scientist Joseph Jordania calls this lack of fear *aphobia*. It can be important to help humans survive.

(☆☆☆☆☆◎◎◎)

【５】Translate the underlined sentences into English.

(1) ワールドカップの決勝トーナメントに初めて出場したラグビーの日本代表チームのスローガン「ONE TEAM」が，この国の今年の流行語大賞に選ばれたと，この賞の主催者の出版社が12月2日に発表した。

(2) プラスチックゴミは世界で最も関心を集める環境問題であり，毎年推定800万トンものプラスチックゴミが海に流れている。ある報告書では，30年以内で海のプラスチックゴミの総重量は海に生息する魚の総重量を超えると予想されている。

(☆☆☆☆◎◎◎◎◎)

【高等学校】

【１】Read the following passage and answer the questions below.

If the Pilgrims had been like many people today and simply tossed their empty bottles and wrappers over the side, Atlantic waves and sunlight [①] all that plastic into tiny bits. And those bits might still be floating around the world's oceans today, sponging up toxins to add to the ones already in them, ②wait to be eaten by some hapless fish or oyster, and ultimately perhaps by one of us.

We should give thanks that the Pilgrims didn't have plastic, I thought recently ③<u>as</u> I rode a train to Plymouth along England's south coast. I was on my way to see a man who would help me make sense of the whole mess we've made with plastic, especially in the ocean.

Because plastic wasn't invented until the late 19th century, and production really only took off around 1950, we have a mere 9.2 billion tons of the stuff to deal with. Of that, more than 6.9 billion tons have become waste. And of that waste, a staggering 6.3 billion tons never made it to a recycling bin—a figure that stunned the scientists who crunched the numbers in 2017.

No one knows how much unrecycled plastic waste ends up in the ocean, Earth's last sink, In 2015, Jenna Jambeck, a University of Georgia engineering professor, caught everyone's attention with a rough estimate: between 5.3 million and 14 million tons each year just from coastal regions. Most of it isn't thrown off ships, she and her colleagues say, but is dumped carelessly on land or in rivers, mostly in Asia. It's then blown or washed into the sea. Imagine five plastic grocery bags stuffed with plastic trash, Jambeck says, sitting on every foot of coastline around the world—that would correspond to about 8.8 million tons, her middle-of-the-road estimate of what the ocean gets from us annually. It's unclear how long it will take for that plastic to completely biodegrade into its constituent molecules. Estimates range from 450 years to never.

Meanwhile, ④<u>ocean plastic is estimated to kill millions of marine animals every year</u>. Nearly 700 species, including endangered ones, are known to have been affected by it. Some are harmed visibly—strangled by abandoned fishing nets or discarded six-pack rings. Many more are probably harmed invisibly Marine species of all sizes, from zooplankton to whales, now eat microplastics, the bits smaller than one-fifth of an inch across. On Hawaii's Big Island, on a beach that seemingly should have been pristine—no paved road leads to it—I walked ankle-deep through microplastics. They crunched like Rice Krispies under my feet. After that, I could understand why some people see ocean plastic as a looming catastrophe, worth mentioning in the same breath as climate change. At a global summit in Nairobi last December, the head of the United Nations Environment Programme spoke of an "ocean Armageddon."

And yet there's a key difference: Ocean plastic is not as complicated as climate change. There are no ocean trash deniers, at least so far. To do something about it, we don't have to remake our planet's entire energy system.

"This isn't a problem where we don't know what the solution is," says Ted Siegler, a Vermont resource economist who has spent more than 25 years working with developing nations on garbage. "We know how to pick up garbage. Anyone can do it. We know how to dispose of it. We know how to recycle." It's a matter of building the necessary institutions and systems, he says—ideally before the ocean turns, irretrievably and for centuries to come, into a thin soup of plastic.

(1) Choose the most appropriate expression for [①] from the four choices below.

A. would wear　B. would be worn　C. would have worn

D. would have been worn

(2) According to the context, write the appropriate conjugated form of the word underlined ② with one word.

(3) Which one of the following includes the same usage of the word underlined ③?

A. Many of us suffer visual problems as we age.

B. In the nineteenth century, as in the seventeenth, great social changes took place.

C. My elder sister likes wrestling as I do not.

D. I saw him as he was coming out of the house.

(4) Choose the most appropriate number from A-F which the following explanations ①-⑤ express.

① the number estimated to be the amount of plastic which finally reach the ocean after being thrown on the land area of the Earth.

② the amount of plastic production we have used since the time it was invented.

③ the time when plastic was first made and its production started to be used around the world.

④ the length of time it takes plastic thrown away and brought into the ocean to change back to a harmless natural state by the action of bacteria.

⑤ the amount of plastic production which has become waste without being used for its second life.

A. from 450 years to never

B. 6.3 billion tons

C. 9.2 billion tons

D. from the late 19th century to around 1950

E. about 8.8 million tons every year

(5) From a viewpoint of "visibly" and "invisibly", explain what the part underlined ④ indicates in detail with 100-120 Japanese letters.

(6) Complete the following partial summary about the problem in the sea with the designated number of words.

> Although there are some people who think the problem of microplastics as ____A(1)____ as that of climate change, the two are different ____B(1)____ how we should deal with it. We have to make our energy system entirely ____C(2-3)____ to struggle with climate change, but on the other hand, we have ____D(1-2)____ ocean plastic and have come up with a simple way to ____E(1-2)____ it.

(☆☆☆☆◎◎◎◎◎)

【2】Read the following passage and answer the questions below.

1 Another problem in assessing proficiency is that any evaluation ought to consider both grammatical competence and communicative competence.

Grammatical competence is what the ordinary person thinks of when we talk about "knowing a language". It's what this ordinary person calls "speaking properly". More technically, grammatical competence refers to speakers'ability to recognize and produce what are considered well-formed utterances in the language in question. That is, when given a pair of sentences, grammatical competence enables you to say, "Yes, that's how we say it in our language" or, "No, that doesn't sound right". Such grammaticality judgments are often used in testing grammatical competence in a language.

[2] Communicative competence refers to the ability to ***use*** those utterances in ways that are considered unmarked or appropriate in one situation as opposed to another in the relevant society. What is unmarked depends on who the participants are, the topic, and the setting, as well as other factors. Our communicative competence also enables us to recognize marked usages and what the speaker intends by such utterances. What someone says is marked if it is ***not*** what most people in your society would say in a given situation; instead, a marked choice of words or the entire conversational contribution is appropriate in some other situation altogether. For example, knowing when you can say *Hey, dude* to someone rather than *Good morning, sir* reflects our communicative competence. Speakers don't make many marked choices, but when they do, such a choice is a comment on how that speaker views the situation and may want others to view it.

[3] Communicative competence is sometimes referred to as pragmatic or sociolinguistic competence, especially when the emphasis is on how to interpret the speaker's intended social meaning in a particular utterance, a meaning that is not the same as the utterance's literal meaning. Thus, when someone stops you on the street and says, "Do you know where the main library is?", chances are good that he or she does not expect you to answer "yes" or "no", but to take this utterance as a request for directions to the library.

[4] Note that the native speakers of a language (or someone who learns the

language as a young child) does not need to be "taught" either grammatical competence or communicative competence. They acquire both types of competence with no obvious effort. This acquisition requires some exposure to the language in use in the speaker's community, and it is based on some innate mechanism or innate learning principles that all humans have.

5 When L2s are taught in a formal setting, the emphasis generally is on teaching—as much as it can be taught—what native speakers know as their grammatical competence. That is, most programs that teach a language in an explicit way concentrate on teaching grammatical constructions. However, more and more second language programs are recognizing the need to pay attention to communicative competence. But because of the belief that "grammar" is "the language", most L2 speakers have paid more attention to studying grammar in their language learning.

6 For this reason, many L2 speakers have more control of the L2 grammar than of its appropriate use. For example, an international student from a culture that is stereotypically considered to be very "polite" once came into my office to find out the results of a quiz that I had given the previous day. But what he said was, "I want my quiz back." I said to myself, "Why is he being so rude?" Any American student would never have said that! Instead, an American might have phrased her or his directive as a pseudo-question ("Have you graded the quizzes yet?" or "Could I find out my grade on the quiz?"). Because I'm a sociolinguist, I could answer my own question: He had learned how to ask for something in English, but didn't realize that although there are various ways to make requests, only certain ways are appropriate in an American student-professor exchange.

7 This international student spoke very grammatically correct English, but because he was lacking in communicative competence, can we say he was a "full" bilingual? Certainly, he would face a rocky road in an English-speaking society.

(1) According to the text, which of the following explanations are referring

to either grammatical competence or communicative competence? Write the letters A-F for each competence.

A. Generally, people think that if someone knows a language, that means that he/she has this competence.

B. If someone has this competence, he/she can tell an expression is right or not in the language.

C. This competence enables you to tell marked utterances from unmarked utterances in a situation.

D. This competence refers to the ability to speak accurately with well-formed utterances.

E. If you have this competence, you judge who is taking part in the conversation and how you should speak to him/her.

F. This competence enables you to know the point of view of the speaker from his/her marked utterance.

(2) Write a brief summary about how two competences, grammatical competence and communicative competence, are acquired by native speakers of a language, starting with "Grammatical competence and communicative competence" and using about 30-40 English words including the key words below. The verb can be conjugated.

Key words: effort, acquire, society, innate learning mechanism

(3) Answer the following questions related to paragraph [6].

(a) What was the problem the international student had when he spoke to the author? Explain it with about 50 Japanese letters.

(b) As a teacher, what kind of activities do you want to do in your classes in order for your students to communicate appropriately in various situations? Express your own idea with concrete examples and reasons, using about 150 words in English.

(☆☆☆☆☆◎◎◎◎)

【3】Read the following passage and answer the questions below.

Which simulation should a writer immerse himself in when composing a piece for a more generic readership, such as an essay, an article, a review, an editorial, a newsletter, or a blog post? The literary scholars Francis-Noël Thomas and Mark Turner have singled out one model of prose as an aspiration for such writers today. They call it classic style, and explain it in a wonderful little book called *Clear and Simple as the Truth.*

The guiding metaphor of classic style is seeing the world. The writer can see something that the reader has not yet noticed, and he orients the reader's gaze so that she can see it for herself. The purpose of writing is presentation, and its motive is ①<u>disinterested truth</u>. It succeeds when it aligns language with the truth, the proof of success being clarity and simplicity. The truth can be known, and is not the same as the language that reveals it; prose is a window onto the world. The writer knows the truth before putting it into words; he is not using the occasion of writing to sort out what he thinks. Nor ②<u>[of / have / the writer / does / to / for / argue / classic prose]</u> the truth; he just needs to present it. That is because the reader is competent and can recognize the truth when she sees it, as long as she is given an unobstructed view. The writer and the reader are equals, and ③<u>the process of directing the reader's gaze takes the form of a conversation</u>.

A writer of classic prose must simulate two experiences: showing the reader something in the world, and engaging her in conversation. The nature of each experience shapes the way that classic prose is written. The metaphor of showing implies that there is something to see. The things in the world the writer is pointing to, then, are *concrete*: people (or other animate beings) who move around in the world and interact with objects. The metaphor of conversation implies that the reader is *cooperative*. The writer can count on her to read between the lines, catch his drift, and connect the dots, without his having to spell out every step in his train of thought.

Classic prose, Thomas and Turner explain, is just one kind of style, whose invention they [④] to seventeenth-century French writers such as Descartes and La Rochefoucauld. ⑤The differences between classic style and other styles can be appreciated by comparing their stances on the communication scenario: how the writer imagines himself to be related to the reader, and what the writer is trying to accomplish.

Classic style is not a contemplative or romantic style, in which a writer tries to share his idiosyncratic, emotional, and mostly ineffable reactions to something. Nor is it a prophetic, oracular, or oratorical style, where the writer has the gift of being able to see things that no one else can, and uses the music of language to unite an audience.

Less obviously, classic style differs from practical style, like the language of memos, manuals, term papers, and research reports. (Traditional stylebooks such as Strunk and White are mainly guides to practical style.) In practical style, the writer and reader have defined roles (supervisor and employee, teacher and student, technician and customer), and the writer's goal is to satisfy the reader's need. Writing in practical style may conform to a fixed template (a five-paragraph essay, a report in a scientific journal), and it is brief because the reader needs the information in a timely manner. Writing in classic style, in contrast, takes whatever form and whatever length the writer needs to present an interesting truth. The classic writer's brevity "comes from the elegance of his mind, never from pressures of time or employment."

(1) Which one of the following is alternative to the underlined ①?

A. distinctive truth　B. destructive truth　C. objective truth

D. amusing truth

(2) Put the words from the underlined ② in the correct order.

(3) According to the text, what is the underlined ③ means? Explain it with about 100 Japanese letters.

(4) Choose the most appropriate word to put into [④].

A. create　B. credit　C. criticize　D. crock

(5) Translate the underlined ⑤ into Japanese.

(6) Write a summary about the difference between classic style prose and practical style prose with about 100 Japanese letters.

(☆☆☆☆◎◎◎◎◎)

解答・解説

【中高共通】

【1】(1) C (2) C (3) A (4) B (5) D (6) B (7) C (8) D (9) A (10) D (11) B (12) A (13) D (14) B (15) D (16) C (17) D (18) B (19) A (20) B

〈解説〉(1) 「and he did」が過去形になっていることに着目する。 (2) 「時期尚早」の意である。 (3) 「～せざるをえない」の意のイディオムである。 (4) 「～したかもしれない」の意である。 (5) 仮定法の倒置の形である。 (6) 「～するとはうかつである」の意である。 (7) 「実用的でない，実行不可能な」の意である。 (8) 知覚動詞の受動態の形であることに着目する。 (9) 主節が過去である分詞構文になっていることに着目する。 (10) 「証明する」の意である。 (11) 「～のように読める」の意である。 (12) 「救出する」の意である。 (13) 「～の結果になる」の意である。 (14) 「理解する」の意である。 (15) 「as soon as」に続くのは副詞節であるため，現在形または現在完了形とする。 (16) 「楽天家」の意である。 (17) 「どちらも使用されない」の意である。 (18) 「～の代わりに」の意である。 (19) 「(時間的に)どのくらい早く」の意である。 (20) 「疑いなく」の意である。

【2】(1) A (2) B (3) and this is where sorry becomes permanently lost in translation (4) A (5) イギリス人は，少なくともことば

では，思っていることを言っていないように見えるという理由で，受動的でありながら攻撃的であるとされている。　(6)　D

(7)　A　sincerely or not (3words)　B　they are seemingly polite to her (6words)　C　be estimated too much (4words)　D　Finney's friend's words that Americans believe in respecting people (8words)　(8)　C

(9)　A

〈解説〉(1)「用途が広い」の意である。　(2)「(意味や意思を)伝達する」の意である。　(3)　並べ替えた英文は「そして，これによって翻訳における "sorry" の意味が永久に失われてしまう」の意である。

(4)　下線部の前後の文に着目するとよい。イギリスにおけるsorryの意味は受動的な攻撃行動であるが，アメリカ人の友人はそのことを理解していなかったのである。　(5)　文構造はあまり複雑ではないので，基本に忠実に和訳をすればよい。seem to be ～ingが「～しているように見える」の意であることに注意したい。　(6)　第7パラグラフの2～4文目に着目するとよい。イギリス人からすると，アメリカ人は意味のない社交的なお世辞などを言っている点が，言動不一致のように思えるのである。　(7)　第8パラグラフの内容を言い換えていることに着目する。できるだけ英文中の表現を用いて書きたいところだが，英文の表現をそのまま使用できない箇所が多いので，注意したい。

(8)　第11パラグラフの1～2文目に着目するとよい。「イギリス文化では，自分の立場をわきまえるのが当然と見なされるが，現実はどうだろうか」と述べている。　(9)　本文と一致しないものを選ぶ。第10パラグラフでは「アメリカ人は他人と共通のところを探そうとする傾向がある」と，Aと逆のことを述べている。

【中学校】

【１】(1)　A　(2)　C　(3)　B　(4)　D　(5)　B

〈解説〉(1)「目立つ」の意である。　(2)「見直す・再点検する」の意である。come at「～に達する」，catch at「～に飛びつく」。　(3)「持ち出す」の意である。make away withで「～を持ち逃げする」，make bold withは「～を勝手に使う」である。　(4)「きっぱり」の意である。(5)「無駄だった」の意である。up in the airは「未定で」。

【2】(1)　①→③→④→②→⑤　(2)　⑤→①→④→②→③
(3)　②→⑥→⑤→④→①→③　(4)　③→②→①→④→⑥→⑤
(5)　③→⑤→①→②→④

〈解説〉(1)　wait A to doの形で「Aが～するのを待つ」の意になる。
(2)　倒置になっているために名詞と動詞が逆になっているが，元の文はMari's anger was such that she lost control of herself.の形である。
(3)　itがto以下の形式主語になっていることに着目する。　(4)　much to one's dismayで「～にとって落胆したことには」の意である。また，on(upon)～ingで「～するとすぐに」の意であることにも着目するとよい。　(5)　無生物主語の基本的な形である。

【3】(1)　B　(2)　B　(3)　C　(4)　B　(5)　I think we need to train students to learn English by themselves. They work on their homework hard, but they are not good at finding what they need to learn by themselves. During class time, there should be a scaffolding technique that encourages students to learn English by themselves. We should give students more opportunities to build their confidence through speeches and conversations with ALTs. This will give students the boost they need to see that what they are learning can be put to good use. This will motivate them to learn more by themselves. By doing so, we can make students eager to learn English. (106 words)

〈解説〉(1)　空所を含む文は，CBLTと伝統的教授法を対比させて述べていることに着目したい。whereas「～であるのに対して」は，2つの事柄に大きな差があるときに用いられる。　(2)　与えられた文は，「教師がたくさんの例や同義語の使用に加え，繰り返しや言い換えを行うことによって，伝えたいことを様々な方法で表現する」ということを述べている。これは第4パラグラフで言及されている，英語教師が行うscaffolding(足場かけ)の具体例であり，空所Bの直後の文In tandem with their verbal input,…のverbal inputに対応する。 (3) 空所の後に直接的に続くのは，just the right amount of support to make the target language comprehensible「目標言語を理解可能にするのに適切な量の支援」であるので，C「教師が提供するにあたり，微妙なバランスを取らなければならない」が適切。 (4) 第4パラグラフの3～4文目に，ボディランゲージやゼスチャー，表情などのパラ言語が生徒の理解に役立つと述べている。 (5) 本文の内容を踏まえて，日本の英語教育に求められるのは何であると考えるかを100字程度で記述する。本文中で述べられているCBLTに基づいた指導法を具体的に書けば良いだろう。本文で使用されている表現を用いながら，ポイントを絞ってまとめていくのが書きやすいと思われる。

【4】恐怖は人間や動物の生存に寄与してきた。危険が迫ると脳が特別なホルモンを作り，危機に対する対応の仕方を判断させる。様々な実験により恐怖を感じたときの脳の働きは明らかになっているが，直面している危機の状況によって恐怖の度合いは変化し，その度合いにより状況への対応の仕方も異なる。(147字)

〈解説〉英文を150字以内の日本語で要約する問題である。要約を作成するには，元の英文のメインアイデアを特定した上で，不要なものは削除したり，関連しているものは統合したりして整理する。メインアイデアを特定する際は，具体例そのものについての記述は含めず，その具体例が説明している内容に着目するとよいだろう。本問では，最初のパラグラフの内容を簡潔にまとめた上で，それ以降のパラグラフについては，恐怖に関する具体的な実験の内容や，実際に起こったできごとに関する記述は削除し，これらのことからわかったことに絞ってまとめていけばよい。

【5】(1) "One Team," the motto for the Japan national rugby team that made the World Cup knockout phrase for the first time, has been selected as the country's top buzzword for this year. (2) One report has predicted that all the weight of plastic waste in the oceans will exceed that of fish in just thirty years.

〈解説〉基本的な和文英訳の問題である。和文英訳を行う際には，英語の文構造を意識しながら書く。本問の(1)は主部が，(2)は述部が長くなるが，文構造を考えれば対応できる問題である。また，与えられた日本語が英訳しにくい場合は，英訳しやすいように日本語の文を解釈する。例えば，(2)の「ある報告書では，～予想されている」を「ある報告書は，～と予想している」と解釈すれば，文構造が定まって書きやすくなるだろう。

【高等学校】

【1】(1) C (2) Waiting (3) D (4) ① E ② C ③ D ④ A ⑤ B (5) 捨てられた漁の網などによって目に見える形で傷つけられる海洋生物もいれば，その身体の大きさに関わりなくマイクロプラスチックを食べて目に見えない形で危害を被っている生物もさらにたくさんおり，その種類は絶滅危惧種も含めて700近い。(112字) (6) A serious (1words) B in (1words) C new or different (3words) D noticed (1words) E tackle

〈解説〉(1) 仮定法過去完了形は，条件節は過去完了形，帰結節は助動詞の過去形＋have＋過去分詞となる。また，空所後の後に目的語が続いていることから，能動態の形が適切である。 (2) 下線部②は，直前にあるsponging up～の節と並列して主節を修飾している。
(3) 「～する時に，～している間に」の意味を表すasの用法である。
(4) ①「地球上に捨てられ，最終的に海に到達するプラスチックの量」は，第4パラグラフの5文目より，年間約880万トン。 ②「プラスチックの発明以後，私たちが使用してきたプラスチックの量」は，第3パラグラフの1文目より，92億トン。 ③「プラスチックが最初に作られ，世界中で生産され始めた時期」は，第3パラグラフの1文目より，19世紀後半に発明され1950年ごろに世界中で生産が始まった。
④「廃棄され海に運ばれたプラスチックが，バクテリアの働きによって，無害な自然の状態に戻るまでにかかる時間」は，第4パラグラフの6～7文目より，450年以上，あるいは永久に戻らない。　⑤「再利用されずに廃棄物となるプラスチックの量」は，第3パラグラフの3文目より63億トン。　(5)　下線部④の文意は「海を漂うプラスチックは，年間数百万もの海洋生物を殺していると推定される」。visiblyとinvisibly(プラスチック製品による負傷などの目に見える被害と，プラスチックの誤食・誤飲などによる目に見えない被害)に着目しながら，第5パラグラフの2～5文目の内容をまとめればよい。　(6)　要約文の空所に指定の語数で適切な語を記入する問題。第6パラグラフと第7パラグラフの内容の要約である。

【2】(1)　Grammatical competence…A，B，D　Communicative competence… C，E，F　(2)　(Grammatical competence and communicative competence) can be acquired without any effort by the native speakers of a language based on an innate learning mechanism, and he/she has to be exposed to the language used in the speaker's society.(33 words)
(3)　(a)　文法的には正しい英語だが，普通ネイティブスピーカーである学生が教授に対して使う表現ではなかった。(48字)　(b)　I think I should give them a lot of opportunities to practice reading a context, imagining the situation and focusing on appropriate expressions.

For example, while reading the text, students can think about the character's positions in the situation and focus on the expressions used by working on answering some quiz questions individually or in a group discussion. Also, they can create a story, set a situation and make the characters use appropriate expressions. This kind of activity can be an opportunity to acquire communicative competence in English.

In Japanese, we usually consider who we are talking to and what kind of expression we should use. We can do that because we have experienced various situations and how people use the language in our everyday lives. However, we lack time to experience this in English. So, it is necessary for students trying to learn English as a foreign language to do those kinds of things consciously in English lessons. (159 words)

〈解説〉(1) grammatical competenceは第1パラグラフで，communicative competenceについては第2パラグラフと第3パラグラフで述べられている。前者は文法的な正確さに関わる能力を，後者は社会言語学的能力や談話能力を指す。 (2) ネイティブスピーカーは，grammatical competenceとcommunicative competenceをどのように身につけるか，簡潔に要約せよという問題。第4パラグラフに記述があるが，英文の書き出しと，使用するキーワードが指定されているので，それらに合わせて表現を工夫しなければならない。 (3) (a) 「international studentが著者に話しかけたときの問題は何だったか」を，50字程度の日本語で記述する問題。指定の文字数が少ないので，第6パラグラフの最終文と第7パラグラフの1文目をまとめればよい。 (b) 設問は「学習者が様々な状況下で適切にコミュニケートできるようにするには，教師としてどのような教室活動をするか」。自分の意見を150語程度の英語で記述する問題。語数が多く，英文に書かれている内容に基づいて，自分で例を挙げつつ答える必要がある。おさえるべきポイントとしては，第6パラグラフに述べられているように，知識としては様々な表現を知っていても，ポライトネス(言語的配慮)に注意が向けられない学習者にならないよう，状況によって適切な表現が異なることを体験的に学ばせるような工夫を書けるとよいだろう。

【3】(1) C (2) does the writer of classic prose have to argue for
(3) 筆者によって示されようとしていることに読者が目を向ける過程は，読者が，筆者が書いたものの行間を読み，点をつなぎ，思考をたどるという作業を通じて，その真意をつかむという意味で，会話と比喩されている。(98字) (4) B (5) 伝統的(標準的)な様式とそう

でないものの違いは，コミュニケーションのシナリオにおけるそれぞれのスタンスを比べることによって理解できる。つまり，筆者がいかに読者とのつながりを想像するか，そして，筆者が何を目指しているか，だ。　(6)　実用的な様式では，筆者と読者の立場や役割がはっきり決まっており，筆者は読者に必要な情報を，ひな型を用いて簡潔に与えることが目的となっているのに対し，伝統的な様式では，興味深い事実を示すために，どんな形式にも，どんな長さにもなる。(114字)

〈解説〉(1)「公平な(立場での)真実」の意であるため，「客観的な真実」を意味する選択肢が適切。　(2)　Norが文頭に来ていることから，倒置にすることに注意する。整序後の文意は「古典散文の作者もまた真実について議論する必要はない」。　(3)　下線部は，「作者が読み手の視線を誘導するプロセスが会話の形式をとる」の意であり，この内容について具体的に説明しているのは，第3パラグラフの5～6文目である。　(4)　credit to～は「(功績などを)～に帰する」の意である。残りの選択肢の多くは他動詞で使用されることが多いこともヒントになるだろう。　(5)　英文の構造は複雑なものではなく，最初の文は主部がThe differences between classic style and other stylesであり，動詞がcan be appreciatedである。また，コロン(：)の後ろの文についても，基本的な間接疑問文になっている。コロンの後は前の文の補足説明になっていることがわかれば，あとは基本に従って丁寧に和訳をすればよい。
(6)　classic style(伝統的な形式)とpractical style(実用的な形式)の違いを，100字程度の日本語で記述する問題。前者は第6パラグラフの主に4文目，後者は同パラグラフの2～3文目に述べられている。これらの違いが分かるように対比を意識しながらまとめればよい。

2020年度　実施問題

【中高共通】

【１】Choose the answer that best completes the sentences from the four choices.

(1) If it (　　) for any misunderstanding between us, we would have got along with each other.

A. were not　B. had not been　C. is not　D. has not been

(2) When I was a student, I (　　) stay up late at night in order to study for the exam, but now, I never do that because it is not good for my health.

A. got used to　B. was used to　C. used to　D. wouldn't

(3) (　　) learning French, learning English is a little easier for me.

A. When it comes to　B. Compared with　C. As for
D. Compromised with

(4) I really wanted to know (　　) or not he had done something right.

A. whether　B. if　C. whatever　D. either

(5) He teaches me the way (　　) I should speak French.

A. in which　B. which　C. where　D. of what

(6) Both groups are (　　) that their lives are misrepresented or misunderstood by the outside world.

A. convicted　B. convinced　C. converged　D. convected

(7) Walking around in town sometimes (　　) you to find an interesting custom locally carried on.

A. lets　B. makes　C. has　D. enables

(8) It was not (　　) I came here that I realized how hard this work was.

A. before long　B. until　C. by　D. as long as

(9) I (　　) to him that he should consider the plan before carrying it out.

A. told　B. ordered　C. spoke　D. suggested

(10) Their late arrival was (　　) the rain.

A. for the purpose of　B. owing to　C. according to

D. on the faith of

(11) The news of new drug development (　　) many researchers.

A. surprise　B. are surprisingly　C. were surprised by

D. surprised

(12) That song (　　) me that I enjoyed my school life long time ago.

A. remembers　B. recalls　C. reminds　D. reacts

(13) I'd rather play golf than (　　).

A. swim　B. swam　C. swimming　D. to swim

(14) It is estimated that the number of people who visit the site is about 20,000 (　　).

A. frequently　B. slowly　C. gradually　D. annually

(15) The four-year drought has caused widespread (　　).

A. family　B. famine　C. fable　D. fabric

(16) Karl has (　　) experience in modern methods of diagnosis.

A. considerable　B. considerate　C. consideration

D. considering

(17) The system brings both financial and environmental benefits, (　　) being especially welcome.

A. the last　B. the latter　C. later　D. the latest

(18) I had an appointment. Otherwise, I (　　) with you.

A. went　B. would go　C. would have gone

D. would like to go

(19) When something wrong happens here, if it's not big, no one will be any the (　　).

A. wiser　B. longer　C. participant　D. witness

(20) They made a great change on that plan without (　　) just before carrying it out.

A. a second thought　B. the first impression　C. another idea

D.　the last decision

(☆☆☆◎◎◎◎)

【2】Read the following passage and answer the questions below.

There are both positive and negative aspects to the functions of silence in Japan. To begin with, it is important to note exactly when Japanese people are silent. Silence occurs when people have nothing to say, of course, but it does not always mean that they have no ideas. Silence is commonly thought to indicate thoughtfulness or hesitation in trying to find a good way to communicate smoothly; therefore, even though people have something to say, they may not express ①[leave / everything / true intentions / that they / their / have / and / may / in mind] unspoken. This kind of silence is known as *enryo-sasshi* (i.e., reserve and restraint). In high-context Japanese culture (Hall, 1970), direct verbal expression, especially negative forms of communication such as anger, hate, refusal, disagreement, and defiance are avoided:

②Ideas and feelings that might hurt the other person or damage the general atmosphere when expressed are carefully sent back for reexamination in an internal self-feedback process. Only those ideas judged safe and vague are allowed to be sent out through the small exit that functions as a screen filter. This message-screening process ...is *enryo*; it makes the Japanese appear silent, vague, and awkward in communicating with superiors, strangers, and people from different cultures. (Ishii & Bruneau, 1994)

Japanese TV commercials provide a good illustration of *enryo-sasshi* in communication. In ads promoting pharmaceutical drugs, for example, it is common to have famous actors or TV personalities play the role of "warm family members" in promoting a medicine rather than to clearly explain its efficacy because this tends to be felt as "wordy" or "pushy" by Japanese [　③　]. People prefer being appealed to gradually in a more "feeling" atmosphere in Japanese forms of communication (Akiyama, 1994).

Japanese silence occurs not only in public but also ④in private interactions, particularly in conjugal relationships, because "the couple are in love but too embarrassed to express their feelings in speech" (Lebra, 1987). Husbands and wives in Japan tend not to use overt verbal communication and try to understand each other by nonverbal means, especially when they attempt to express tender emotions (ibid.). Silence in this case may reflect their feelings of embarrassment caused by closeness or intimacy, or it may have to do with a specific Japanese way of thinking related to *ishin denshin* and *enryo-sasshi*. Silence thus functions as a kind of lubricating oil to create smoother communication because it can help to avoid hurting others and contributes to a peaceful and harmonious atmosphere, allowing people to overcome difficult situations in a calm and unhurried way.

On the other hand, silence can frequently cause misunderstandings, even in Japanese interactions. In fact, it is not unusual for people to feel irritated and impatient when they cannot understand each other because their expressions are too indirect to follow. It is also true that in Japan, actions or judgments tend to be delayed, so it often takes too much time to clarify the facts and solve problematic situations.

The Japanese may also be silent not only to avoid conflict with others but also to hurt someone or to keep them at a distance. When people feel angry or are in disagreement with others, they may not directly express their feelings but often just keep silent and ignore the other person. [1] [2] [3] [4]

Even in communication among the Japanese themselves, it is sometimes difficult to understand the actual meaning and function of silence. In communication with people from other countries, silence can become a serious obstacle to intercultural understanding.

For one thing, as has been explained, when the Japanese are silent, it may imply a wide range of meanings, such as consideration or sympathy, modesty, agreement, patience, embarrassment, resentment, lack of forgiveness or defiance, and apathy. ⑤<u>This can cause confusion for non-Japanese</u>, as they usually do not have similar cultural values that help them to interpret the meaning of silence. In fact, sometimes they will have totally opposite attitudes and values.

Generally speaking, Western cultures have long emphasized verbal expression and communicating opinions and emotions clearly and openly:

> The Western tradition is relatively negative in its attitude toward silence and ambiguity, especially in social and public relations. People seldom recognize that silence does have linking, affecting revelational, judgemental, and [⑥] communicative functions in Western cultures. (Jensen; cited in Ishii & Bruneau, 1994)

At the same time, there may be a different concept of time, depending on the communication style. According to Naotsuka (1996), many people from other countries consider the Japanese communication style, which is characterized by silence and indirectness, as "wasting time." Japanese society is based on the smooth maintenance of relationships among group members, [⑦] relationships in the West put more emphasis on individualism, so that time spent in silence or for indirect purposes may be seen as not very productive (ibid.).

However, Westerners are not always more talkative and frank than the Japanese. In some situations, the Japanese can ask certain kinds of blunt peasonal questions, such as "How old are you?" or "Are you married?" ⑧<u>Although Western people may consider these kinds of questions impolite or "intrusions of privacy" (ibid.), in Japanese relationships, where people are attuned to depending on one another, personal information of this nature is needed in order to get along with others.</u>

Judging from the above, although there are a number of important cultural differences in communication styles, people may not consciously be aware of them and will judge or criticize others according to their own values or standards of communication. ⑨<u>This</u> can be one of the most troublesome obstacles to intercultural understanding.

(1) Put the words from the underlined ① in the correct order.

(2) Translate the underlined ② into Japanese.

(3) Choose the best word for [③] from the four choices below.

A. consumers　B. producers　C. executors　D. composers

(4) According to the text, what is NOT the function of silence in the situation of the underlined ④ ? Choose the most appropriate one from the four choices.

A. to reflect their feelings of embarrassment

B. to create smoother communication as a kind of lubricating oil

C. to avoid overcoming difficult situations in a calm and unhurried way

D. to contribute to a peaceful and harmonious atmosphere

(5) Choose the best sentence for each of [1] ～ [4] from the four choices below to complete the part of this text. You have to use each choice only once.

A. If students see someone being bullied, they may not mention anything about the fact and just try to keep a distance from both the assailant and the victim, for fear of being mixed up in the bullying themselves.

B. In short, silence also means defiance and indifference in Japanese life.

C. Similarly, in a train, if people recognize that someone is being molested, they may not say anything to help the victim, because they are afraid of disapproval for their forward behavior, or simply because they are apathetic.

D. This behavior characterizes bullying, which has recently become a much more serious problem among Japanese children.

(6) As for the underlined ⑤, what can cause the confusion? And why? Explain with 70-80 Japanese letters.

(7) Choose the best word for [⑥] and [⑦] from the four choices below.

⑥ A. activating　B. progressive　C. settling

D. stabilizing

⑦ A. because B. if C. therefore
D. whereas

(8) Translate the underlined ⑧ into Japanese.

(9) According to the text, what is the underlined ⑨ means? Explain with 50-60 Japanese letters.

(☆☆☆◎◎◎◎)

【中学校】

【1】Choose the most appropriate sentence from the four alternatives below to fill in each blank.

(1) A: We've run out of staples.
B: (　　)
ア Right after the meeting.
イ I'll bring some more envelopes.
ウ That's good exercise.
エ Have you checked the stationery cabinet?

(2) A: She's being promoted next week, isn't she?
B: (　　)
ア No, she did it herself.
イ Yes, Emma said so.
ウ She should be proud of you.
エ She hasn't gone far.

(3) A: How often do you work overtime?
B: (　　)
ア Hardly ever.
イ Not so fast.
ウ It's been a long time.
エ We'll need quite a bit.

(4) A: Would you like me to call Bobby, or would you rather speak to him

yourself?

B: (　　)

ア　He probably won't attend it.

イ　Could you take care of that?

ウ　Let's meet at the lobby then.

エ　I call him Bob.

(☆☆◎◎)

【2】Read the following passage and choose the best sentence for each of [1] ~ [5] from the seven choices below.

A: Hi, my name is Richard, and I'm calling because I think I left my bag at the theater earlier this evening at the five thirty performance. [1]

B: This is the ticket office, but maybe I can help you. Well...it looks like there's a small bag here. [2]

A: My bag is also that color. What's inside of it? [3]

B: Let's see... [4] What else did you put in your bag?

A: I don't remember, but the one I'm missing is black, with a zipper.

B: [5] Well, our cleaning staff is going through the theater right now. If you can leave me your phone number, I'll call you immediately if anything turns up.

A: I need my bag. I can't drive a car without that card.

A.　I can't find it.

B.　Oh, maybe we have the one you're missing.

C.　Is this where I can ask?

D.　What does your bag look like?

E.　This bag doesn't, have it.

F.　It's black with a key chain.

G.　It's got my wallet with my driver's license inside.

(☆☆◎◎)

【3】Read the following passage and answer the questions below.

Motivation in language-learning plays a vital role. It is motivation that produces effective second-language communicators by planting in them the seeds of self-confidence. It also successfully creates learners who continuously engage themselves in learning even after they complete a targeted goal. In order for English instructors to motivate them, a number of methods are needed both in and outside of class. According to Hussin, Maarof, and D'Cruz, "positive self-concept, high self-esteem, positive attitude, clear understanding of the goals for language learning, continuous active participation in the language learning process, the relevance of conductive environment that could contribute to the success of language learning" (2001). They state that six factors influence motivation in language learning: attitudes, beliefs about self, goals, involvement, environmental support, and personal attributes (2001). Above all, three specific elements are strongly believed to build motivation towards language-learning: self-confidence, experiencing success and satisfaction, and good teacher-learner relationships as well as relationships between learners. All three factors are believed to be correlated to each other in the process of motivation development. This paper demonstrates analysis of three factors that have a solid connection with motivation.

Self-confidence is the most significant in language-learning. It provides learners with the motivation and energy to become positive about their own learning. It also creates the ①drive in them to acquire the targeted language, enjoy the learning process, and experience real communication. "At the heart of all learning is a person's belief in his or her ability to accomplish the task" (Atsuta, 2003). "In general, successful language learners appear to have higher self-esteem than those who are unsuccessful" (Richard-Amato, 2003). Lack of belief in one's ability hinders him from achieving that task—pursuing a targeted language accomplishment. Moreover, it is widely believed that once students gain self-confidence, it progressively expands, in conjunction with experiencing success and satisfaction as well as good relationships.

Experience of success provides students with more power to pursue a new goal. It allows language learners to understand the purpose of trying and have pleasure in communicating with others. Some people might feel successful when they can communicate their thoughts to people; others might feel the sense of success when they complete a challenging task in a targeted language. The feeling of success time and again emerges specifically when he realizes the degree of his improvement and achievement. Some people, on the other hand, appreciate compliments from others. Subrahmanian suggests that external praise for one's improvement is strongly related to fomenting the sense of success (2001). There is a similarity between the experience of success and satisfaction; the experience of success at all times satisfies people not only in language-learning but also in anything. To make it short, it is strongly believed that the experience of success comes hand in the hand with the sense of satisfaction.

According to Lile, "a student will find it difficult to perform in a stressful environment" (2002). He also mentions that "the lessons must be very simple, yet fun and interesting, with a lot of changes from a writing exercise, to a speaking, listening, back to writing, and so on" . Nunan states that "students need to be able to use the skills taught in the classroom to do things other than those that they had been specifically taught" (1999). This implies that in order for language learners to experience success and become satisfied, ②<u>[is / for / to / essential / create / environment / it / a / relaxing / instructors / learning</u>] so that students can perform successfully. Moreover, a language class needs to contain a variety of materials and activities focusing on all necessary skills. By encouraging students to practice not only one skill but all, the class will become more challenging and effective.

According to Hussin, Maarof, and D'Cruz, "teachers need to find creative ways to teach the language and increase the student's motivation to learn the language and to eventually appreciate the language" (2001). There are a number of methods that English instructors can use to motivate students in class, and instructors should flexibly employ the most suitable method for the class. Furthermore, Kabilan indicated that “Teachers should develop a mutual relationship with their learners” (2000). In order to develop a mutual relationship with their learners, teachers need to understand students who are from different backgrounds, have different interests, future goals, aims for English learning, and most importantly, different personalities. Once they understand them better, teachers are able to apply specific teaching and communicating strategies tailored to each student, thereby creating a trusting relationship between a teacher and student. Once a [③] develops, the classroom will become comfortable and enjoyable enough for students to learn positively from the teacher without any hesitation.

Hussin, Maarof, and D’Cruz mention that “what occurs in the language classrooms must be extended beyond the walls of the classroom so that a link is created between what is learned in the classrooms with what occurs outside of the classrooms” (2001). Languages cannot be learned merely in classrooms. Learning a language requires communication in real life situations. Thus, students need to acquire an array of communication skills that they can use with various kinds of people. It is essential that they learn not only how to communicate in the target language but also the background, history, and culture that defines it.

“Students who remain silent in groups of ten or more will contribute actively to discussions when the size of the group is reduced to five or three. Type of communicative task can also influence students’ willingness to speak” (Nunan, 1999). According to Richard-Amato, “In classrooms in which mutual respect is lacking, differing values can lead to conflicts between student and teacher, and between student and peer” (2003). The classroom size and the size of group are to be carefully considered. Language learners tend to feel frightened to make a speech in front of a big group. Thus, teachers need to aid students who need support and encourage them to understand that no one can be as perfect as native speakers. In addition, teachers are required to teach all the students the importance of having respect for one another in a classroom so that each of the students can actively participate in lesson.

(1) Choose the word that is the closest in meaning to the underlined word ① from the four alternatives below.

A. action　B. goal　C. movement　D. will

(2) Put the words from the underlined ② in the correct order.

(3) Choose the most appropriate word ③ from the text to make a comprehensible sentence.

(4) According to the text, which of the following is NOT true?

A. Learners can be positive if self-confidence leads to the motivation and the energy for them to make a denial of opportunities for learning language.

B. If the students experience success and become satisfied, they make more challenging and effective classes.

C. Languages should be learned not only in the classroom but also in daily life so that students need to get communication skills that they can use with many people.

D. Teachers need to tell students how important it is to respect each other if they want students to participate actively in lesson.

(5) Considering what is written in the passage, how do you motivate students to learn English? Write your answer with concrete reasons in approximately 100 words in English.

【4】Read the following passage and summarize this passage within 100 Japanese letters.

Do you ever feel that as you get older, every year seems to go by quicker? This speed only seems to be increasing, especially with social media. Every news feed, status update, comment and "like" floods us with information about someone's success, their amazing holiday or the delicious food they've eaten. And it can sometimes feel like everyone else's lives are electronically flashing past your eyes, leaving you behind.

For some people, when they see all these experiences, they can feel a lot of pressure to keep up with the lives of others. They don't want to miss any opportunities to be social, to try unusual things or to make or save money. A person with a bad case of this anxiety is a person with FOMO—the fear of missing out. They tend to be worried that they will make the wrong decision, not have the latest gadget, or not share the latest and greatest experience.

The pressure not to miss out on the latest thing is something I've noticed in Japan particularly. On a lot of food and drink packaging are four kanji: FOR A LIMITED TIME ONLY. And in many restaurants, I now notice another four kanji: LIMITED NUMBER AVAILABLE. It's a great way to get customers to buy these things, as we're often told to live life to its fullest and to grab every opportunity that we can, because we could die tomorrow.

I've developed a new perspective on this need to never miss an opportunity ever since an encounter with a pack of Nara deer. I wouldn't call it a near-death experience, but it was pretty frightening.

I had wandered away from my friends to take some photos, and as I was checking my shoe for deer droppings, I heard a bang and then what sounded like rolling thunder. I looked up to see a large herd of deer running directly towards me at full speed. I froze and thought: "Is this it? Is this how I'm going to die? Trampled by panicking Nara deer while checking my shoes for deer poop? Not even killed by a predatory animal? Really?"

Thankfully, the deer were smarter than me and turned away at the last second. I didn't see my life, or anyone else's flash past my eyes. I only felt grateful that I had spent most of my day with friends. And it made me realize — we never really miss out on anything, because life is already full of everything. So, instead of trying to look for something new, we should pay attention to what we can enjoy from something now. Yes, life is for a limited time only, but the ways to fill it?　Well, those are unlimited.

(☆☆☆☆◎◎)

【5】Translate the sentences into English.

(1) もし宝くじが当たったら，新しい車を買おう。

(2) 私たちは2人とも東京に行ったことがあるが，どちらも北海道に行ったことはない。

(☆☆☆◎◎◎◎)

【高等学校】

【1】Read the following passage written by the British broadcaster Ms. Sarpong and answer the questions below.

[1] In March 2017 Theresa May unveiled her plans to set aside £320 million to fund 140 free schools, the majority of which would be grammar schools; a new scheme which would create 70,000 new school places. Within days a cross-party alliance between former Conservative education secretary Nicky Morgan, Liberal Democrat and former deputy prime minister Nick Clegg, and ex-shadow education minister Lucy Powell was set up to oppose Theresa May's plans. This new gang of three presented their argument in a joint op-ed in the *Observer* newspaper:

> All the evidence is clear that grammar schools damage social mobility. Those championing selection as the silver bullet for tackling social mobility, or as the panacea for creating good new school places, are misguided. Whilst they can boost attainment for the already highly gifted, they do nothing for the majority of children, who do not attend them. Indeed, in highly selective areas, children not in grammars do worse than their peers in non-selective areas.

As a state-school-educated kid myself, I'm inclined to agree with the 'gang of three'. I understand Theresa May's faith in grammar schools, of course: that style of education set her on the path to leadership, just as it did with Margaret Thatcher and countless other grammar-school-educated success stories, but ①that was then and this is now. There was a time when grammar schools acted as an effective social mobility pipeline for gifted children from lower-income families to enter white-collar jobs. However, this system of benefiting the top 20 per cent of children in the state-school system worked when we had enough low-skilled manual jobs to go round for the remaining 80 per cent.

2 As we know, this is no longer the case, so we are going to need ②an education system that benefits the majority of kids, not just the gifted few. What is the modern answer to grammar schools? Something tells me it isn't more grammar schools. We must seek to raise the aspirations and academic attainment levels of a wider range of children — if we fail, this will only worsen our growing income inequality and further entrench our class divides.

3 I would argue that through our education system we have an opportunity to tackle the issues we have with the 'other' class by creating a class in common — by producing generations of open-minded young people who neither fear nor discriminate against 'others', but instead have an understanding and appreciation of their history, culture, and value. I believe our schools should be microcosm of society, so educating children selectively and separately based on attainment, background, gender, ethnicity, religion, or any other distinction feels counterproductive to me. In reality, we have schools divided along various lines due to legislative history, tradition, catchment area, income, and of course class. But without too much upheaval we can mitigate these divisions by adding to the national curriculum the opportunity for all students to learn alongside others from different backgrounds, as they would have to do in the workplace. This would be in the form of a national twinning programme between state and private schools, which is underpinned by an annual cross-school project. This would take the form of a diversity module in the curriculum that all students work on every academic year, which increases in difficulty each year but is designed to

require a wide range of talents and learning styles and experiences. At present, most of the interaction pupils have with other pupils from different schools usually takes the form of competitions where they are pitted against each other — whether this be through sport, debating or chess tournaments. There is not much room for collaboration with the 'other class'. A state and private school twinning model would encourage social mobility and make schools a true representation of what we need to achieve in our workplaces.

4 An in-depth exploration into the history of modern-day inequality can be taught with a focus on the emotional and psychological impact that historical moments have had on various groups, not for the purpose of attributing blame or benefit, but more as a way of understanding that we are all collectively living with the legacy and that it can be addressed if the will is there. ③This can be a vital aid to fostering cross-cultural understanding.

5 The discussion about inequality, social mobility, and inclusion needs to stop being the sole domain of liberal middle-class university academics. These same academics should be enlisted to develop the diversity module, to go into schools to help teachers disseminate this information. The conversations and the data need to be shared and studied in all schools so that our children interact with some of the smartest minds and brainstorm how best to address some of our most entrenched structural barriers. ④All this will enable students to see 'other' students as people and potentially friends, rather than demographics or statistics.

6 To some these discussions may seem too philosophical for our classroom, or not so worthy of time as reading, writing, and arithmetic. I would argue that to create the society we want, we need to make the time and effort. It will require politicians, teachers, and parents to agree that our classrooms should become hubs of debate as well as learning.

7 In society at large, we tend to exclude the other class from these discussions out of an inherent snobbery that they may lack the sophistication, relevant education, or capacity to understand or be objective. ⑤This is

something that can be eradicated using the classroom, so that children from all backgrounds can come together and help shape a new tomorrow, the better future that they will be living in as adults.

(1) According to the text, what the underlined ① means? Explain within 100 Japanese letters.

(2) According to the author, what kind of generations should be produced through the education system which is mentioned in the underlined ②? Explain with 40-50 Japanese letters.

(3) According to the text, what is the underlined ③ means? Explain within 100 Japanese letters.

(4) According to the text, which one of the following is NOT included in what the underlined ④ means? Choose the most appropriate one from the four choices.

A. to have students interact with others to think about our entrenched structural barriers

B. to share what people think and talk to each other in all schools

C. to help teachers spread the information about inequality, social mobility, and inclusion

D. to put each academic separately as different domains in middle-class universities

(5) According to the text, what is the underlined ⑤ means? Explain within 80 Japanese letters.

(6) According to the text, what is the words which mean the following explanation? Search in Paragraph [3] for the three sequent words and quote them.

A thing, a place or a group that has all the features and qualities of something much larger. In this text, it means somewhere children should learn what would happen in their future workplace and have interaction with others from various cultural backgrounds.

(7) According to the text, which one of the following is true?

A. The author has the same opinion as Theresa May's on the issue of grammar schools because she was educated in public schools.

B. The author insists that school students should have opportunity to work on solving problems collaborating with the 'other' class.

C. The author believes that there are a lot of opportunities for students to make a team with others from different backgrounds for social mobility.

D. The author thinks that students should spend much more time for reading, writing, and arithmetic at school than for fostering cross-cultural understanding.

(☆☆☆◎◎◎◎)

【2】Read the following passage and choose all of the items below which are true to the text.

You now may be saying to yourself, "Okay, diversity happens, but wouldn't life be simpler for everyone if we eliminated languages with only a few thousand speakers so that everyone would speak either the same language or one of several major languages?" Communication might be simpler with fewer languages, but most groups are not willing to give up their languages. The reason is that each language does "social work" for its speakers. Here, suffice it to say that languages often are the single most important symbol of group identity. And this is not just a pre-modern view that's lost when a group modernizes. Evidence that people consider their languages as essential symbols is that there are more official languages (serving as national symbols) in Europe today than existed in the nineteenth century.

Although the spread of international commerce and communication via long-distance phones, faxes, email, and the web may have shrunk the importance of geographical distances as an impediment to communication, linguistic diversity is here to stay. We can distill the reasons from the discussion about groups, their penchant for distinctiveness and their use of borders. As long as groups wish to distinguish themselves from other groups, many different languages will continue to be spoken. This is especially true for any language that is the official language of a nation — simply because nations have the funds to nurture a chosen official language at home. And sometimes nations go so far as to use funds to promote their L1s elsewhere as second languages; this is the case with the major European languages, especially English and French. They seek to develop or strengthen cultural and economic ties through a common language.

What is the attraction for a group of having its own language? It serves as a positive badge of identification. When groups are in contact, they both value their own language, but typically the less powerful group learns the other group's language, not vice versa. Or, sometimes near-peers communicate in a neutral language, giving no deference to either group's badge of identification. Either way, language's function as a badge promotes bilingualism because it promotes maintaining L1s and learning at least a neutral L2.

Bilingualism is a natural outcome of the socio-political forces that create groups and their boundaries. There are two reasons why bilingualism grows in the soil in which culturally distinct groups and their languages flourish.

First, this distinctiveness means that some groups command more social or economic prestige than others; when persons wish to join an attractive group, the entry fee is becoming bilingual in the language of the attractive group. Think what happens to immigrants all over the world; they almost always must learn the dominant language of their new home if they are to survive in this new setting. If a group is so attractive that others wish to cross into its territory — whether permanently or temporarily — then the group reminds those others whose territory it is that is hosting them. In most cases, this reminder comes in the form of the expectation — or the requirement, for long-term visitors — that the newcomers will learn the host's language.

Second, some groups are more powerful than others, meaning they control desirable resources. Previously, the source of such power was often military or colonial might; today, the source is more often technological expertise or economic clout. To interact with today's powerful groups, others often have to learn the languages of those groups. To take some relatively recent examples, think about such results of colonialism as the spread of Spanish and Portuguese in South America from the fifteenth century onwards, or Italian in the early twentieth century in the Horn of Africa (Eritrea, Ethiopia, and Somalia). Today, think about the need to learn English to conduct business via computers in much of the world, or the need to read critical textbooks, or the need to interact with fellow workers if your company has an international scope.

Some people learn a second language just because they like to learn languages or are attracted to a certain culture, but most L2 learners expect to benefit by improving their lives in a material way. Still, learning a language that facilitates self-improvement does not have to mean that speakers quickly lose their L1. If the immigrant group is large enough and speakers have strong networks composed of fellow immigrants who speak their language, then an L1 can be maintained for years for in-group talk with family and friends. Also, if people who have become bilingual because their jobs demand it live in nations or regions where their L1 is the main local language, many opportunities remain to speak their L1. All the activities outside of work hours can be in their L1. And even in the offices of foreign-owned conglomerates around the world, the chatter in the cafeteria is in the local language.

A. Most groups usually don't accept to stop using their languages, even though they know there is another way to make communication simpler.

B. Languages are not enough for many groups to identify themselves and to make themselves different from others.

C. Major European languages are sometimes spread through other countries in order to connect the countries culturally or economically.

D. When people go into a new place, which has another language and culture that are attractive for them, they usually try to make themselves understood in their own language in order to survive there.

E. One of the reasons of bilingual development in the places having many different groups and languages is that people need to learn the languages of the groups that have power in controlling desirable resources.

F. When people start to learn a second language, most of them must hardly be motivated to learn it by desiring to improve their material lives.

G. If people are required to become bilingual at their jobs, they usually forget their home language even though there are some opportunities to use it outside of their workplaces.

(☆☆☆◎◎◎◎)

【3】Read the following passage and answer the questions below.

Fluency is often discussed in relation to accuracy. While most second language professionals tend to agree on what it means to be accurate in a language, the concept of fluency is not as easy to define. Hartmann and Stork (1976) state that a person is fluent when he or she uses the language's structures accurately while at the same time concentrating on meaning, not form. The fluent speaker uses correct patterns automatically at normal conversational speed. Interestingly, here accuracy is seen as a major part of fluency.

An early advocate of the fluency-accuracy polarity was Brumfit (1984). He [①] the two in pedagogical contexts and makes the distinction that "accuracy will tend to be closely related to the syllabus, will tend to be teacher-dominated, and will tend to be form-based. Fluency must be student-dominated, meaning-based, and relatively unpredictable towards the syllabus". Brumfit further points out that fluency is meant "to be regarded as natural language use, whether or not it [②] in native-speaker-like language comprehension or production". It involves maximizing the language so far [③] by the learner by creating natural use in the classroom as much as possible.

Fillmore (1979) proposes that fluency [　④　] four abilities: (1) the ability to talk without awkward pauses for relatively long periods of time; (2) the ability to talk in coherent and semantically dense sentences that show mastery of syntax and semantics; (3) the ability to say appropriate things in a variety of contexts; and (4) the ability to use language creatively and imaginatively. These are abilities that language users all possess to varying degrees. Fillmore's categories are interesting in that they relate to language but also to personality. ⑤<u>They also show that there is an interaction between language use and knowledge of the world.</u> In particular, this is seen in the third and fourth characteristics.

Hedge (1993) describes fluency as "the ability to link units of speech together with facility and without strain or inappropriate slowness or undue hesitation". Similarly, ⑥<u>Richards and Schmidt</u> (2010) describe fluency as "the features which give speech the qualities of being natural and normal, including native-like use of pausing, rhythm, intonation, stress, rate of speaking, and use of interjections and interruptions". These descriptions emphasize a smoothness of language delivery, without too many pauses or hesitations. They suggest natural language use, not necessarily speaking quickly.

⑦<u>Thornbury</u> (2005) describes features of fluency centered primarily around pausing. A speaker's rate of speech is important, but it is not the only factor or even the most important one. Research on listeners' perceptions of a speaker's fluency suggests that pausing is equally important. Thornbury's four features of fluency are:

1. Pauses may be long but not frequent.
2. Pauses are usually filled.
3. Pauses occur at meaningful transition points.
4. There are long runs of syllables and words between pauses.

Fluency as a concept, it seems, includes many perspectives, and the features that make it up are still being debated.

(1) Choose the best word for each blank of [①]−[④] from the choices below. Also, make each one of them inflect appropriately if necessary. You can use each word only once.

include　acquire　result　contrast

(2) According to the text, what is the underlined ⑤ means? Explain within 100 Japanese letters.

(3) Compare the positions which the underlined ⑥ and ⑦ describe, and summarize within 100 Japanese letters.

(4) What do you think is fluency in speaking English? And how do you want to create learning conditions where the fluency can be developed? Expressyour own idea in approximately 150 words in English.

(☆☆☆☆◎◎◎◎)

解答・解説

【中高共通】

【1】(1) B　(2) C　(3) B　(4) A　(5) A　(6) B
(7) D　(8) B　(9) D　(10) B　(11) D　(12) C
(13) A　(14) D　(15) B　(16) A　(17) B　(18) C
(19) A　(20) A

〈解説〉(1) if it had not been for ～「～がなかったら」。仮定法過去完了。
(2) used to ～「以前は～したものだ」。 (3) compared with ～「～と比べて」。 (4) whether or not ～「～かどうか」。ifと交換不可。
(5) the way in which ～「～する方法」。 (6) be convinced that「～を確信している」。 (7) enable O to ～「Oに～することを可能にする」。
(8) it is not until ～ that …「～になってはじめて…する」。

(9)　suggest to O that ～「Oに～を提案する」。提案・要求・決定を表す動詞に続くthat節ではshouldが用いられる。　(10)　owing to ～「～のために」。　(11)　surprise「驚かす」。　(12)　remind O that～「Oに～を思い出させる」。　(13)　would rather ～ than …「…よりむしろ～したい」。　(14)「その遺跡を訪れる人数は年間約2万人であると推定されている」。annually「毎年」。　(15)「4年にわたる干ばつが大規模な飢饉を引き起こした」。famine「飢饉」。　(16)　considerable experience「かなりの経験，豊富な経験」。considerate「思いやりのある，熟考した」と混同しないように。　(17)「そのシステムは経済的，環境上両方の恩恵をもたらすが，後者が特にありがたい」。the latter「後者」。(18)「私には約束があった。そうでなければ(約束がなかったら)あなたと一緒に行っていただろう」。　(19)　No one will be any the wiser.「誰も気づかないだろう」。　(20)　without a second thought「考えずにすぐ」。

【2】(1)　everything that they have in mind and may leave their true intentions
(2)　表現されたときに他人を傷つけたり，全体の雰囲気を損なったりするかもしれない考えや感情は，心の中で自ら振り返る過程において，入念に再検討される。　(3)　A　(4)　C　(5)　1　D　2　A　3　C　4　B　(6)　日本人の沈黙には，幅広い意味合いが含まれていて，普通，似たような文化的価値観を持たない外国人にとって，沈黙の意味を理解するのは難しいので，困惑する。(74字)
(7)　⑥　A　⑦　D　(8)　西洋人たちは，このような質問を失礼だとか，プライバシーの侵害だとか考えるかもしれないが日本人の人間関係においては，お互いに頼りにし合う習慣があり，このような性質の個人情報は，人とうまくつき合っていくのに必要なのだ。
(9)　コミュニケーションにおいて，異文化間の違いを意識せず，自分の価値基準で他者を判断する可能性があるということ。(54字)

〈解説〉(1)「人々は言うべきことがあっても」に続く文。整序後の文意は「心の中にあるすべてのことを表現するわけではないし，本音を言わないでおくかもしれない」。 (2) when (they are) expressed「(それら＝考えや感情が)表現されたときに」。reexamination「再検討」。
(3) 日本の薬のテレビコマーシャルで，はっきりと効き目を説明しない理由を述べている部分である。冗漫で厚かましく感じられるからとある。したがって，by consumers「顧客によって」が適切。 (4) 個人的なやり取りの状況で，沈黙の機能ではないものを選ぶ。A「困惑の感情を表すこと」，B「潤滑油の一種としてスムーズなコミュニケーションを創出すること」，D「平和的で仲のよい雰囲気に役立つこと」は第3段落に記述がある。Cは同段落の最終文に逆のことが書かれているので誤り。 (5)「日本人は他人に腹を立てたり，意見が合わなかったりするとき，黙って無視をする」という内容から，Dの「いじめ」に話が及んでいる。→A「いじめを目撃するとき生徒がどのように振る舞うか」について述べられている。→C「同様に，電車内でのふるまい」に言及している。→B「沈黙は日本社会の中で無視と無関心をも意味する」と段落のまとめの文がくる。 (6) 下線部の文意は「このことが日本人ではない人に困惑を引き起こす」。「このこと」の具体的な内容は前文に，理由は下線部に続くas以下にある。内容と理由を70～80字でまとめる。 (7) ⑥「沈黙は伝達機能を持つと人々は認識していない」という内容。communicative functionsにかかる語として適切なものを選択する。activating「促進するような」。 ⑦ 空所前後で，日本社会における人間関係と西洋における人間関係について述べている。それらをつなぐ接続詞として，whereas「…だが一方」が入る。
(8) consider O C「OをCとみなす，考える」。intrusion「侵入，侵害」。be attuned to ～「～に慣れる」。 (9) 異文化理解を妨げる要因を，前文の記述から50～60字でまとめる。

【中学校】

【1】(1) エ (2) イ (3) ア (4) イ

〈解説〉(1) A「ホッチキスの針を切らしてしまいました」。B「文具棚を調べましたか？」。 (2) A「彼女は来週昇進するんですよね？」。

B「ええ，エマがそう言っていました」。　(3)　A「どれくらいの頻度で超過勤務をしますか？」。B「めったにしません」。　(4)　A「ボビーに私から電話してほしいですか，それともあなたが自分で彼に話したいですか？」。B「あなたにお願いできますか？」。take care of ～「～を引き受ける，対処する」。

【2】1　C　　2　F　　3　G　　4　A(E)　　5　E(A)

〈解説〉1　リチャードが忘れ物の件で電話をしている。C「ここで(忘れ物の)問い合わせができますか？」。　2　電話口の者が，すでに届けられているかばんの特徴をリチャードに伝えている。F「キーチェーンのついた黒いものです」。　3　リチャードが自分のかばんの中身について説明している。G「中に運転免許証の入った財布があります」。　4　中身を聞いてA「それは見つかりません」，またはE「このかばんにはそれはありません」。　5　リチャードはさらに特徴を伝えるが，A「それは見つかりません」，またはE「このかばんにはそれはありません」。

【3】(1)　A　　(2)　it is essential for instructors to create a relaxing learning environment　　(3)　relationship　　(4)　A　　(5)　I think that motivation is very important to learn something. If students have motivation to learn something new, they can understand it deeply. I think motivating students is not easy but it is important to do. For that, I have to make materials that make students want to learn. If they like the materials, they will learn English more. I think I have to give students chances to use English. If they can use the English that they learned, they will gain confidence. If they have confidence, they will try to learn English more and have motivation to learn it. (100 words)

〈解説〉(1)　自信が言語学習においてどのように作用するかを述べている箇所である。自信は，学習者に目標言語を獲得させ，学習過程を楽しませ，真のコミュニケーションを経験させるという内容から考える。

driveは「活動，運動」。　(2)　整序後の文意は「リラックスした学習環境をつくることが指導者にとって必須である」。　(3)　空所のある第5段落では，学習意欲を高めるために教師と学習者の関係作りが大切であると述べている。よって，空所にはrelationshipが入り，文意は「一度関係ができると」となる。　(4)　A「自信が言語学習の機会を拒絶するモチベーションやエネルギーにつながれば，学習者は積極的になることができる」の「拒絶する」が誤り。　(5)　生徒が英語を学ぶよう教師としていかに動機づけをするか100語程度で書く。公開解答では，教材の工夫や英語を使う機会を生徒に与えることを挙げている。本文の内容を踏まえると，自信や成功体験などがキーワードとなる。自信を持たせるためにCan-do listを用いて生徒が自分の進歩を実感できるようにすることなども解答として考えられる。

【4】人は新しいことや珍しいことを求め，日々の生活にそれらがないと不安になりがちだ。しかし，普段過ごしている生活の中にすでに人生を楽しめる要素は含まれている。そういったことにまずは目を向けるべきである。(98字)

〈解説〉100字以内の日本語で要約する問題である。文章構成によっては，各段落の要約をつなぎ合わせることで要約文を完成させる場合もある。本問で提示されている文は第1，2段落で問題提起，第3～5段落は筆者の体験，第6段落がまとめとなっているので，要約にあたっては第1，2，6段落を中心にまとめればよい。

【5】(1)　If I win the lottery, I will buy a new car.　　(2)　Both of us have been to Tokyo, but neither of us has been to Hokkaido.

〈解説〉(1)　仮定法で表すと，If I won the lottery, I would buy a new car.となる。　(2)「私たちは2人とも」はwe bothとも表現できる。neither of usは基本的に単数扱いである(ただし，インフォーマルな会話などの場面では複数扱いすることもある)。

【高等学校】

【1】(1)　低所得家庭の有能な子どもたちの社会階層移動のために，グラマースクールが効果的な時代もあったが，それは上位20%を支えるその他80%の子どもたちに，単純労働の職が行き渡る時代のことで，今は状況が異なる。(98字)　(2)　他の階級の人々に恐れや差別意識を抱かず，彼らの歴史，文化や価値観をよく理解しようとする世代。(46字)　(3)　不平等を深く説明するには様々な集団に及ぼした感情的，心理的影響に焦点が当てられるが，それは責任や恩恵の追究が目的ではなく我々は遺産とともに生き，意思があればその遺産を語れると知る手段であるということ。(100字)　(4)　D　(5)　一般に，こういった議論の時に，自分とは異なる階級の人々は洗練性や適切な教養，理解力や客観性に欠けるのだろうという生来の優越感から，我々は排除する傾向があること。(80字)　(6)　microcosm of society

(7)　B

〈解説〉(1)　下線部は「それは昔のことであって，今はそうではない」の意。グラマースクールがその役割を果たしていた時代もあったが，今は状況が異なることを指す。下線部以降の2文の内容を100字以内でまとめる。　(2)　下線部は「恵まれたわずか(の子ども)だけでなく大多数の子どもに恩恵のある教育システム」の意。問いは，「この教育システムを通してどのような世代が生み出されるべきか」。第3段落1文目 by producing generations以下を訳出する。　(3)　下線部を含む文意は「これが異文化理解の育成に重大な助けとなりうる」。「これ」とは第4段落の内容を指す。　(4)　「生徒が他の生徒を人として，友人として見るのを可能にすることは何か」に対する答えとしてA，B，Cは本文に合致する。D「中流階級の大学でそれぞれの教育機関を異なるドメインとすること」は，第5段落1文目で述べられていることと真逆である。　(5)　下線部を含む文意は「これは授業で根絶できることである」。「これ」は直前の文を指す。out of ～「～が原因で」。inherent「生来備わっている」。snobbery「お高くとまること」。　(6)　問いは，「以下の説明文が示す連続した3語を第3段落から探して書け」。説明文の文意は「はるかに大きなものの全ての特徴や量を持つもの，場所または集団。この文章では，子どもたちが将来の職場で起こるだろうことを学び，様々な文化的バックグラウンドを持つ人と交流すべき所を意味する」であるので，第3段落2文目のmicrocosm of society「社会の縮図」が適切。　(7)　A　文意は「筆者は，グラマースクールの問題について，テリーザ・メイと同意見である」だが，第1段落後半で筆者は「テリーザ・メイに反対の3人組に賛同する」と述べているので，一致しない。　C　文意は「異なる階級やバックグラウンドの生徒が交流する機会は十分ある」だが，第3段落後半で「現在，学校は様々な線で分けられ，他の階級と協力する余地はない」と述べているので，一致しない。　D　文意は「異文化理解を促進するよりも，読み書き算数の時間をより多く設けるべきである」だが，第6段落1文目，2文目で「不平等，社会階層移動，多様性の受け入れに関する議論は哲学的すぎて，読み書き算数のような時間ほど価値があると思えないという人もいるかもしれないが，我々の望む社会の実現には，そのような時間と努力が必要なのだ」と述べているので，一致しない。

【2】A，C，E

〈解説〉A「コミュニケーションをもっと単純にする別の方法があると知っていても，ほとんどの集団はたいてい自分たちの言語を使わないことを受け入れない」は，第1段落2文目と一致する。　B「自分自身を特定したり，他者と異なったものとしたりするために多くの集団にとって言語は十分ではない」は第1段落の4文目と不一致。　C「文化的，経済的に国を結びつけるために，他国を通して主要なヨーロッパ言語は時に広がる」は，第2段落の最後の2文と一致する。　D「人々が新しい場所にくるとき，そこは彼らにとって魅力的な言語と文化をもつのだが，そこで生きるために自身の言語で自分のことを理解してもらおうとする」は第5段落1，2文目と不一致。　E「多くの異なる集団や言語をもつ場所でバイリンガルが発達する理由の1つは，魅力的な資源を支配するのに力のある集団の言語を学ぶ必要があるからだ」は，第6段落の1文目と一致する。　F「人々が第2言語を学び始めるとき，多くの人が物質的生活を向上させたくてそれを学ぼうとするのではない」は，第7段落の1文目と不一致。　G「人々が仕事でバイリンガルになることを要求されると，職場外で使う機会があってもたいてい母語を忘れる」は，第7段落4，5文目と不一致。

【3】(1)　①　contrasts　②　results　③　acquired　④　includes　(2)　フィルモアの言う流暢さが，言語に関する知識のみに基づいた能力ではなく，文脈に応じて発言したり，言語を独創的に使用したりする能力と関わっていて，世の中と言語使用との間に相互作用があることを示している。(99字)　(3)　リチャードとシュミッドの言う流暢さが，余計なポーズや躊躇がなく，自然にスムーズに話すことであるのに対し，ソーンベリーは，ポーズとその前後のことばの使い方が，発話のペースと同時に重要であると述べている。(100字)　(4)　I think fluency makes our communication smooth. Even though it is not perfectly smooth, fluency should enable us to have meaningful conversations. Of course sometimes it is difficult to convey our true feelings or what we really want to say, however, if we have strategies to continue our conversation, it can be easier to understand each other. For example, asking or repeating to make sure of the speakers' intention.

So, in order to have meaningful conversation fluently, I would like to give lessons where students can practice using strategies of communication. The most important thing for students is to focus on what information they are going to exchange. If they have the purpose of their conversation, they have to try hard and make an effort to convey their ideas and feelings or to understand what others want to say by using different strategies. Therefore, teachers should help students have an appropriate purpose or goal when having a conversation in the target language. (162words)

〈解説〉(1)　①　ブラムフィットは流暢さと正確さを対立したものとして考えている。よって空所はcontrast「対比する」。　②　ブラムフィットは流暢さを「自然な言語使用」と表現し，ネイティブスピーカーのような言語理解や発話であるかは問題ではないとしている。空所はresult in ～「～という結果になる」。 ③ 空所を含む文意は「教室内で可能な限り自然な使用をすることにより，学習者によってそれまでに獲得された言語を最大限引き出すことを伴う」。acquire「獲得する」。④ フィルモアは，流暢さは4つの能力を含むという仮説を立てている。include「含む」。 (2) 下線部の文意は「それら(フィルモアのカテゴリー)は言語使用と世の中の知識の間に相互作用があることも示している」。それは特に，「(3)様々な文脈で適切なことを言う能力，そして(4)創造的に，想像力を働かせて言語を使う能力に見られる」とあるので，それらの内容を盛り込み100字以内でまとめる。 (3) 両者ともにポーズについて言及している点は同じだが，前者は「余計なポーズや躊躇がないこと」とし，後者は「ポーズをとること」を中心に据えて，流暢さの特徴を述べている。 (4) 問いは「英語を話すことにおいて流暢さはどういうものだと思うか，流暢さを伸ばせる学習状況をどのようにつくりたいか，150語程度の英文で書け」。公式解答では，前者の問いについて「会話を続けることができる方策をもっていること」，後者について「会話をするときに適切な目的や目標を生徒にもたせるよう支援する」としている。

2019年度　実施問題

【中高共通】

【１】Choose the answer that best completes the sentence from the four choices.

(1) My parents never allowed me (　　) alone at night.

A. go out　B. going out　C. to go out　D. to going out

(2) You all are such nice people. I've been (　　) by how kind and caring all of you here are.

A. organized　B. loved　C. overwhelmed　D. fooled

(3) The car drove off (　　) the direction of 5th Avenue.

A. in　B. to　C. from　D. for

(4) (　　) I to tell you about my trip in India, one night would not be enough.

A. Am　B. Are　C. Have　D. Were

(5) (　　) the hypothesis, the results of the study showed that there was no significant difference in total speaking time between the two groups of children.

A. Contrary to　B. Except for　C. Instead of　D. Even if

(6) Please help yourself to more salad (　　) you like.

A. whoever　B. whichever　C. whenever　D. whatever

(7) In Ms. Tanaka's absence, all inquiries (　　) the Bellevue project should be taken care of by her assistant.

A. consuming　B. assuming　C. concerning　D. comparing

(8) I've heard Bob rejected the offer. What (　　) he possibly want?

A. shall　B. must　C. oughtn't　D. can

(9) What my teacher said to me was very (　　) and it gave me a lot of energy.

A. encouraging　B. encouraged　C. being encouraged

D. encouragement

(10) I'm a night owl. I'm used to (　　) up late at night.

A. stay　B. be stayed　C. have stayed　D. staying

(11) If you need to tell someone something (　　), you should not use email. Email can be forwarded, printed or copied and sent to other people.

A. authentic　B. confidential　C. pharmaceutical

D. international

(12) a) "Oh, no! I've totally forgotten about this cake in the fridge. It's gone bad."

b) "(　　)! That was from your favorite dessert store!"

A. It's a deal　B. Don't mention it　C. Never say never

D. What a shame

(13) This is the place (　　) I have long wanted to visit.

A. where　B. which　C. what　D. in which

(14) (　　) is to blame for the accident?

A. Who do you think　B. Do you think who

C. Whom do you think　D. Who do you know

(15) Thank you for your order, but we no longer carry that particular item. We would like to (　　) you for the inconvenience with our special discount coupon.

A. compensate　B. decorate　C. precede　D. reconvene

(16) a) "Let's throw away some of your books."

b) "(　　). Those remind me of my precious college life."

A. Now that's your business　B. Now that's a tough call

C. That can't be helped　D. That's beyond my knowledge

(17) "Please remain (　　) until the airplane comes to a complete stop."

A. seat　B. seated　C. seating　D. having seated

(18) I'd like all of you to (　　) small groups to discuss the topic of the next debate.

A. break off　B. break through　C. break out　D. break into

(19) He (　　) for school only ten minutes ago.

A. left　B. has left　C. has gone　D. had gone

(20) (　　) our school, I would like to say a few words to celebrate our friendship between Binton High School and our school.

A. As far as　B. In spite of　C. On behalf of

D. In contrast to

(☆☆☆◎◎◎◎)

【中学校】

【１】Read the following passage and answer the questions below.

In January of 2011, Brazil's state of Rio de Janeiro suffered an enormous sediment-related disaster. It caused over 800 deaths and left 400 people missing. It also destroyed the homes of approximately 20,000 people, turning out to be the worst natural disaster in Brazil's history.

"The rainstorm started suddenly and reached its heaviest around 4 a.m. ①(　　)" reflects Joáo Mori, who was then the chief firefighter of Nova Friburgo City, which is located in the region that was severely struck by the disaster. Nova Friburgo City is hilly and mountainous, and a landslide occurred on hillsides because of the rainstorm, causing heavy casualties. "Back then, we did not have any system for predicting landslides or warning against them," Mori says. "No one could predict that such a serious disaster would happen."

In response, the government of Brazil announced a policy to strengthen its disaster risk-management system. In December of 2011, to reinforce the country's capacity to predict and monitor rainfall, the government established the National Center for Monitoring and Early Warning of Natural Disasters (CEMADEN) within the Ministry of Science Technology, Innovations and Communications. In 2012, Brazil also set up the National Center for Risk and Disaster Management (CENAD) within the Ministry of National Integration to address disaster risk evaluation and disaster response. However, despite the establishment of these centers, the country still faced numerous problems, such as lack of infrastructure to prevent disasters, urban development plans that did not take disaster risks into consideration, and, most of all, no risk map to identify vulnerable spots. ②The Brazilian government requested Japan's cooperation to help improve these shortcomings. In 2013, a four-year disaster risk reduction (DRR) project was launched.

"This is such a huge project. It's like running several technical cooperation projects at the same time," says Toshiya Takeshi from Japan's Ministry of Land, Infrastructure, Transport and Tourism. He is an expert who worked on the project as Chief Advisor for two years, starting from its launch. One major feature of this project is that it covers a broad range of fields: risk mapping, urban planning, prevention and rehabilitation, as well as prediction and warning. The project's aim is to make manuals for each respective field and to conduct pilot projects based on those manuals. Another unique aspect of the project is that it involves many different agencies, including four ministries of the Brazilian federal government (Ministry of Cities, Ministry of National Integration, Ministry of Science Technology, Innovations and Communications, and Ministry of Mines and Energy), and the governments of two states and three cities where the pilot projects are to be conducted.

"Since Brazil is a federal state, state and municipal governments have almost the same authority as does the federal government. So they used to issue warnings and predictions separately, and I found this system to be quite complicated," says Takeshi. "This is why I put special emphasis on reinforcement of cooperation across agencies and fields."

As part of this effort, Takeshi organized weekly liaison meetings where lead staff from federal agencies in each field could meet up. When conducting the meetings, Takeshi was careful not to push Japanese methods, but to find ways that best catered to local needs. He carefully considered pros and cons of both Japanese and ③(　　) ways. "Instead of just introducing methods that were successful in Japan, I ④[challenges / explained / had / how / Japan /

tackled] that are similar to what Brazil faces now, highlighting Japan's experiences and processes," he explains.

Even the name of the project is an important example of this. Takeshi says that referring to the project as a 'JICA project' led some ③(　　) staff members to perceive it as a Japan-initiated project, and to feel as if it were something external. "I encouraged the members to give a nickname to the project, and we decided to call it GIDES, an acronym for Comprehensive Sediment Disaster Management in Portuguese," he says. "I felt that this name generated a sense of ownership over the project among the staff members."

The project members also held technical meetings organized by field once every two or three months, inviting not only federal government officials, but also officials of state and municipal authorities, as well as experts and researchers from the academia. As a result of these liaison meetings, cooperation across agencies became more intense, and in some meetings, federal government staff members even took the lead. Marcel Sant'Ana, an officer of the National Secretariat for Urban Development under the Ministry of Cities, says, "Since there was no opportunity for us, members of four different ministries, to collaborate together, we did not know how other ministries processed their work or what technologies they used. Now we clearly know the role of each agency and are able to consider measures based on that knowledge." He adds, "It's a great advancement."

(1) Choose the best sentence for ①(　　) from the four alternatives below.

A. I was watching out for the rainstorm,

B. It was still completely dark,

C. It was just after noon,

D. It was lighter than last year's rainstorm,

(2) Translate the underlined ② into Japanese, clarifying what "shortcomings" refers to.

(3) Choose the best answer for both ③(　　) from the four choices.

A. Japanese　B. English　C. Spanish　D. Brazilian

(4) Put the words from ④[ ] in the text in the correct order.

(5) According to the text, what is the improvement mentioned by Marcel Sant'Ana?

A. The prevention of damage from extreme weather.

B. The merging of all the ministries into one new ministry that oversees the entire project.

C. The knowledge of what each agency does and the ability to take action with that.

D. The addition of researchers and experts to the collaborative efforts.

(6) According to the text, which of the following is true?

A. Takeshi had been working on the project as Chief Advisor until it was finished.

B. Takeshi named this new project "JICA project."

C. Takeshi strongly encouraged cooperation between the agencies, the fields and the ministries.

D. Takeshi organized annual meetings with federal government staff members.

(☆☆☆◎◎◎)

【2】This is a part of President Obama's speech. Read it and answer the questions below. The passage is based on President Obama's speech but it is rewritten for clarity.

At the end of the day, we can have the most dedicated teachers, the most supportive parents, and the best schools in the world—and none of it will matter unless all of you fulfill your responsibilities: unless you show up to those schools, pay attention to those teachers, listen to your parents, grandparents and other adults and put in the hard work it takes to succeed. That's what I want to focus on today: the responsibility each of you has for your education. 【 A 】 I want to start with the responsibility you have to yourself. Every single one of you has something that you're good at. Every single one of you has something to offer. You have a responsibility to yourself to discover what that is. That's the opportunity an education can provide. Maybe you could be a great writer; maybe even good enough to write a book or articles in a newspaper, but you might not know it until you write a paper for your English class. Maybe you could be an innovator or an inventor; maybe even good enough to come up with the next iPhone or a new medicine or vaccine, but you might not know it until you do your project for your science class. Maybe you could be a mayor or a senator or a Supreme Court justice, but you might not know that until you join student government or the debate team. 【　B　】 And no matter what you want to do with your life, I guarantee that you'll need an education to do it. You want to be a doctor, a teacher, or a police officer? You're going to need a good education for every single one of those careers. You cannot drop out of school and just drop into a good job. You've got to train for it and work for it and learn for it.

You'll need the knowledge and problem-solving skills you learn in science and math to cure diseases like cancer and AIDS, and to develop new energy technologies and protect our environment. You'll need the insights and critical thinking skills you gain in history and social studies to fight poverty and homelessness, crime and discrimination, and to make our nation more fair and more free. You'll need the creativity and ingenuity you develop in all your classes to build new companies that will create new jobs and boost our economy.

We need every single one of you to develop your talents, skills and your intellect so you can help us old folks solve our most difficult problems. If you don't do that, if you quit on school, you're not just quitting on yourself, you're quitting on your country. Now I know it's not always easy to do well in school. I know a lot of you have challenges in your lives right now that can make it hard to focus on your schoolwork.

Where you are right now doesn't have to determine where you'll end up. No ①[your / you / written / one's / destiny / for]. You write your own destiny.

You make your own future.

So today, I want to ask all of you, what's your contribution going to be? What problems are you going to solve? 【 C 】 What will a president who comes here in twenty or fifty or one hundred years say about what all of you did for this country? Now, your families, your teachers and I are doing everything we can to make sure you have the education you need to answer these questions. I'm working hard to fix up your classrooms and get you the books, equipment and computers you need to learn, but you've got to do your part, too. So I expect all of you to get serious this year. I expect you to put your best effort into everything you do. 【 D 】 I expect great things from each of you. So don't let us down. Don't let your family down, or your country down. Most of all, don't let yourself down. Make us all proud.

(1) According to the text, complete the following sentence by choosing the best answer.

The responsibilities mentioned in the text include the responsibility to __________________.

A. Supreme Court justices
B. become an educator
C. discover what one has to offer
D. make the adults in one's life proud

(2) Choose the best answer to the following question from the four choices.
Which of the following jobs is NOT mentioned in the text?
A. Firefighter. B. Doctor. C. Writer. D. Senator.

(3) Put the words from ①[ ] in the text in the correct order.

(4) Choose the most appropriate place from 【 A 】～【 D 】 in the text, to put the sentence below.
What discoveries will you make?

(5) Answer the following question with one word.
Who is the intended audience of the speech?

(6) According to the text, which of the following is NOT true?

A. You gain basic knowledge to make the next iPhone in home economics class.

B. You gain basic knowledge to cure diseases in math and science class.

C. You gain basic knowledge to fight poverty and homelessness in social studies and history class.

D. You gain basic knowledge to create new companies from every class.

【３】Read the following passage and answer the questions below.

Edgar Allan Poe wrote stories and poems of mystery and terror, insanity and death. His life was short and seemingly unhappy. He was born Edgar Poe on January 19th, 1809 in Boston, Massachusetts. His parents were actors. He was a baby when his father left the family and he was two when his mother died. At that time, they were in Richmond, Virginia. Edgar went to live with the family of a wealthy Richmond businessman named John Allan. John Allan never officially adopted him as a son, but the boy became known as Edgar Allan Poe. He attended schools in England and in Richmond. He also attended the University of Virginia in Charlottesville. He was a good student. But he had a problem with alcohol. Even one drink seemed to change his personality and make him drunk. Also, he liked to play card games for money. Edgar was not a good player. He lost money that he did not have. John Allan refused to pay Edgar's gambling losses.【　A　】He also refused to continue paying for his education. So the young man went to Boston and began working as a writer and editor for monthly magazines.

Poe served in the Army for two years, before entering the United States Military Academy at West Point to become an officer. He was dismissed from the academy in 1831 after six months. By then, he had already published three books of poetry. He began writing stories while living with his aunt in the city of Baltimore, Maryland. In October of 1833, he won a short story contest organized by a local newspaper. He received fifty dollars in prize money and got a job editing the Southern Literary Messenger in Richmond. He published many of his own stories.

In 1834, Poe married Virginia Clemm. They moved to Philadelphia, Pennsylvania, in 1838. There, Poe served as editor of Burton's Gentleman's Magazine and continued to write. He published many of his most frightening stories during this time. 【 B 】 Edgar Allan Poe did something unusual for writers of his time: he used a narrator in a story to describe what was happening. A good example is the short story "The Tell-Tale Heart." The narrator claims that he is not mad, yet reveals that he is a murderer. Police officers arrive after getting reports of noises from the house. The murderer shows them around the house and is proud of the way he has hidden all the evidence. But he begins to hear a sound. The others in the room cannot hear it.

Edgar Allan Poe is also remembered for the kind of literature known as detective fiction. These are stories of an investigator who has to solve murders and other crimes. In fact, Edgar Allan Poe is considered the father of the modern detective novel. His fictional detective C. August Dupin first appeared in his story "The Murders In the Rue Morgue" in 1841. Dupin also appeared in two later stories, "The Mystery of Marie Roget" and "The Purloined Letter." Arthur Conan Doyle, creator of the fictional detective Sherlock Holmes, wrote about Poe's influence on other crime writers: "Each may find some little development of his own, but his main art must trace back to those admirable stories of Monsieur Dupin, so wonderful in their masterful force, their reticence, their quick dramatic point."

Jeff Jerome is the curator of the Edgar Allan Poe House and Museum in Baltimore. He says Poe's influence can also be seen in the work of H.G. Wells and Alfred Hitchcock, to name a few. Poe's influence extends to plays, movies, operas, music, cartoons, television, paintings just about every kind of art. Poe's creation of the detective novel is recognized by the Mystery Writers of America. The writers group presents the yearly Edgar Awards to honor the best detective and suspense books, movies and TV shows. An award also goes to an individual, organization or business for working to continue the influence of Edgar Allan Poe.【　C　】The award is named for Poe's most famous work. This year, the Edgar Allan Poe Society and the Poe House in Baltimore will receive the Raven Award.

Edgar Allan Poe became famous after "The Raven" was published in 1845. The poetry is rich in atmosphere. The rhythm suggests music. The narrator of "The Raven" is a man whose love has died. He sits alone among his books late at night. He hears a noise at the window. The ①[asks / it / finds / man /large / bird / questions / black / and / a]. The raven answers with a single word: "Nevermore." At the end of the poem, the man has quite clearly gone mad from ②grief.

The sadness and honor in Poe's writing might lead readers to suspect a disordered mind. Yet people who knew him reported him to be a nice man. Some even called him a real gentleman. His wife died in 1847. Virginia Clemm Poe had suffered from tuberculosis for many years. At the same time, Poe's magazine failed, and so did his health. He died on October 7th, 1849, under mysterious conditions. He was found in a tavern in Baltimore. He did not know where he was or how he got them. He was dressed in rags. He died four days later in a hospital. He was forty years old.

Over the years, historians and medical experts have tried to explain the cause of Poe's death. Some say he killed himself with drink. Others say he developed rabies from an animal bite. Mary in Baltimore believe he was beaten by local criminal gangs.【　D　】Eves year about two thousand people visit Edgar Allan Poe's grave at the Westminster Hall and Burying Ground in Baltimore. Additionally, every year on January 19th, Poe's birthday, people watch for a man dressed in black to appear. His face is covered. He places a bottle of French cognac and three roses on the grave. No one in Baltimore really wants to know the visitor's identity. They prefer that it remain a mystery, much like Edgar Allan Poe himself.

(1) Choose the most appropriate place from 【 A 】～【 D 】 in the text, to put the sentence below.

These included "The Black Cat," "The Fall of the House of Usher" and "The Pit and the Pendulum."

(2) Choose the best answer to the following question from the four choices.

Which of the following is NOT a story that C. August Dupin appeared in?

A. The Tell-Tale Heart.

B. The Purloined Letter.

C. The Mystery of Marie Roget.

D. The Murders In the Rue Morgue.

(3) Choose the best answer to the following question from the four choices.

Who awards individuals, organizations or businesses with the Raven Award?

A. Edgar Allan Poe Society.

B. Poe House.

C. Westminster Hall and Burying Ground.

D. Mystery writers of America.

(4) Choose the best answer to the following question from the four choices.

According to the text, who is Jeff Jerome?

A. Edgar Allan Poe's adoptive father.

B. The creator of Sherlock Holmes.

C. A personal friend of Edgar Allan Poe.

D. The person who is in charge of Edgar Allan Poe House and Museum.

(5) Put the words from ①[ ] in the text in the correct order.

(6) Paraphrase the underlined ② by filling a word [ア] and [イ].

grief= a [ア] of great [イ]

(☆☆☆◎◎◎◎)

【４】Translate the underlined sentences into English.

(1)　歩きながらのスマートフォンの使用が問題になっている。<u>もっとみんなでマナーの向上を目指そう</u>。

(2)　2020年に東京オリンピック・パラリンソピックの開催を控えた私たちにとってグローバルな視点を持つことが求められている。<u>私たちにとって一番大切なことは，単に英語力を身につけるだけではなく，日本の古くからの伝統や文化をもっと諸外国へ向けて発信していくことだ</u>。

(☆☆☆◎◎◎◎)

【５】In the New Course of Study guidance, it was clearly stipulated that English classes at junior high school should be taught in English. What do you think about this? Write your opinion with concrete reasons in approximately 100 words.

(☆☆☆☆◎◎◎◎)

【高等学校】

【１】Read the following passage and answer the questions below.

[1] If I touch a hot stove and burn my hand, I immediately learn that touching a hot stove results in a burned hand. My brain makes the connection almost simultaneously. There's little need for reflection because the "hot stove＝burn" connection is one that my mind makes almost immediately.

[2] Academic learning however is seldom ①<u>that obvious</u>.

[3] Let's pretend I'm a fourth grade student, distracted by everything from cafeteria food to the playground outside my classroom window. If I fail a math test, am I immediately able to tell you why? Most kids aren't self-aware enough or mature enough to tell you why they failed at something (or in some cases, why they got in trouble). The younger the student, the more difficult this is. More than [　②　], since I'm not sure exactly WHY I failed a test, the only connection my brain makes is "Math＝F". Since

most kids really do want to be successful, students also equate "F=Failure" and "Failure=Bad". They don't understand that failure is a part of [③], largely because we as teachers don't allow students to re-do work and learn from mistakes. ④<u>As a result, they come to hate the subject or the teacher, never really knowing why other than "I am bad at Math."</u>

4 This is precisely why reflection is so important. Although it's a ⑤<u>cumbersome</u> and time-consuming practice to teach to kids, without reflection it is almost impossible for actual "learning" to occur. Faced with increasing demands to "cover" as much material as possible to prepare for state tests, teachers【 A 】, electing to instead "cover" the material. We often accuse kids of having "forgotten" material they "learned" the year before, but in reality, they never really learned it at all. The teacher "covered" it and perhaps the students memorized it for the short term before being lost forever. Reflection is a key ingredient to move knowledge from short-term to long-term memory.

5 If the goal is not just coverage but actual learning, then reflection is no longer optional—it's an [⑥] piece for transforming a classroom from "covering material" to being "focused on learning".

6 After all, if I touch a hot stove and burn my hand, but never make the connection that the hot stove is what burned my hand, I'm likely to repeat that mistake. This is an absurd example—of course it's the stove that burned my hand—but often times in life "What went wrong?" is a question without an obvious answer. And unfortunately, it's a question that the vast majority of our students never even think to ask.

7 And while many colleges talk about the importance of being a "reflective practitioner" in their teacher training programs, there seems to be little "reflection" taught in the classroom.

8 For some silly reason it's not cool to talk about "reflecting". It's difficult for teachers, who as a result of their position as the "distributor of knowledge" in the mind of most students and parents, feel obligated to be

"right" all the time. This is of course, absurd. However, because of this need to be right we get very defensive and struggle to admit when we're wrong.

9 There's something about the word "reflection" that seems to make teachers [⑦]. Maybe because it's too "touchy-feely" for some. Maybe it's because it requires adults to show humility, and admit they can improve. Regardless, if we【 B 】, how can we ever hope to see them reflect on their own mistakes?

10 Reflection is an integral part of the learning process. It allows us to learn more about ourselves and how we learn, but it also aids us in improving academic skills. Consider sports teams that watch film of the previous night's game. They are able to identify mistakes and correct them at practice. Looking at a failed math test can have the same result if we help students to notice "Oh! I forget to carry the one every time I borrow!" Then, we【 C 】, and help students discern which activities worked well for them and which ones didn't.

11 Teaching students to reflect on their work by noticing and correcting their own mistakes as well as which activities and behaviors allowed them to be successful is a vital part of the learning experience that far too many classrooms leave out of the equation. As teachers, we should model this expectation by reflecting ourselves and involving students in our own reflections. ⑧Only then [students / we / not / to / understand / help / can] touch a hot stove, as opposed to simply making them afraid of all stoves forever.

(1) Explain the meaning of the underlined ①in Japanese, including the answers to the questions "WHAT is obvious?" and "HOW obvious is it?"

(2) Choose the best word for [②], [⑥], and [⑦] from the four choices below.

② A. all　　B. likely　　C. once
D. often

⑥ A. essential B. optimistic C. utilizable
D. initiative

⑦ A. undisciplined B. unskilled C. uncomfortable
D. unrestrainted

(3) Choose an appropriate phrase <u>with three words from Paragraph 7 ~ 10</u> that best fits [③].

(4) Translate the underlined ④<u>into Japanese</u>, <u>explaining what "why" refers to</u>.

(5) Substitute the underlined ⑤ with the best alternative from the four choices below.

A. skilled B. burdensome C. indispensable D. advanced

(6) Choose the best phrase for each of【 A 】~【 C 】from the three choices below. <u>You have to use each choice only once.</u>

[1] are not willing to practice it ourselves and model it for our students

[2] can look back on the learning process as well

[3] often skip teaching students to reflect on their work

(7) According to Paragraph 8, why is it difficult for teachers to admit when they are wrong? Explain the reason <u>within 60 Japanese letters</u>.

(8) Put the words from the underlined ⑧ in the correct order.

(9) According to the text, which of the following is NOT true?

A. Teachers tend to think they have to cover the materials in order to meet the request for the state test and have the misunderstanding that covering leads to the real learning for students.

B. Without making the cause and effect connections, we are likely to repeat our mistakes. However, most students don't even try to think about why they made a mistake.

C. Reflection is quite useful for realizing what the mistake is and correcting it concretely not only in academic learning but also for the sports team.

D. Reflection is useful and necessary only for learners, and all teachers have to do is to give students time to reflect their work to foster their learning in their class.

(☆☆☆◎◎◎◎)

【２】 Read the following passage and answer the questions below.

When we look in the mirror, we see some of the "instruments" necessary for choice. Our eyes, nose, ears, and mouth gather information from our environment, while our arms and legs enable us to act on it. We depend on these capabilities to effectively negotiate between hunger and satiation, safety and vulnerability, even between life and death. Yet our ability to *choose* involves more than simply reacting to sensory information. Your knee may ①twitch if hit in the right place by a doctor's rubber mallet, but no one would consider this reflex to be a choice. To be able to truly choose, we must evaluate all available options and select the best one, making the mind as vital to choice as the body.

Thanks to recent advances in technology, such as functional magnetic resonance imaging (MRI) scans, we can identify the main brain system engaged when making choices: the *corticostriatal network. Its first major component, the *striatum, is buried deep in the middle of the brain and is relatively consistent in size and function across the animal kingdom, from reptiles to birds to mammals. It is part of a set of structures known as the *basal ganglia, which serve as a sort of switchboard connecting the higher and lower mental functions. The striatum receives sensory information from other parts of the brain and has a role in planning movement, which is critical for our choice making. But its main choice-related function has to do with evaluating the reward associated with the experience; it is responsible for alerting us that "sugar = good" and "root canal = bad." Essentially, it provides the mental connection needed for wanting what we want.

［　1　］［　2　］［　3　］［　4　］ It is involved in making complex cost-benefit analysis of immediate and future consequences. It also enables us to exercise impulse control when we are tempted to give in to something that we know to be detrimental to us in the long run.

The ability to choose well is arguably the most powerful tool for controlling our environment. After all, it is humans who have dominated the planet, despite a conspicuous absence of sharp claws, thick hides, wings, or other obvious defenses. We are born with the tools to exercise choice, but just as significantly, we're born with the desire to do so. Neurons in the striatum, for example, respond more to rewards that people or animals actively choose than to identical rewards that are passively received. As the song goes, "Fish gotta swim, birds gotta fly," and ②we all gotta choose.

This desire to choose is so innate that we act on it even before we can express it. In a study of infants as young as four months, researchers attached strings to the infants' hands and let them learn that by tugging the string, they could cause pleasant music to play. When the researchers later broke the association with the string, making the music play at random intervals instead, the children became sad and angry, even though the experiment was designed so that they heard the same amount of music as when they had activated the music themselves. ③These children didn't *only* want to (ア) music; They really desire to have the power to (イ).

Ironically, while the power of choice lies in its ability to unearth the best option possible out of all these presented, sometimes ④the desire to choose is so strong that it can interfere with the pursuit of these very benefits. Even in situations where there is no advantage to having more choice, meaning that it actually raises the cost in time and effort, choice is still instinctively preferred. In one experiment, rats in a maze were given the option of taking a direct path or one that branched into several other paths. The direct and the branched paths eventually led to the same amount of food, so one held no advantage over the other. Nevertheless, over multiple trials, nearly every rat preferred to take the branching path. And though humans can consciously override this preference, this doesn't necessarily mean we will. In another experiment, people given a casino chip preferred to spend it at a table with two identical roulette-style wheels rather than at a table with a single wheel, even though they could bet on only one of the wheels, and *all three* wheels were identical.

The desire to choose is thus a natural drive, and though it probably developed because it is a crucial aid to our survival, it often operates independently of any concrete benefits. ⑤In such cases, the power of choice is so great that it becomes not [something / a / an end / means / but / valuable / merely / intrinsically / to] and necessary. So what happens when we enjoy the benefits that choice is meant to confer but our need for choice itself is not met?

*corticostriatal　皮質線状体　　*striatum　線状体

*basal ganglia　大脳基底核　　*prefrontal cortex　前頭葉皮質

(1) Paraphrase the underlined ①with 6～10 English words, including "make", "movement" and "control" in that order.

＝ Your knee may ______________________________ if hit in the right place by a doctor's rubber mallet, ...

(2) Choose the best sentence for each of [1] ～ [4] from the four choices below to complete the paragraph.

A. This is where the other half of the corticostriatal network, the *prefrontal cortex, comes into play.

B. We must also make the connection that under certain conditions, too much of a sweet thing can eventually lead to a root canal.

C. Yet the mere knowledge that sweet things are appealing and root canals excruciating is not enough to guide our choices.

D. Located directly behind our foreheads, the prefrontal cortex acts as the brain's command center, receiving messages from the striatum and other parts of the body and using those messages to determine and execute the best overall course of action.

(3) Choose the most appropriate meaning of the underlined ② from the four

choices below.

A. Humans don't necessarily like any rewards. They especially don't like rewards which are given to them regardless of their preference.

B. It is necessary for humans to exercise the ability to choose to control our environment just as fish swim and birds fly to control their habitats.

C. Every time humans encounter the enemies, they have to choose because they don't have any defenses such as sharp claws, thick hides, and wings.

D. Choosing is not only an ability for survival but also the desire with which humans are born. In other words, they cannot help choosing.

(4) Choose the best combination of words for (ア) and (イ) from the four choices below and complete the underlined ③.

A.	ア hear	イ survive		B.	ア hear	イ choose	
C.	ア learn	イ survive		D.	ア learn	イ choose	

(5) Explain the meaning of the underlined ④ within 80 Japanese letters, using one of the examples mentioned in the same paragraph.

(6) Put the words from the underlined ⑤ in the correct order.

(☆☆☆☆◎◎◎◎)

【3】Read the following passage and answer the questions below.

If a student thinks she can learn, she will. There is now no doubt that student's own self-efficacy as a learner has an influence on how well she actually does in school. According to Hattie's research (2009), a student's self-reported grades are the greatest indicator of improved learning. In many ways, this is a self-fulfilling prophecy. "If I think I can learn, I will; if I believe I am incapable of learning, I will fail." As Hattie points out, a child's willingness to invest in learning, openness to experiences, and the general reputation she can build as a "learner" are keys to success (2009), and this self-efficacy is prejudiced by the way the teacher makes the child feel. Why, then, don't all teachers make it their first act to instill a sense of self-confidence in their students?

As Hattie tells us, some teachers believe that their students are limited in their potential because of poor genes, low socioeconomic status, or other negative preexisting conditions. Since they don't believe the student can learn, they teach in such a way that the student does not learn: ①a vicious circle. A student believes she is a learner when she has experienced a pattern of successes in learning environments. When she's been told, "You're quick!" "You're smart!" "You have talent!" and "You're clever!" many times in her formative years, these affirmations also become a self-fulfilling prophecy. "I can learn; I am a learner; I can figure this out!" is the best thing a child can tell herself. However, many children don't feel this level of empowerment, and worse yet, they may not believe the people who encourage them because the words aren't accompanied by actions worthy of praise.

If most of us know all of this from our life experiences, why do so many of us teachers fail to build up our students' self-perceptions as learners? As I correct papers and write feedback to my students, I realize that two things challenge me as I try to balance out my comments. First, after correcting the same mistakes over and over, I'm almost angry at having to reteach items that I'm sure I taught (well) before. I'm annoyed that I have to spend time on concepts that were supposedly taught weeks ago. Why did they fail to learn in the first place? How did I fail to teach this right the first time? ②This [leave / is/ leads / feedback / me / frustration / to / that / than / less] gentle (e.g., "I recommend you review the previous feedback and go over the support documents in the classroom" instead of "you've made a lot of progress. To continue improving, I recommend that you reread previous feedback and reread the documents related to this assignment"). Second, I find it easier to note the mistakes ("Citations are not in APA format") than to try to motivate the student ("I know you're smart and will be able to learn this if you spend a bit more time reviewing exercises similar to number 3").

Positive feedback works only when it's sincere and based on praiseworthy deeds. Self-esteem is evident in risk-takers, and risk-takers are born of secure environments and high self-efficacy. How can we promote this virtuous cycle in the classroom? One way is to create ③climate in which students believe that it's okay to make errors ("I can always try again; I am not my failures but rather my successes"). ④In the U.S. there is the belief that "if I try hard, it doesn't matter if I'm behind, and if I pick myself up at least one time more than the times I fall, I will be a success." When a learner meets with success, she develops a positive self-image, and this colors all of her future learning endéavors. Teachers can influence this element by building up students' self-esteem and helping them believe they all have the potential to learn.

Books can be fabulous influence, but books alone often cannot foster a "can do" attitude; there are myriad factors in an individual's life that come into play when shaping the fragile self-image of small children. Children form an image of themselves as learners partly based on inspiration from literary characters, but they also learn from the real people who surround them. Did the child have models in her life that showed her the rewards of being smart, or were the prizes in her environment given to lazy people who cheated and beat the system? Was *The Little Engine That Could* read to her at bedtime, or did she sit in front of the TV watching shows celebrating low achievers? As Costa and Kellick (2009) note, the habits of mind form early. If a child sees that learning is rewarded (you can advance to a higher-paying job; you are praised by your parents or peers; you simply feel good because people acknowledge your intelligence), then her brain craves that good feeling repeatedly.

We now know that "self-concept is a structural product of reflective activity, but it is also susceptible to change as the individual encounters new roles, situations, and life transitions" (Demo, 1992), many of which occur in school settings. When viewed from a sociological perspective, ⑤this information can be devastating. For instance, telling a certain racial group that they will likely not go to college, or telling girls they're not as capable of doing math or science, often turns into a self-fulfilling prophecy. I once knew a teacher who told his entire class that there are some groups that are cut out for math and others that are not, and unfortunately, this group was not. The result? An entire class that failed.

I firmly believe in the power of one: one teacher, one student at a time. An important battle is won for each student empowered to believe she is a learner. Levine (2002) used to preach that our job as teachers is to help students find success every day so that they develop a perception of themselves as learners. With each little battle won, self-confidence improves. While students can drive their own self-efficacy if they have strong personalities, most rely on teacher guidance to develop this positive inner vision.

(1) Explain what the underlined ① refers to in this text <u>within 70 Japanese letters.</u>

(2) Put the words from the underlined ② in the correct order.

(3) Substitute the underlined ③ with the best alternative from the four choices below.

A. atmosphere　　B. relationship　　C. weather

D. curriculum

(4) Translate the underlined ④<u>into Japanese.</u>

(5) Choose the most appropriate answer that explains the meaning of the underlined ⑤ from the four choices below.

A. The idea that self-concept is easily changed by encountering new circumstances or roles especially in school is not so strong but is vulnerable.

B. Teachers can change their students' self-concepts for the worse if they tell their students something that dampens their enthusiasm.

C. Students can be influenced by new roles and situations especially in their school lives, so teachers have to give students time to get accustomed to them.

D. Teachers are able to improve students' motivations by denying their potential with negative words rather than praising their efforts too much.

(6) Read the following passage about "self-efficacy" and choose the best word for [⑥]－[⑩] from the four choices below the grid.

> Self-efficacy is defined as people's beliefs about their [⑥] to produce designated levels of performance that exercise influence over events that affect their lives. Self-efficacy beliefs determine how people feel, think, [⑦] themselves and behave.
>
> A strong sense of efficacy enhances human accomplishment and personal well-being in many ways. People with high [⑧] in their capabilities approach difficult tasks as challenges to be mastered rather than as threats to be [⑨]. Such an efficacious outlook fosters intrinsic interest and deep engrossment in activities. They set themselves challenging goals and maintain strong commitment to them. They heighten and sustain their efforts in the [⑩] of failure. They quickly recover their sense of efficacy after failures or setbacks. They attribute failure to insufficient effort or deficient knowledge and skills which are acquirable. They approach threatening situations with [⑧] that they can exercise control over them. Such an efficacious outlook produces personal accomplishments, reduces stress and lowers vulnerability to depression.

⑥ A. diversities　B. capabilities　C. responsibilities
　D. personalities

⑦ A. define　B. evacuate　C. instruct
　D. motivate

⑧ A. skills　B. assurance　C. influence
　D. initiative

⑨ A. avoided　B. overcome　C. tackled
　D. handled

⑩ A. fear B. sake C. face D. benefit

(☆☆☆☆◎◎◎◎)

【4】 Read the following passage and answer the questions below.

One image for teaching English as a second language or foreign language (ESL/EFL) is that of a tapestry. The tapestry is woven from many strands, such as the characteristics of the teacher, the learner, the setting, and the relevant languages (i.e., English and the native languages of the learners and the teacher). For the instructional loom to produce a large, strong, beautiful, colorful tapestry, all of these strands must be interwoven in positive ways. For example, the instructor's teaching style must address the learning style of the learner, the learner must be motivated, and the setting must provide resources and values that strongly support the teaching of the language. However, if the strands are not woven together effectively, the instructional loom is likely to produce something small, weak, ragged, and pale—not recognizable as a tapestry at all.

In addition to the four strands mentioned above—teacher, learner setting, and relevant languages—other important strands exist in the tapestry. In a practical sense, one of the most crucial of these strands consists of the four primary skills of listening, reading, speaking, and writing. This strand also includes associated or related skills such as knowledge of vocabulary, spelling, pronunciation, syntax, meaning, and usage. The skill strand of the tapestry leads to optimal ESL/EFL communication when the skills are interwoven during instruction. This is known as the integrated-skill approach.

If this weaving together does not occur, the strand consists merely of discrete, segregated skills—parallel threads that do not touch, support, or interact with each other. This is sometimes known as the segregated-skill approach. Another title for this mode of instruction is the language-based approach, because the language itself is the focus of instruction (language for language's sake). In this approach, the emphasis is not on learning for authentic communication.

Two types of integrated-skill instruction are content-based language instruction and task-based instruction. The first of these emphasizes learning content through language, while the second stresses doing tasks that require communicative language use. Both of these benefit from a diverse range of materials, textbooks, and technologies for the ESL or EFL classroom.

With careful reflection and planning, any teacher can integrate the language skills and strengthen the tapestry of language teaching and learning. When the tapestry is woven well, learners can use English effectively for communication.

(1) Summarize this passage within 100 Japanese letters.

(2) In order to enable your students to use English effectively for authentic communication, what kind of tapestry are you going to weave? In other words, how are you going to integrate the four language skills in your English class? Express your own idea in approximately 150 words in English.

(☆☆☆☆◎◎◎◎)

解答・解説

【中高共通】

【1】(1) C (2) C (3) A (4) D (5) A (6) C (7) C (8) D (9) A (10) D (11) B (12) D (13) B (14) A (15) A (16) B (17) B (18) D (19) A (20) C

〈解説〉(1) allow O to～「Oが～することを許す」。 (2) be overwhelmed by～「～に圧倒される」。 (3) in the direction of ～「～

の方向に」。　(4)　未来のことを表す仮定法。If I were to tell …のIfが省略され，倒置が起きている。　(5)　Contrary to～「～に反して」。(6)　whenever you like「いつでも好きなときに」。　(7)　concerning～「～に関して」。　(8)「いったい彼は何を望んでいるのか」。possiblyはcanとともに用いて強意。　(9)　encouraging「励みになる，(人を)勇気づける」という能動の意味。encouragedは「勇気づけられた」という受動の意味。　(10)　be used to～ing「～することに慣れている」。night owl「夜型の人」。　(11)　confidential「秘密の，マル秘の」。(12)　What a shame!「何てことだ，気の毒に」。　(13)　先行詞のthe placeが動詞visitの目的語にあたるので，目的格の関係代名詞が適切。(14)「誰がその事故の責任を負うべきだと思いますか」。「誰だと思うか」という意味の文では疑問詞が文頭に出る。　(15)　compensate O for～「Oに～を償う」。　(16)　tough call「難しい決断」。
(17)　remain seated「座ったままでいる」。　(18)　break into small groups「小グループになる」。　(19)　ten minutes agoから過去時制と判断できる。　(20)　on behalf of～「～を代表して」。

【中学校】

【1】(1)　B　　(2)　災害を防ぐためのインフラの欠如や，災害リスクを考慮していない都市開発，被害を受けやすい場所の災害マップがないことなどの問題点を改善するためにブラジル政府は日本の協力を要請した。　　(3)　D　　(4)　explained how Japan had tackled challenges
(5)　C　　(6)　C

〈解説〉(1)　Joá Moriの回想部分。「暴風雨は突然始まり，午前4時頃最も強くなった」に続く文として「まだ真っ暗だった」。
(2)　shortcomings「問題点，欠点」については前文に具体的な記述がある。lack of infrastructure「インフラの欠如」。take～into consideration「～を考慮する」。vulnerable「脆弱な，傷つきやすい」。　(3)　第6段落の内容から，Toshiya Takeshi氏が日本のやり方を押し付けるのではなく，ブラジル現地のニーズに応じた方法を模索していたことがわかる。

また第7段落では，彼が「JICAプロジェクト」と呼ぶと日本主導であるとブラジルのスタッフが感じると述べている。 (4) 整序した部分以下の文意は「私は日本の経験と手順を強調しながら，今ブラジルが直面していることと似通った課題に日本がいかに取り組んできたかを説明した」。 (5) Marcel Sant'Anaが第7段落の最後の1文で「政府機関それぞれの役割がはっきりして，知識に基づいた方法を考えることができるようになった」と明らかにしている。 (6) 第3段落の最後の1文と第4段落の3文目から，Toshiya Takeshi氏は4年のプロジェクトの内2年携わったことがわかるのでAは誤り。第7段落の3文目より，メンバーがGIDESと名付けたとあるのでBは誤り。第6段落の1文目より，週に1度会合をもったとあるのでDは誤り。

【2】(1) C (2) A (3) one's written your destiny for you
(4) C (5) students あるいは children (6) A

〈解説〉(1) 「誰にでも得意なことがある。誰にでも人に与えられるものがある。それが何であるか見つける責任がある」と第1段落の4文目から6文目にある。 (2) 第1段落に作家，革新者，発明者，市長，上院議員，最高裁判事，医者，教師，警察官などが挙げられている。
(3) 直後に「あなたがあなた自身の運命を決めるのだ。あなたが自分自身の将来を作るのだ」とある。同様の内容となるように整序する。
(4) 挿入すべき文「あなたはどんな発見をするだろうか」は，将来についていくつかの問いかけをしている第5段落の前半がふさわしい。
(5) 問いは「スピーチの対象となる聴衆は誰か」。スピーチの内容やscience class，schoolworkなどの語彙からも児童・生徒対象だと考えられる。 (6) 第1段落の9文目より，A「家庭科の授業で次のiPhoneを作る基礎的な知識を得る」は，「家庭科」が誤り。正しくは科学の授業。

【3】(1) B (2) A (3) D (4) D (5) man finds a large black bird and asks it questions (6) ア feeling イ sadness

〈解説〉(1)　挿入文は「これらは『黒猫』,『アッシャー家の崩壊』,『落とし穴と振り子』を含んでいた」。「彼はこの時期に恐ろしい作品をたくさん出版している」の後の空欄Bがふさわしい。恐ろしい作品の例を挙げている。　(2)　質問は「C・オーギュスト・デュパンが登場する話ではないものはどれか」。第4段落の4，5文目に彼が登場する作品として『モルグ街の殺人』,『マリー・ロジェの謎』,『盗まれた手紙』が挙げられている。　(3)　質問は「誰が個人，組織または企業に大鴉賞を授与するのか」。第5段落の4文目と5文目にMystery writers of Americaという作家団体が授与すると述べられている。　(4)　第5段落の1文目に「Jeff Jeromeはボルチモアにあるエドガー・アラン・ポー博物館の館長だ」とある。　(5)　直後に「大鴉が答える」という件がある。よって「男が大鴉に質問する」というような内容にすればよい。(6)　grief「深い悲しみ」。

【4】(1)　Let's all aim for better manners. あるいは Let's improve our manners. あるいはLet's make our manners better.　(2)　The most important thing for us is not only to acquire English skills, but also to disseminate Japan's old traditions and culture to more foreign countries.

〈解説〉日本語の言い回しにとらわれすぎず，平易な英語で書くことを心がける。「発信する」を上手く表現する。disseminate「広める，普及させる」はspread, get～knownなどでも可。traditionには「伝承されてきている」という意を含むので,「古くからの」はoldで済ませる。

【5】I think English teachers should try to teach in English. I know it is difficult to use English in English classes but I think it is important for students. Students should use English as much as they can to raise their English ability. They need to get familiar with English to use it. If teachers use English in English classes, students will be given a lot of opportunities to have exposure to English. Teachers should try to brush up on their communication skill to raise students' English ability. I hope many Japanese students enjoy English classes and raise their English ability. (101 words)

〈解説〉「新学習指導要領では，中学校で英語の授業は英語で行われるべきであると明記された。これについてどう考えるか。正しい理由とともに意見を100語程度で書け」という問いである。ねらいは生徒が授業の中で「英語に触れる機会」を最大限に確保することと，授業全体を英語を使った「実際のコミュニケーションの場面」とすることである。これらを踏まえて自分自身の考えを書く。

【高等学校】

【1】(1) 手がストーブに触れると火傷をするという因果関係が，脳が瞬時に学習できるほど明確であるということ。 (2) ② B ⑥ A ⑦ C (3) the learning process (4) 結果として，生徒はその教科か担当の教師のことが嫌いになるだけで，「数学が苦手だ」ということ以外に，なぜ不合格だったのかという理由については，ついに理解することはない。 (5) B (6) A [3] B [1] C [2] (7) 生徒や保護者にとっては「知識を与える人」と捉えられていることで，常に正しくあるべきとの束縛を受けているから。(54字) (8) can we help students understand not to (9) D

〈解説〉(1) 下線部①を含む文意は「しかしながら学問的な学びは，そんなに明確であることはめったにない」。質問は「何がどのように明確であるかを含めて下線部を説明せよ」。第1段落の3文目を使って解答する。 (2) ② more than likely「ほぼ間違いなく」。 ⑥ ダッシュ前の「振り返ることはもはや任意ではない」と同意となるようにする。よってessential「不可欠な」。 ⑦ 空欄後の「振り返ることが教師にとっては気恥ずかしく，謙虚さを示し，改善の余地があると認める必要がある」から，教師の気持ちに合うものを選ぶと，uncomfortable「心地よくない」。 (3) 空欄を含む文意は「主に，教師である私たちが生徒に勉強をやり直させたり，間違いから学ばせたりしないという理由で，彼らは失敗が［ ③ ］の一部であると理解しない」。同様の主張を述べている文を探す。第10段落の1文目の「振り返ることは学びの過程に不可欠な部分である」と内容が一致する。(4)　下線部④はwhyの後に，I failed a testが省略されている。それを補って日本語訳をする。　(5)　cumbersome「厄介な」なのでburdensome「重荷となる」が適切。　(6)　A「振り返ることは厄介で時間がかかることである」という第4段落の内容から，[3]の「生徒に自分の勉強を反省することを教えるのを教師はしばしば省く」が続く。　B　教師が振り返りをしたがらないという第8段落や9段落の内容を受けて，[1]の「それでも，私たちがそれを進んで実行し，生徒のために手本を示さなければ」。　C　スポーツ同様，間違った数学のテストを見直すことが有効だという第10段落の流れから，[2]の「学びの過程も振り返ることができる」。　(7)　問いは「教師が間違っていると認めることはなぜ難しいのか」。答えにあたるのは第8段落の2文目。

(8)　下線部の文意は「その時初めて私たちは，永遠にストーブ全てを怖がらせるのに対し，生徒が熱いストーブに触らないことを理解させることができる」。文頭のonly then V＋Sは否定語による倒置。「その時初めてV＋Sする」という強調の意味となる。　(9)　Dの「学習者のみに有効で必要である」という部分が誤り。

【２】(1)　make a sudden quick movement that you can not control (10words)

(2)　1　C　　2　B　　3　A　　4　D　　(3)　D　　(4)　B

(5)　ネズミが迷路において餌に到達する経路を調べる実験で，多くの個体がわざわざ脇道を選択するのは，最終の利益よりも選択することへの願望が優先されている証である。(77字)　　(6)　merely a means to an end but something intrinsically valuable

〈解説〉(1)　twitch「ぴくぴく動く」を，make，movement，controlを使って6～10語で言い換える。　(2)　第2段落では，「線状体の選択に関わる機能が，経験から考えられる価値，例えば「砂糖は善だが歯根には悪」などを私たちに知らせてくれている」という内容である。それに続く文は，C「しかし甘いものは魅力的で，歯根がひどい状態だという単なる知識だけでは私たちの選択を導くには十分ではない」→B

「ある条件下では多量の甘いものが結局は歯根に至るという，結び付けもしなければならない」→A「それが，もう一つの皮質線状体ネットワークである前頭葉皮質が作用する場所である」→D「前頭葉皮質は額のすぐ裏に位置し，線状体や体の他の部分からメッセージを受け取り，全般的な一連の行動を決定，実行するためにそれらのメッセージを使いながら，脳の指令センターのような働きをする」。
(3) 「選択能力は周りを支配するための手段で，人間はその手段を持って生まれ，選択したいという願望を持って生まれた」という第4段落の内容から，D「選択は生き延びるための能力というだけでなく，人間が生まれながらに持って生まれた願望である。言い換えると選択しないではいられないのだ」。 (4) 幼児の手にひもをつけ，ひもをひっぱると心地よい音楽が流れるようにした。ひもとは無関係に音楽を流したところ不機嫌になったという結果から，選択願望が生まれつきであることを確かめた。よって下線部③は「子どもたちは音楽がただ聞きたかったのではない。選択する力を持つことを望んだのだ」となる。 (5) 問いは，「同段落の中の例を使って下線部④の意味を説明せよ」。第6段落の3文目～5文目のネズミの実験内容を例とする。
(6) 「選択願望は具体的な利益とは無関係にしばしば作用する」という前文を受けて，⑤を整序する。「そのような場合，選択の力はとても大きいので，それは単に目的を達成するための手段ではなく，本質的に貴重で必要なものになるのだ」。a means to an end「目的を達成するための手段」。

【3】(1) 生まれつきの能力や経済的な状況などから生徒の能力が限られていると考える教師が，生徒の学びが期待できない方法で授業を行うという悪循環のこと。(69字) (2) frustration leads me to leave feedback that is less than (3) A (4) アメリカ合衆国では，「もし私が頑張って取り組めば，負けてしまっても問題ではない。そして，何回失敗しても，少なくとも1回以上それを越える回数困難を乗り越えて向上できれば，勝者と言えるのだ」という考えがある。学習者が

成功を体験すると，彼女は自己に対して肯定的なイメージを強くし，これが彼女のその後の学習に対する努力全般に影響を与えるのだ。

(5)　B　(6)　⑥　B　⑦　D　⑧　B　⑨　A　⑩　C

〈解説〉(1)　a vicious circle「悪循環」について70字以内で説明する。下線部①の前に言い換えや説明の意を持つコロンがあるので，前文に答えを求める。　(2)　何度も同じ間違いのテストを採点していると腹が立ってくるという内容を受けて，②「このフラストレーションが決して優しくないフィードバックを書き残させるのだ」。　(3)　climate「雰囲気，風潮」。　(4)　behind「遅れをとって，負けて」。pick oneself up「立ち直る，向上する」。color「影響を及ぼす」。　(5)　社会学的な観点から見ると，⑤「その情報は破壊的にもなりうる」。第6段落では，自己概念は変化しやすく，多くの場合学校という環境の中で起こること。例として，数学に向いているグループとそうではないグループがあると間違ったことを告げた教師の行動とその結末を挙げている。Bの「教師は生徒の熱意をくじくようなことを言えば，悪い方に自己概念を変えてしまうことがある」が正しい。　(6)　self-efficacy「自己効力感」についての一節である。空欄を含む文の意味はそれぞれ以下のようになる。　⑥　自己効力感は日常生活の出来事に影響する必要な行動ができるという可能性を信じることと定義されている。⑦　自己効力感を信じることが人の感情，考え，動機づけや行動を決定している。　⑧　能力を信頼している人は習得されるべき課題として難しいタスクに取り組む。　⑨　避けられるべき脅威というよりも　⑩　彼らは失敗に直面しても，さらに努力を重ねる。なお，2つ目の空欄⑧を含む文は，彼らは良くないことが起こりそうな状況にも自信を持って近づくので，それらをコントロールすることができるのだ，の意味である。

【4】(1)　英語指導はタペストリーを編むようだ。指導者，生徒，環境，言語，そして4技能の糸を効果的に織る，つまり統合することで美しいタペストリー＝効果的に英語を使用するコミュニケーションの担い

手を作り上げられる。(100字)　(2) In order to improve the students' abilities for authentic communication in English, I'd like to introduce "presentation" activities into my English lesson, because it can include the four primary skills as follows: The students read authentic materials to gain knowledge and information about the theme given by the teacher. After discussing with their co-workers, they write essays which convey their own opinions and ideas. They practice how to present their opinions and the perform in front of the audience, and at the same time they listen to the other students' performances. Of course, they are required to express their opinions or questions about their presentations. If the students are able to, some free discussion will make them more deeply involved in the topic.

The advantages of this activity are that students can have enough time to prepare, which allows students with various academic levels to join in the activity, and that it requires students not to talk as prepared but also to express their own words impromptu. (166 words)

〈解説〉(1)　英語指導を織物を織ることに例えた一節である。多くの場合，筆者の主張は最初と，最後に結論として繰り返される。それを念頭に置き，パラグラフごとに重要なところに下線を引くなどしながら読み進めていく。　(2)　問いは「英語の授業でどのように4技能を統合させるのか，自分自身の考えを150語程度で書け」である。解答例のように1つ活動を取り上げて書くこともできるが，教師のスモールトークや生徒のスピーチからやり取りに発展させたり，話題の新聞記事を読んだりビデオを見て感想を書いたりするなど，日々の授業で複数技能を統合させた活動を少しずつ盛り込み，質を高めながら，繰り返し行うことの意義などについても書くことができる。

2018年度　実施問題

【中高共通】

【１】Choose the answer that best completes the sentence from the four choices.

(1)　(　　) of the three jeans fit me. These are all too tight.

A.　All　　B.　Each

C.　Neither　　D.　None

(2)　I (　　) to an athletic club near the office, and I make it a rule to exercise there after work.

A.　am belonging　　B.　belong

C.　was belonging　　D.　will belong

(3)　There (　　) no bus service, you have to take a taxi to get to the town.

A　being　　B.　is

C.　maybe　　D.　was

(4)　You should put a shawl around your shoulders (　　) you get cold.

A.　in case　　B.　so that

C.　unless　　D.　until

(5)　"Don't you watch that popular TV drama every Friday?"

"(　　). I look forward to watching it every week."

A.　No. absolutely not　　B.　No, I can't miss it

C.　Yes, I dislike it　　D.　Yes, of course

(6)　The information society as we know it today (　　) if it had not been for the invention of the printing press.

A.　does not exist　　B.　will not exist

C.　would not exist　　D.　would not have existed

(7)　We must keep our boss (　　) if schedule changes cannot be avoided.

A.　informed　　B.　informing

C.　informs　　D.　to inform

(8) We ( ) when gasoline prices went up to $4 per gallon.

A. have been surprising B. surprised

C. were surprised D. were surprising

(9) My brother is a good person. He is proud of ( ) scolded by his teacher at school when he was a student.

A. having B. having been

C. never having D. never having been

(10) "Do you ( ) my turning on the radio?"
"No, it doesn't bother me at all. Please enjoy listening to it."

A. admit B. disagree

C. like D. mind

(11) Don't tell us that you didn't know it's illegal. ( ) of the law is no excuse.

A. Assurance B. Endurance

C. Ignorance D. Remembrance

(12) They observed the ( ) of deforestation and, in response, developed the practice of planting and cultivating trees for food and for timber.

A. affection B. consequences

C. definition D. indifference

(13) In order to keep politics from influencing sports events, the rules of the soccer games ( ) political banners at any stadiums.

A. forbid B. forecast

C. foretell D. formalize

(14) His work really ( ) from the rest, so he will win the first prize in the design contest.

A. calls for B. comes across

C. looks up to D. stands out

(15) The word "punch" ( ) the Hindustani word "pancha."

A. brings about B. derives from

C. stands for D. takes root in

(16) Emma was so tired that she couldn't walk, (　　) run.

A all the more　　B. by far

C. much less　　D. to make matters worse

(17) The population of Tokyo is relatively (　　) for its size.

A. large　　B. many

C. much　　D. wide

(18) (　　) I used to think was simple has turned out to be complicated.

A. Although　　B. That

C. What　　D. Which

(19) British Parliament consists (　　) two Houses, the House of Commons and the House of Lords.

A. among　　B. in

C. of　　D. with

(20) The improvement of survival rates of cancer patients was (　　) to a combination of new treatments and earlier diagnosis.

A. attributed　　B. contributed

C. distributed　　D. redistributed

(☆☆☆◎◎◎)

【中学校】

【１】Read the following speech and answer the questions below.

Hello, I'm Severn Suzuki speaking on behalf of ECO, the Environmental Children's Organization. We're a group of twelve- and thirteen-year-olds from Canada trying to make a difference. We raised all the money ourselves to come six thousand miles to tell you adults you *must* change your ways. Coming up here today, I have no hidden agenda. I am fighting for my future. Losing my future is not like losing an election or a few points on the stock market.

I am here to speak for all future generations. I am here to speak on behalf of the starving children around the world whose cries go unheard. I am here to speak for the countless animals dying across this planet because they have nowhere left to go.

I am afraid to go out in the sun now because of the holes in the ozone. I am afraid to breathe the air because I don't know what chemicals are in it. I used to go fishing in Vancouver with my dad until just a few years ago we found the fish full of cancers. And now we hear about animals and plants becoming extinct every day — vanishing forever. 【 A 】

In my life, I have dreamt of seeing great herds of wild animals, jungles and rainforests full of birds and butterflies, but now I wonder if they will even exist for my children to see. Did you have to worry about these things when you were my age? All this is happening before our eyes and yet we act as if we have all the time we want and all the solutions. I'm only a child and I don't have all the solutions, but I want you to realize, <u>neither do you!</u>

You don't know how to fix the holes in our ozone layer. You don't know how to bring salmon back to a dead stream. You don't know how to bring back an animal now extinct. And you can't bring back the forests that once grew where there is now a desert. If you don't know how to fix it, please stop breaking it!

Here you may be delegates of your governments, businesspeople, organizers, reporters or politicians. But really you are mothers and fathers, sisters and brothers, aunts and uncles. And each of you is somebody's child. I'm only a child yet I know we are all part of a family, five billion strong — in fact, thirty million species strong — and borders and governments will never change that. I'm only a child yet I know we are all in this together and should act as one single world towards one single goal. In my anger I am not blind, and in my fear I'm not afraid to tell the world how I feel. 【 B 】

In my country we make so much waste. We buy and throw away, buy and throw away. And yet northern countries will not share with the needy. Even when we have more than enough, we are afraid to lose some of our wealth, afraid to let go. In Canada, we live a privileged life with plenty of food, water and shelter. We have watches, bicycles, computers and television sets — the list could go on for days.

Two days ago here in Brazil, we were shocked when we spent time with some children living on the streets. And this is what one child told us: "I wish I was rich. And if I were, I would give all the street children food, clothes, medicine, shelter and love and affection." If a child on the street who has nothing is willing to share, why are we who have everything still so greedy? I can't stop thinking that these children are my own age, and that it makes a tremendous difference where you are born. I could be one of those children living in the **favellas* of Rio, I could be a child starving in Somalia, a victim of war in the Middle East or a beggar in India. I'm only a child yet I know if all the money spent on ***war*** was spent on ending poverty and finding environmental answers, what a wonderful place this Earth would be. 【　C　】

At school, even in kindergarten, you teach us how to behave in the world. You teach us: "Not to fight with others. To work things out. To respect others. To clean up our mess. Not to hurt other creatures. To share, not be greedy."
【　D　】

Do not forget why you are attending these conferences, who you are doing this for — we are your own children. You are deciding what kind of world we will grow up in. Parents should be able to comfort their children by saying, "Everything's going to be all right" ; "We're doing the best we can" and "It's not the end of the world." But I don't think you can say that to us anymore. Are we even on your list of priorities? My dad always says, "You are what you *do*, not what you *say*." Well, what you do makes me cry at night. You grown ups say you love us. I challenge you, *please*, make your actions reflect your words.

Thank you for listening.

【Notes】 **favellas*　貧民街

(1)　Choose the most appropriate place, from 【　A　】～【　D　】 in the text, to put the sentence below.

Then why do you go out and do the things you tell us not to do?

(2) Paraphrase the underlined text using 7 words or less.

(3) Complete the following sentence by choosing the best answer.

Severn is only a child ________.

A. but she can solve all the major problems because she has a lot of time

B. but she understands that humans, including herself, are all part of a family together and should act as one single world towards a single goal

C. yet she knows that governments are not responsible for the present condition of the earth

D. yet she believes firmly that it is better to spend money on war than on ending poverty and environmental problems

(4) According to the text, which of the following is NOT mentioned by Severn?

A. The environment is polluted by the behavior of the human race.

B. Deserts can't be turned back into forests.

C. The amount of money needed to fix the environment is enormous.

D. Lots of animals are dying because they don't have places to live in.

(5) According to the text, which of the following is true?

A. Severn was paid by the government of Brazil to participate in the conference.

B. Severn met a boy living on the street in Brazil who would like to share what he has with all the street children if he were rich.

C. Severn thinks that children the same age have the same opportunities no matter where they are born.

D. Severn demands that people attending the conference educate children how to behave in the world.

(☆☆☆◎◎◎)

【2】Read the following passage and answer the question below.

NASA's Spitzer Space Telescope has revealed the first known system of seven Earth-size planets around a single star. Three of these planets are firmly located in the habitable zone, the area around the parent star where ①(　　).

The discovery sets a new record for greatest number of habitable-zone planets found around a single star outside our solar system. All of these seven planets could have liquid water — key to life as we know it — under the right atmospheric conditions, but the chances are highest with the three in the habitable zone.

"This discovery could be a significant piece in the puzzle of finding habitable environments, places that are conducive to life," said Thomas Zurbuchen, associate administrator of the agency's Science Mission Directorate in Washington. "Answering the question 'are we alone' is a top science priority and finding so many planets like these for the first time in the habitable zone is a remarkable step forward toward that goal."

At about 40 light-years (235 trillion miles) from Earth, the system of planets is relatively close to us, in the *constellation Aquarius. Because they are located outside of our solar system, these planets are scientifically known as exoplanets.

This exoplanet system is called TRAPPIST-1, named for The Transiting Planets and Planetesimals Small Telescope (TRAPPIST) in Chile. In May 2016, researchers using TRAPPIST announced they had discovered three planets in the system. Assisted by several ground-based telescopes, including the European Southern Observatory's Very Large Telescope, Spitzer confirmed the existence of【　i　】of these planets and discovered【　ii　】additional ones, increasing the number of known planets in the system to【　iii　】.

Using Spitzer data, the team precisely measured the sizes of the seven planets and developed first estimates of the masses of six of them, allowing their density ②(　　),

Based on their densities, all of the TRAPPIST-1 planets are likely to be rocky. Further observations will not only help determine whether they are rich in water, but also possibly reveal whether any could have liquid water on their surfaces. The mass of the seventh and farthest exoplanet has not yet been estimated—scientists believe it could be an icy, "snowball-like" world, but further observations are needed.

"The seven wonders of TRAPPIST-1 are the first Earth-size planets that have been found orbiting this kind of star," said Michael Gillon, lead author of the paper and the principal investigator of the TRAPPIST exoplanet survey at the University of Liege, Belgium. "It is also the best target yet for studying the atmospheres of potentially habitable, Earth-size worlds."

In contrast to our sun, the TRAPPIST-1 star — classified as an *ultra-cool dwarf — is so cool that liquid water could survive on planets orbiting very close to it, closer than is possible on planets in our solar system. All seven of the TRAPPIST-1 planetary orbits are ③[to / than / is / their host star / closer to / Mercury] our sun. The planets also are very close to each other. If a person was standing on one of the planet's surface, they could gaze up and potentially see geological features or clouds of neighboring worlds, which would sometimes appear larger than the moon in Earth's sky.

The planets may also be tidally locked to their star, which means the same side of the planet is always facing the star, therefore each side is either perpetual ④(　　) or ⑤(　　). This could mean they have weather patterns totally unlike those on Earth, such as strong winds blowing from the day side to the night side, and extreme temperature changes.

Spitzer, an *infrared telescope that trails Earth as it orbits the sun, was well-suited for studying TRAPPIST-1 because the star glows brightest in infrared light, whose wavelengths are longer than the eye can see. In the fall of 2016, Spitzer observed TRAPPIST-1 nearly continuously for 500 hours. Spitzer is uniquely positioned in its orbit to observe enough crossing — transits — of the planets in front of the host star to reveal the complex architecture of the system. Engineers optimized Spitzer's ability to observe transiting planets during Spitzer's "warm mission," which began after the spacecraft's coolant ran out as planned after the first five years of operations.

"This is the most exciting result I have seen in the 14 years of Spitzer operations," said Sean Carey, manager of NASA's Spitzer Science Center at *Caltech/ *IPAC in Pasadena, California. "Spitzer will follow up in the fall to further refine our understanding of these planets so that the James Webb Space Telescope can follow up. More observations of the system are sure to reveal more secrets."

【Notes】*constellation Aquarius　みずがめ座　　*ultra-cool dwarf　超低温矮星　　*infrared telescope　赤外線望遠鏡　　*Caltech　カリフォルニア工科大学　　*IPAC　Infrared Processing and Analysis Centerの略

(1)　Choose the best sentence for ①(　　) from the four alternatives below.

A.　the temperature ranges are stable

B.　the temperature ranges will not support life

C.　a rocky planet is most likely to have liquid water

D.　liquid water cannot exist on the surface of a planet

(2)　Choose an answer from the four alternatives below to complete【　i　】～【　iii　】. (Each answer can only be used once.)

A.　two　　B.　three　　C.　five　　D.　seven

(3)　Choose the one that best completes ②(　　) from the four alternatives below.

A.　estimates　　B.　estimated　　C.　to estimate

D.　to be estimated

(4)　Put the words from ③[　　] in the text in the correct order.

(5)　Choose the best answer for ④(　　) and ⑤(　　) from the four alternatives below.

A.　④　mountains　⑤　sea　　B.　④　day　⑤　night

C.　④　high　⑤　low　　D.　④　large　⑤　small

(6)　According to the text, which of the following is true?

A.　All of the TRAPPIST-1 planets orbit the sun in our solar system.

B. The discovery of the planets of TRAPPIST-1 answers a top science priority "are we alone" .

C. The "warm mission" of Spitzer is the searching for the existence of Earth size planets and reveal the details of them.

D. More observations of the TRAPPIST-1 system by the James Webb Space Scope Telescope will definitely reveal more secrets.

(☆☆☆◎◎◎)

【3】Read the following passage written by Helen Keller and answer the questions below.

I have often thought it would be a blessing if each human being were stricken ①(　　) and ②(　　) for a few days at some time during his early adult life. Darkness would make him more appreciative of sight; silence would teach him the joys of sound.

③Now and (　　) I have tested my seeing friends to discover what they see. Recently I was visited by a very good friend who had just returned from a long walk in the woods, and I asked her what she had observed. 'Nothing in particular,' she replied.

How was it possible, I asked myself, to walk for an hour through the woods and see nothing worthy of note? I who cannot see find hundreds of things to interest me through mere touch. I feel the delicate symmetry of a leaf. I pass my hands lovingly about the smooth skin of a *silver birch, or the rough, shaggy bark of a pine. In spring I touch the branches of trees hopefully in search of a bud, the first sign of awakening Nature after her winter's sleep. I feet the delightful, velvety texture of a flower, and discover its remarkable *convolutions; and something of the miracle of Nature is revealed to me. ④Occasionally, if I am very fortunate, I place my hand gently on a small tree and feel the happy quiver of a bird in full song. I am delighted to have the cool waters of a brook rush through my open fingers. To me a lush carpet of pine needles or spongy grass is more welcome than the most luxurious

*Persian rug. To me the pageant of seasons is a thrilling and unending drama, the action of which streams through my finger tips.

⑤At (　　) my heart cries out with longing to see all these things. If I can get so much pleasure from mere touch, how much more beauty must be revealed by sight. Yet, those who have eyes apparently see little. The panorama of color and action which fills the world is taken for granted. It is human, perhaps, to appreciate little that which we have and to long for that which we have not, but it is a great pity that in the world of light the gift of sight is used only as a mere convenience rather than as a means of adding fullness to life.

If I were the president of a university I should establish a compulsory course in 'How to Use Your Eyes.' The professor would try to show his pupils how they could add joy to their lives by really seeing what passes unnoticed before them. He would try to awake their dormant and *sluggish faculties.

Perhaps I can best illustrate by imagining what I should most like to see if I were given the use of my eyes, say, for just three days. And while I am imagining, suppose you, too, set your mind to work on the problem of how you would use your own eyes if you had only three more days to see. If with the oncoming darkness of the third night you knew that the sun would never rise for you again, how would you spend those three precious intervening days? What would you most want to let your gaze rest upon?

I, naturally, should want most to see the things which have become dear to me through my years of darkness. You, too, would want to let your eyes rest long on the things that have become dear to you so that you could take the memory of them with you into the night that loomed before you.

I who am ①(　　) can give one hint to those who see — one admonition to those who would make full use of the gift of sight: Use your eyes as if tomorrow you would be stricken ①(　　). And the same method can be applied to the other senses. Hear the music of voices, the song of a bird, the mighty strains of an orchestra, as if you would be stricken ②(　　)

tomorrow. Touch each object you want to touch as if tomorrow your tactile sense would fail. Smell the perfume of flowers, taste with relish each *morsel, as if tomorrow you could never smell and taste again. Make the most of every sense; glory in all the *facets of pleasure and beauty which the world reveals to you through the several means of contact which Nature provides. But of all the senses, I am sure that sight must be the most delightful.

【Notes】 *silver birch　白樺　　*convolution　ぐるぐる巻いた状態
*Persian rug　ペルシャじゅうたん　　*sluggish　物ぐさな
*morsel　ひと口　　*facet　物事の様相，面

(1) Write one word that best fits ①(　　) and one word that best fits ②(　　).

(2) In ③(　　) and ⑤(　　) write one word that makes the underlined ③ and ⑤ match the meaning of the underlined ④. (③(　　) and ⑤(　　) should not be the same word.)

(3) According to the passage, complete the following sentences ① and ② by choosing the best answers.

① Helen finds ________.

A. nothing interesting in nature through touch
B. nothing interesting in nature through sound
C. many things in nature interesting through touch
D. many things in nature interesting through sound

② Those who have eyes ________.

A. always see the pageant of seasons thrillingly
B. take it for granted that the color and the action fill the world
C. cry out with yearning to see all things
D. get much pleasure because the beauty is revealed by sight

(4) According to passage, which of the following is true about Helen Keller.

A. Helen states that people should use their senses as if they could be lost in three days.
B. Helen gets no pleasure because she is not only able to see anything but

she also lacks a sense of touch.

C. Helen takes it for granted that only one hour's walk in the woods would not give anyone anything interesting in particular to observe.

D. Helen believes that sight is used only as a mere convenience for most people who can see because they often think that sight is a means to add fullness to their lives.

(☆☆☆◎◎◎)

【４】Translate the underlined sentences into English.

(1) 自転車は健康的だし，地球に優しい。歩行者にも優しい走りをぜひ。

(2) 音楽の効果は気晴らしの域を超えるが，その癒やしは万能ではない。

(☆☆☆◎◎◎)

【５】Many junior high schools in Kyoto prefecture have "Can-Do" lists for English education. How do you think these lists are useful? How can you use the lists? Write your answer with concrete reasons in approximately 100 words.

(☆☆☆◎◎◎)

【高等学校】

【１】Read the following passage and answer the questions below.

In the early part of the twentieth century, the American naturalist William Beebe came upon a strange sight in the Guyana jungle. A group of army ants was moving in a huge circle. The circle was 1,200 feet in circumference, and it took each ant two and half hours to complete the loop. The ants went around and around the circle for two days until most of them dropped dead.

What Beebe saw was what biologists call a "circular mill." The mill is created when army ants find themselves separated from their colony. ①Once they're lost, they obey a simple rule: follow the ant in front of you. The result is the mill, which usually only breaks up when a few ants straggle off by chance and the others follow them away.

As Steven Johnson showed in his illuminating book *Emergence*, an ant colony normally works remarkably well. No one ant runs the colony. No one issues orders. Each individual ant knows, on its own, almost nothing. [②] the colony successfully finds food, gets all its work done, and reproduces itself. But the simple tools that make ants so successful are also responsible for the ③demise of the ants who get trapped in the circular mill. ④Every move [what / an ant / depends / do / fellow ants / its / makes / on], and an ant cannot act independently, which would help break the march to death.

I've assumed that human beings are not ants. [⑤] , I've assumed that human beings can be independent decision makers. Independence doesn't mean isolation, but it does mean relative freedom from the influence of [⑥] . If we are independent, our opinions are, in some sense, our own. We will not march to death in a circle just because the ants in front of us are.

(1) Translate the underlined ① into Japanese, explaining what "they" refers to.

(2) Choose the best word or phrase for [②] , [⑤] and [⑥] from the four choices below.

② A. Likewise B. Naturally C. Therefore D. Yet

⑤ A. Eventually B. In other words C. In the meantime D. Nevertheless

⑥ A. ants B. others C. ourselves D. the colony

(3) Substitute the underlined ③ with the best alternative from the four choices below.

A. death B. discord C. happiness D. misunderstanding

(4) Put the words from the underlined ④ in the correct order.

(☆☆☆◎◎◎)

【2】Read the following passage and translate the underlined sentence into Japanese.

Even while recognizing (how could they not?) the social nature of existence, economists tend to emphasize people's autonomy and to downplay the influence of others on our preferences and judgments. Sociologists and social-network theorists, by contrast, describe people as *embedded* in particular social contexts, and see influence as inescapable. Sociologists generally don't view this as a problem. They suggest it's simply the way human life is organized. And it may not be a problem for everyday life. But what I want to argue here is that the more influence a group's members exert on each other, and the more personal contact they have with each other, the less likely it is that the group's decisions will be wise ones.

(☆☆◎◎◎)

【3】Read the following passage and answer the questions below.

What makes information cascades interesting is that they are a form of aggregating information, just like a voting system or a market. And the truth is that they don't do a terrible job of aggregation. 【 A 】 In classroom experiments, where cascades are easy to start and observe, cascading groups pick the better alternative about 30 percent of the time, which is better than any individual in the groups can do. The fundamental problem with cascades is that people's choices are made sequentially, instead of all at once. There are good reasons for ①this — some people are more cautious than others, some are more willing to experiment, some have more money than others. But roughly speaking, all of the problems that cascades can cause are the result of the fact that some people make their decisions before others. If you want to improve an organization's or an economy's decision making, one of the best things you can do is make sure, as much as possible, that decisions are made simultaneously rather than one after the other.

An interesting proof of ②this can be found in one of those very classroom experiments I just mentioned. This one was devised by economists Angela Hung and Charles Plott, and it involved the time-honored technique of having students draw colored *marbles from *urns. 【　B　】 In this case, there were two urns. Urn A contained twice as many light marbles as dark ones. Urn B contained twice as many dark marbles as light ones. At the beginning of the experiment, the people in charge chose one of the two urns from which, in sequence, each volunteer drew a marble. The question the participants in the experiment had to answer was: Which urn was being used? A correct answer earned them a couple of dollars.

To answer that question, the participants could rely on ③<u>two sources of information</u>. First, they had the marble they had drawn from the urn. If they drew a light marble, chances were that it was from Urn A. If they drew a dark marble, chances are that it was from Urn B. This was their "private information," because no one was allowed to reveal what color marble they had drawn. All people revealed was their guess as to which urn was being used. This was the second source of information, and it created ④<u>a potential conflict</u>. If three people in front of you had guessed Urn B, but you drew a light marble, would you still guess Urn A even though the group thought otherwise?

Most of the time the student in that situation guessed Urn B, which was the rational thing to do. And in 78 percent of the trials, information cascades started. This was as expected. But then ⑤<u>Hung and Plott changed the rules</u>. The students still drew their marbles from the urn and made their decisions in order. But this time, instead of being paid for picking the correct answer, the students got paid based on whether the group's collective answer — as decided by majority vote — was the right one. The students' task shifted from trying to do the best they could individually to trying to make the group as smart as it could be.

This meant one thing had to happen: each student had to pay more attention to [　ア　] and less attention to [　イ　]. (Collective decisions are only wise, remember, when they incorporate lots of different information.) People's private information, though, was imperfect. So by paying attention to only his own information, a student was more likely to make a wrong guess. But the group was more likely to be collectively right. Encouraging people to make incorrect guesses actually made the group as a whole smarter. And when it was the group's collective accuracy that counted, people listened to their private information. 【　C　】 The group's collective judgment became, not surprisingly, significantly more accurate than the judgments of the cascading groups.

Effectively what Hung and Plott did in their experiment was remove (or at least reduce) the sequential element in the way people made decisions, by making previous choices less important to the decision makers. That's obviously not something that an economy as a whole can do very easily. 【　D　】 Organizations, on the other hand, clearly can and should have people offer their judgments simultaneously, rather than one after the other. On a deeper level, the success of the Hung and Plott experiment — which effectively forced the people in the group to make themselves independent — ⑥underscores the value and the difficulty of autonomy. One key to successful group decisions is getting people to pay much less attention to what everyone else is saying.

*marble　ビー玉　　*urns　壺

(1)　Find the part of the text the underlined ① refers to and write it down in English.

(2)　Explain what the underlined ② refers to in this text in Japanese.

(3)　Find the two sources of information referred to in the underlined ③, written within 10 words for each, from the text and write them down in English.

(4)　Explain the meaning of the underlined ④ within 70 Japanese letters, using the example mentioned in the text.

(5)　Explain how "⑤Hung and Plott changed the rules" within 80 Japanese letters.

(6) Choose the best combination of phrases for [ア] and [イ] from the two choices below.

A. ア everyone else's information イ his private information

B. ア his private information イ everyone else's information

(7) Choose the most appropriate place, from 【 A 】～【 D 】, to put the sentence below.

We don't want companies to have to wait to launch products until the public at large has voted yea or nay.

(8) Substitute the underlined ⑥ with the best alternative from the four choices below.

A. denies B. emphasizes C. exerts D. overlooks

(☆☆☆◎◎◎)

【4】Read the following passage and answer the questions below.

Mistakes are good

Children make many mistakes when they learn language. What parent hasn't heard 'goed' for 'went' or 'eated' for 'ate'? It's [①] not to listen to a three year old without hearing errors of other types as well — 'scissor it' for 'cut it,' 'let's broom the floor' for 'let's sweep the floor,' 'Can you needle it?' for 'Can you sew it?,' and so on.

Mistakes like these mean just one thing — children are doing what they are supposed to be doing; they are discovering the rules of English. ②<u>We adults may not say 'goed' or 'eated,' but adding '-ed' to a verb IS the basic way to form the past tense in English</u>. Most verbs work that way, and any new verb that enters the language has to form its past tense with '-ed' — that's why the past tense of 'blog' has to be 'blogged.' Figuring out the rule is a prelude to figuring out the exceptions.

The same goes for other mistakes children make. Maybe we don't scissor things, but we do sometimes hammer them. And maybe we don't broom floors, but we do mop them. English allows many words that refer to objects (like *hammer* and *mop*) to be converted into words that refer to actions involving those objects. A child who says 'Scissor it' or 'Let's broom the floor' has started to figure ③this out, and that's a good thing.

Mistakes don't disappear overnight. It may take several hundred exposures to the right past tense form of a verb before all the errors are eliminated. Immature forms may pop up for months or even years before they are finally laid to rest, but there's no reason for concern. Mistakes arise as a normal part of the language acquisition process, and they'll disappear as a normal part of that same process.

It's not [ア], it's [イ] that matters

It's natural to want to help children with something as important as language. But the best way to help may not be what you think. One thing that's quite unlikely to work is trying to correct mistakes. A child whose parents insist on correcting *They no go* ('No, don't say that; say "They ... ARE ... NOT ... goING".') doesn't learn English any faster than a child whose parents respond by saying, 'That's right. They aren't going. They have something else to do at home.'

Using baby talk with a child probably doesn't help either. A lot of mothers speak to very young children in short simple sentences, with higher-than-normal pitch and child-like pronunciation. That certainly doesn't do any harm and it may help get the child's attention, [④] to be crucial for language learning. Children in cultures where mothers don't do this still acquire language without difficulty.

Does this mean that children can learn to talk no matter what their circumstances? Not quite. No one — adult or child — has ever learned a language by listening to the radio. That's because (unless you already speak the language) there's no way to figure out what the voice on the radio is saying. Chances are it isn't talking about what you're looking at or what you're feeling, and that's not good enough.

Children need to hear language being used to talk about things they can see and feel, what they have just experienced or are about to experience, what they are curious about and what they care about. This is the type of speech that provides children with the raw material they need to learn a language — to figure out what words mean, where a subject or a direct object fits into a sentence, how to ask a question, and all the other things that make up language.

In fact, that's the single most important thing that any parent needs to know about language. Talk to children about what matters to them. They will take care of the rest.

(1) Choose the best word or phrase for [①] and [④] from the four choices below.

① A. hard B. harmful
C. lucky D. useful

④ A. and it's fortunate B. and it's likely
C. but it's unfortunate D. but it's unlikely

(2) Translate the underlined ② into Japanese, taking why "IS" is capitalized into consideration.

(3) Explain what the underlined ③ refers to within 50 Japanese letters.

(4) Choose the best phrase for [ア] and [イ] to complete the title of the latter section from the four choices below.

ア A. how you say it B. what you say
C. when you say it D. where you say it

イ A. how you say it B. what you say
C. when you say it D. where you say it

(5) Do you agree or disagree that "mistakes are good," especially in relation to English as a Second Language learners? How do you react when students make mistakes as they are learning language? Explain and provide examples, using 150-200 words in English.

(☆☆◎◎◎)

【５】Read the following passage and summarize the story within 100 Japanese letters.

A young man played, or I should say practiced, football at an Ivy League university. "Jerry" wasn't skilled enough to play more than occasionally in the regular season games, but in four years this dedicated, loyal young man never missed a practice.

The coach, deeply impressed with Jerry's loyalty and dedication to the team, also marveled at his evident devotion to his father. Several times the coach had seen Jerry and his visiting father laughing and talking as they walked arm-in-arm around the campus. But the coach had never met the father or talked with Jerry about him.

During Jerry's senior year and a few nights before the most important game of the season — a traditional rivalry that matched Army-Navy Georgia-Georgia Tech or Michigan-Ohio State in intensity — the coach heard a knock on his door. Opening it, he saw the young man, his face full of sadness.

"Coach, my father just died," Jerry murmured. "Is it all right if I miss practice for a few days and go home?"

The coach said he was very sorry to hear the news and, of course, it was all right for him to go home. As Jerry murmured a "thank you" and turned to leave, the coach added, "Please don't feel you have to return in time for next Saturday's game. You certainly are excused from that, too." The youth nodded and left.

But on Friday night, just hours before the big game, Jerry again stood in the coach's doorway.

"Coach, I'm back," he said, "and I have a request. May I please start the game tomorrow?"

The coach tried to dissuade the youth from his plea in light of the importance of the game to the team. But finally he consented.

That night the coach tossed and turned. Why had he said yes to the youth? The opposing team was favored to win by three touchdowns. He needed his best players in for the entire game. Suppose the opening kickoff came to Jerry and he fumbled. Suppose he started the game and they lost by five or six touchdowns.

Obviously he could not let the youth play. It was out of the question. But he had promised.

So, as the bands played and the crowd roared, Jerry stood at the goal line awaiting the opening kickoff. *The ball probably won't go to him anyway*, the coach thought to himself. Then the coach would run one series of plays, making sure the other halfback and the fullback carried the ball, and take the youth out of the game. That way he wouldn't have to worry about a crucial fumble, and he would have kept carried his promise.

"Oh no!" the coach groaned as the opening kickoff floated end over end right into Jerry's arms. But instead of fumbling, as the coach expected, Jerry hugged the ball tightly, dodged three onrushing defenders and raced to midfield before he was finally tackled.

The coach had never seen Jerry run with such agility and power, and perhaps sensing something, he had the quarterback call Jerry's signal. The quarterback handed off, and Jerry responded by breaking tackles for a 20-yard gain. A few plays later he carried the ball over the goal line.

The favored opponents were stunned. Who was this kid? He wasn't even in their scouting reports, for until then he had played a total of three minutes all year.

The coach left Jerry in, and he played the entire first half on both offense and defense. Tackling, intercepting and knocking down passes, blocking, running — he did it all.

At halftime the underdogs led by two touchdowns. During the second half Jerry continued to inspire the team. When the final gun sounded, his team had won.

In the locker-room bedlam reserved only for teams that have fought the impossible fight and triumphed, the coach sought out Jerry and found him sitting quietly, head in hands, in a far corner.

"Son, what happened out there?" the coach asked as he put his arm around him. "You can't play as well as you did. You're just not that fast, not that strong nor that skilled. What happened?"

Jerry looked up at the coach and said softly, "You see, Coach, my father was blind. This is the first game he ever saw me play."

(☆☆☆◎◎◎)

解答・解説

【中高共通】

【1】(1)　D　(2)　B　(3)　A　(4)　A　(5)　D　(6)　C
(7)　A　(8)　C　(9)　D　(10)　D　(11)　C　(12)　B
(13)　A　(14)　D　(15)　B　(16)　C　(17)　A　(18)　C
(19)　C　(20)　A

〈解説〉(1)「何ひとつ～ない，誰ひとり～ない」のnone。neitherは「(2者のうちの)どちらも～でない」。 (2)　動詞belongは状態を表すため進行形にできない。 (3)　There is ～を分詞構文にする場合，There being ～。 (4)「～の場合に備えて，～するといけないから」という意味のin case。 (5)　否定疑問文の答え方に注意。空欄の後に「毎週楽しみに観ている」と言っているので，空欄には肯定的な答えが入る。

(6)　if節は過去の事実に反する仮定として，仮定法過去完了。主節は，現在の事実に反する仮定。「もし印刷機の発明がなかったら，現在のような情報化社会は存在しないだろう」。 (7)　第5文型keep＋O＋C「OをCの状態にしておく」なので，O = C(our boss is informed)の関係が成り立つ。 (8)　be surprised「驚く」。 (9)　動名詞を否定するnotやneverは動名詞の直前に置く。「彼は学生の頃，学校で先生に叱られなかったことを自慢に思っている」。 (10)　Do you mind～？「～してもいいですか」。　(11)　ignorance「知らないこと，無知」。「法律を知らなかったことは，言い訳にならない」という意味である。
(12)　consequence「成り行き，結果」。　(13)　forbid「禁止する」。
(14)　stand out「目立つ，際立つ」。　(15)　derive from「～に由来する」。
(16)　much less「(否定的語句のあとで)なおさら～でない」。all the more「なお一層」。by far「はるかに」。to make matters worse「さらに悪いことに」。　(17)「人口が多い，少ない」はlargeやsmallで表す。
(18)　関係詞の後にI thinkのようなほかの節が続くときの語順は，I used to think it was simpleのitが節の前に移動したと考える。「単純だと考えていたことが複雑であるとわかった」。　(19)　consist of ～「～からなる」。　(20)　attribute A to B「AをBのせいだと考える」。

【中学校】

【1】(1)　D　　(2)　You don't have all the solutions, either.　(3)　B
(4)　C　　(5)　B

〈解説〉(1)　挿入すべき文は「私たちにしないように言うことを，なぜあなたたちは外でするのですか」の意味である。第9段落で，世の中でいかに振る舞うべきか大人が子どもに教える具体例が6つ羅列されているので，その後に入れるのが適切。　(2)　否定の文を受けて「～ない」と言うときにneitherを使う。neither do youは，I don't have all the solutionsという文を受けて，「あなたも解決策を持っているわけではない」ということを述べている。　(3)　第6段落4文目，5文目のI'm only a child以下に注目する。ここで述べられていることが，Bの「Severnはほんの子どもであるが，彼女自身を含む人間は家族の一部であり，1つの目標に向かう1つの人間社会として行動するべきだと理解している」と合致する。　(4)　環境を修復するために必要なお金についての記述はないのでCは誤り。　(5)　A　第1段落第3文で，自分たちで費用をまかなってやってきたと述べているので誤り。　B　ブラジルで会った少年については，第8段落の2文目，3文目の内容と合致するので正しい。　C　論旨にない。　D　Severnは，大人たちが正しい行動をとるように促しているので誤り。

【２】(1)　C　　(2)【i】A　　【ii】C　　【iii】D　　(3)　D

(4)　closer to their host star than Mercury is to　　(5)　B　　(6)　D

〈解説〉(1)　ハビタブルゾーン(生命居住可能領域)の説明。生命のカギとなるのが水であることから，Cの「親星の周りで，岩石惑星が液状水を持っているだろうエリア」が正解。なお，parent star　は我々の太陽系における太陽に相当し，岩石惑星は地球型の惑星のことを指す。(2)　2016年5月に研究者たちは，「通過惑星及び微惑星小望遠鏡TRAPPIST」を使って3つの惑星を発見したと発表した。「NASAのスピッツアー宇宙望遠鏡がこれらの惑星(3つの惑星)のうち【i】個の存在を確認し，加えて【ii】個発見し，その惑星系で知られている【iii】個に数が増えた」という流れである。よって【iii】は第1段落の1文目から7だとわかる。【i】は3つの惑星のうちという条件を考えると2，【ii】は5であるとわかる。　(3)　their density was estimatedという意味上の関係が成り立つ。to以下はbe estimatedとする。「密度を推定することを可能にした」。　(4)　太陽と対照的に，トラピスト - 1星は温度が低いので，近くで軌道している惑星上で，液状水が存在するとされている。トラピスト - 1星と惑星間の距離は，太陽系の惑星が太陽に限りなく近づけるよりも短いと書かれている。この内容をうけて，「トラピスト - 1星の7つのすべての惑星の軌道は，(太陽系の一番内側の)水星が太陽に近いより親星に近い」となるよう語句を並べる。　(5)　惑星は潮汐ロック，すなわち惑星の同じ面をいつも親星に向けていることから，常にそれぞれの面が昼か夜のどちらかである。　(6)　Dは第12段落の内容と合致しているので正しい。　A　第2段落にplanets found around a single star outside our solar systemと述べているので，「太陽系の太陽の周りを回っている」のではないとわかる。　B　第3段落第2文で「トラピスト - 1の惑星の発見は，目標への顕著な一歩である」と述べている。直接are we alone という疑問への答えになるわけではない。C　warm missionについては，第11段落に述べてられている。赤外線望遠鏡を使って，地球を追いかける形で太陽を回る軌道をとりながら，トラピスト‐1系の複雑な構造を明らかにするのがwarm missionである。地球サイズの惑星が存在するかを調査して詳細を明らかにすることではない。

【3】(1) ① blind ② deaf (2) ③ then ⑤ times
(3) ① C ② B (4) A

〈解説〉(1) 後に続く文で「暗闇は目が見えることを一層ありがたく思わせるし，静寂は音の喜びを教える」と述べていることから，「もし人間が数日間『視覚障害』や『聴覚障害』の状態になれば…」とするのが正解。strike＋人～「人を～の状態にする」。 (2) now and then, occasionally, at timesは，いずれも「ときどき」の意味。 (3) ① 第3段落第2文目以降に，Cの「ヘレンは触ることにより，自然界の面白いものをたくさん見つける」と同じことが述べられている。 ② 第4段落4文目に，Bの「目が見える人は，色や動きが世界を満たしていることを当然だと思っている」と同じことが述べられている。

(4) Aの「人々は3日間(感覚を)失っているかのように，感覚を使うべきだとヘレンは述べている」は第1段落第1文と同義なので正しい。BとCは第3段落の内容に反しており，Dは第4段落の内容に反しているので誤り。

【4】(1) I ask all bicycle riders to be kind to pedestrians, too. (2) While music can do more than relax the listener, its healing power is not omnipotent.

〈解説〉(1) 「(私は自転車に乗る人に)歩行者にも優しい走りを(お願いしたい)」と考えて英訳する。「歩行者に優しい」は，pedestrian-friendly, friendly to pedestrianでも可。 (2) whileは「～だけれども」という譲歩の意味。「気晴らし」「～の域を超える」「万能の」は，それぞれrelaxation, go beyond, almightyなどを使用しても可。

【5】I believe "Can-Do" lists are useful for goal management. It can help students focus on their next goals. Each item on the lists should be easy to understand, so students can check to see what they can or can't do themselves. For teachers, "Can-Do" lists can be a great help when planning lessons for the year. "Can-Do" lists contain the goals for students for the school year. So the teacher doesn't have to develop goals and lesson plans, but only lesson plans. I'd like to use "Can-Do" lists at the end of each term to make sure my students are progressing as they should be. In addition, we should revise the lists every year so that they suit our future students. (121 words)

〈解説〉問題文の意味は「京都府における英語教育のCan-Doリストの有効性とはどのようなものか，あなたならCan-Doリストを授業にどのように活用するかを100字程度で記述せよ」である。Can-Doリストについては，平成25年3月に文部科学省初等中等教育局から出された「各中・高等学校の外国語教育における『CAN-DO リスト』の形での学習到達目標設定のための手引き」を熟読しておくこと。同手引きは，「国際共通語としての英語力向上のための5つの提言と具体的施策」(平成23年6月，外国語能力の向上に関する検討会)において，生徒に求められる英語力を達成するための学習到達目標を「CAN-DOリスト」の形で具体的に設定することについて提言がなされたことを受けて作成されたものである。「CAN-DO リスト」の形で学習到達目標を設定する目的は，「生徒が身に付ける能力を各学校が明確化し，主に教員が生徒の指導と評価の改善に活用すること」，「学習到達目標を，言語を用いて『～することができる』という能力記述文の形で設定することにより，4技能を有機的に結び付け，総合的に育成する指導につなげること」及び「生涯学習の観点から，教員が生徒と目標を共有することにより，言語習得に必要な自律的学習者として主体的に学習する態度・姿勢を生徒が身に付けること」と示されている。目的や趣旨はもちろんのこと，設定手順，活用方法，評価方法及び評価時期，学習到達目標の見直しについて理解をしておくことが必要である。

【高等学校】

【1】(1)　軍隊アリは，一旦道に迷ってしまうと，自分の前のアリに続けという簡単な規則に従う。その結果生み出されるのが，“サーキュラー・ミル”であり，これは大抵，数匹のアリがたまたま列をはずれて，他のアリがそのアリの後について行ったときに初めてくずれるのである。

(2)　②　D　⑤　B　⑥　B　(3)　A　(4)　an ant makes depends on what its fellow ants do

〈解説〉(1)　theyはarmy ants。straggle「(道路から)それる，(隊列などから)はぐれる」。　(2)　②　スティーブン・ジョンソンが，本の中でアリの巣は極めてうまく機能していると書いている。「どれかのアリが指揮や命令しているわけでもなく，個々のアリは，ほとんど何も知らない」と「巣はうまく食べ物を見つけ，全ての仕事を完了させ，子を繁殖させる」をつなぐ接続詞はDの「しかし」が適当。　⑤「人間はアリではない」と「人間は独立した意思決定者になりうる」をつなぐのはBの「言い換えると」。　⑥は「自立」が何を意味するのか述べている文である。「他人の影響から相互の自由」と考えられるのでB。(3)「アリたちを成功させるその単純な技能は，“サーキュラー・ミル”という罠にかかるアリたちの(　③　)の責任をも負う」という文脈なので，Aのdeath(死)が適切である。　(4)　an ant makesに主語のEvery moveを修飾させる。「一匹のアリのどの動きも，仲間のアリが何をするか次第である」。

【2】私がここで主張したいのは，ある集団の構成員たちが互いに及ぼしあう影響が大きければ大きいほど，またその構成員たち同士の個人的な接点が多ければ多いほど，その集団の決定が賢明なものとなる見込みは，ますます低くなるということだ。

〈解説〉下線部を訳す問題である。the more～the less…「～すればするほど…でない」に注意する。本文全訳は，「人間の社会性を認識するときでさえ，経済学者は人々の自主性を強調し，私たちの好みや判断に対する他人の影響は少ないと考える。対照的に，社会学者や社会ネットワーク理論家は，人々は社会的関係にはめ込まれ，その影響は避けられないものと見ている。概して，社会学者はこのことが問題であると見なさず，それは単に人間社会が組織される方法であり，日常生活にとっても問題ではないと言っている」となる。

【３】(1)　①　people's choices are made sequentially, instead of all at once
(2)　②　ある団体，あるいは会社の意思決定を改善したいなら，取り得る最善の策の1つは，決断を次々に下すのではなく，できる限り同時に下すということ。　(3)　・the marble they had drawn from the urn (8 words)　・their guess as to which urn was being used (9 words)
(4)　自分の個人情報に基づくと壺はAだと判断できるが，他人の意見から判断するとBだと判断できるため，2つの答えが対立する可能性があること。(66字)　(5)　質問に個人単位で答えて正解すれば各自に賞金が与えられる規則が，集団の中で多数決で選ばれた答えが正解すれば賞金が集団全員に与えられる規則に変わった。(73字)　(6)　B
(7)　D　(8)　B

〈解説〉(1)　下線部①は「これ(人が一斉にではなく順次に物事を決めること)には十分な理由がある」と解釈することができる。理由がハイフン以下に続く。　(2)　下線部②を含む文の意味は，「これの興味深い証拠は，私が今述べた教室での実験の1つに見ることができる」。「これ」は1文前の内容を指していると判断できる。　(3)　source of informationとは，「情報源」。情報カスケードの実験(自分がどちらの壺からビー玉を抜き取ったか判断する)において，情報源は，「抜き取った玉(の色)」と「推測」である。第3段落の第2文目と第6文目をそれぞれ名詞句にして10語以内で解答する。　(4)　下線部④a potential conflict「対立の可能性」の詳しい説明が，次に続くIf three people以下の文にある。「もし，自分の目の前にいる3人が壺Bだと推測していて，あなたが明るい色のビー玉を抜き取ったとしたら，他の人は壺Bだと考えているのにあなたはそれでも壺Aだと推測するだろうか」という文を70字以内の日本語にまとめる。　(5)　ルールの変更は，第4段落第5文目instead of以下を80字以内の日本語にまとめる。　(6)　多数決による決定になると，前段までに述べられていた情報カスケード(前の人の情報に左右される)とは異なり，自分個人の情報に注意を払うようになる。よってBが正解。個人の情報は不完全であるが，重要であるのが集団としての正確さであるとき，人は個々の情報に耳を傾ける，と話は続く。　(7)　挿入する文の意味は「一般大衆が可否を投票するまで，製品を売り出すのを待つようなことを会社にさせたくない」である。空欄の直前の文章がこの文につながるかどうか調べると，Dの「実験では，結果として起きる要素を取り除いているのだが，これは，明らかに会社全体が簡単にできることではない」が適切とわかる。(8)　「HungとPlottの実験(その実験は集団の中の人を効果的に自立させるのだが)の成功は，自主性の価値と難しさを強調する」の意味なので，Bのemphasizesが適切である。

【4】(1)　①　A　　④　D　　(2)　我々大人は，おそらく「goed」や「eated」とは言わないかもしれないが，動詞に「ed」をつけることは，確かに英語という言語において過去形をつくる基本的な方法である。(3)　英語では物を指す多くの語がその物を用いて行う動作を指す語として転用され得るということ。(43字)　　(4)　ア　A　　イ　B

(5)　I agree with this idea because through mistakes, second language learners can discover aspects of English they normally wouldn't think about. For example, in my English class, a student made a mistake. He wrote "effect" although he should have written "affect". When he found out what he had done wrong, he asked me the differences between the two words. I taught him how they were different and he learned new things through the mistake. Also, we are all second language learners of English. It is impossible to use English without making any mistakes. Therefore, it is important to tell students that teachers also make mistakes. I often say in class, "I make mistakes, too. So let's enjoy making mistakes together and discover new things about English."

Then, students feel like they are allowed to make mistakes. When students make mistakes using English, I say "Thank you for making mistakes. We've got a chance to learn from this." Sometimes I let them correct their mistakes themselves. Mistakes provide chances for students and even teachers to improve their English. I'm sure that we can turn any mistake into an opportunity to learn new things about English. (195 words)

〈解説〉(1)　空欄①を含む文は「『それを切る』の代わりに"scissor it", 『床を掃こう』を "let's bloom the floor", 『それを縫ってくれませんか』を "Can you needle it?" などと言ったり，その他のタイプの間違いをしたりしない3歳の子の話を聞かないことは難しい (＝間違えるのを必ず聞く)」となるのが正しい。空欄④を含む文は「多くの母親は幼い子どもに対し，短く単純な文で，普通より高いピッチの子どものような発音で話す。それは害にはならず，子どもの注意を引きつけるが，言語学習に重大なことではない」となるのが正しい。　(2)　特定の語を大文字にするのは強調したいからである。よって解答例のように「確かに」,「～であることは間違いない」のように訳すとよい。

(3)「"Scissor it" や "Let's bloom the floor" と言う子どもがこのことを理解し始めるのだが，…」。「このこと」とは，直前のEnglish allows以下の文章の内容を指す。50字以内でまとめる。　(4)　後半の内容を要約しているのは，最後から2番目の文Talk to children about what matters to them.「子どもたちが関係すること(子どもが見たり，感じたり，経験したり，経験しようとしていること，興味を持っていること，気にかけていること)について彼らに話しなさい」であることから考える。話し方ではなく話す内容が大切なのである。　(5)　英語を第2言語とする学習者について，間違いをすることがよいという考えに賛成か反対か，また，生徒が間違いをしたらどのように指導するか，100-200語で答えよ，という問題である。言語は間違いをしながら習得される。これを軸に意見をまとめる。解答例のように，授業では間違いを恐れず英語を使える雰囲気を作ることや，自分で間違いに気づかせることを書き入れたい。

【5】誠実で真面目に練習に取り組むが試合にあまり出場できなかった青年が，自分の父の死の後に出場した試合で，今まで盲目であった父が初めて自分の試合を天国から見てくれているのを感じ，実力以上の力を発揮できた話。(100字)

〈解説〉100字以内での要約であるから，多くのことを書くことができない。削るべきところを見極めること。解答例のように，決してうまくはないが練習を休むことのなかった青年。父の死。話の核心である青年からコーチへの言葉「僕の父は目が見えませんでした。僕がプレーするのを父が見た，これが初めての試合なんです」を中心にまとめる。

2017年度　実施問題

【中高共通】

【１】Choose the one that best completes the sentence from the four alternatives.

(1) You must (　　) the traffic rules for your safety and the safety of other drivers.

A. defend　B. infringe　C. observe　D. protect

(2) The music festival was a great success because many artists (　　).

A. participated　B. confessed　C. represented

D. took part in

(3) The doctor wrote a (　　) for some painkillers for Kate to take while her arm was healing.

A. description　B. prescription　C. subscription

D. transcription

(4) It's important to have a few close friends that you can (　　) in when you're in trouble.

A. compose　B. confide　C. disregard　D. dissolve

(5) All parts of the aircraft are closely (　　) for signs of wear or damage.

A. familiarized　B. organized　C. recognized

D. scrutinized

(6) I had to have my husband drive me to the office today because I discovered that my driver's license had (　　).

A. exceeded　B. expanded　C. expired　D. extended

(7) No doubt Sarah meant to lend a helping hand with cooking, but she has only proved to be a (　　).

A. delay　B. hindrance　C. limitation　D. service

(8) The company was accused of (　　) its customers of millions of dollars.

A. defrauding　B. intersecting　C. reclaiming

D. providing

(9) Economic progress has brought about a longer life ( ) for the average person.

A. composure B. expectancy C. expectation

D. guarantee

(10) With its enduring beauty, National Garden Park has been one of the nation's ( ) botanical gardens.

A. astonished B. admitted C. previous D. leading

(11) My wife insisted ( ) the black suit to her sister's wedding.

A. me to wear B. on me to wear C. on my wearing

D. that I should be worn

(12) The more I talk with Ms. Miyata, the more ( ) I am by her personality and capacity for tolerance.

A. impresses B. impression C. impressed D. impress

(13) We highly recommend that the passwords to your bank accounts ( ) once every three months.

A. will change B. has been changed C. be changed

D. to change

(14) The fair held this weekend is intended for ( ) considering moving to the rural area of this town.

A. whoever B. those C. who D. which

(15) I ( ) in France for two years when I was a child, but I can't speak French at all.

A. have been B. have once stayed C. lived D. went

(16) I should not ( ) that ice cream, but I did. Now I have a little stomachache.

A. ate B. be eaten C. be eating D. have eaten

(17) "I'm impressed. Every picture you took is really good."

"Thanks, but I don't think I'm ( ) photographer as you."

A. a good as B. as a good C. as good a D. good as a

(18) Since high blood pressure often goes undetected, it is important to have blood pressure (　　) periodically.

A. check　　B. checking　　C. to check　　D. checked

(19) This is the house (　　) my brother lived about twenty years ago.

A. in that　　B. in which　　C. which　　D. whereas

(20) Today is our wedding. This is the day (　　) we will never forget.

A. about which　　B. that　　C. what　　D. when

(☆☆◎◎◎)

【中学校】

【１】Read the following essay and answer the questions below.

There are many things I enjoy about travelling. Haggling is not one of them.

On a recent trip to Cambodia—my first to this beautiful country, I met many fellow travellers who seemed to take pleasure in bargaining with *tuk-tuk drivers and market stall holders over amounts as small as 50 cents.

It puzzled me because the tourists, many of whom were from developed countries, did not look poor. Some disgusted me because they were downright rude to the mild-mannered and friendly locals.

My travel companion said many guide books encourage bargaining. He explained that some people bargain because they feel they are being overcharged, since goods and services are generally cheaper in Cambodia than in developed countries. Also, even for the exact same service, locals apparently enjoy lower prices than tourists. For example, a tuk-tuk ride might cost less than US【　i　】for a local, but【　ii　】for a foreign tourist.

I could not help but retort, "①(　　)"

To me, the prices were reasonable and affordable, considering that I pay more than that for a similar service in Singapore. I do not think I should be exploiting people for their labor just because I am in a developing country. Locals may pay a lower price than foreigners, but that is logical because they are earning unfairly low wages.

According to a 2010 socio-economic survey by Cambodia's National Institute of Statistics, the average monthly income in the capital city, Phnom Penh, is about【　iii　】. The average national income is even lower at around $1 a day.

I was more than happy to pay a higher price than the locals, and offer a tip when appropriate. It was the ②(　　) I could do to show my gratitude for great service. It was also the bare minimum I could do to make a pathetic attempt at reducing the income inequality between developed and developing countries.

American writer Anne Elizabeth Moore, who has lived and worked in Cambodia, described ③similar sentiments in her book, Cambodian Grrrl: "It's going to be much easier for me to replace that dollar than ④[of / would / in /shopkeeper / for / front / the / it / be / me]. It is not worth a dollar for me to strong-arm her into lowering her prices in order to feel like I won this shopping experience."

At the end of the day, it is about treating people decently, no matter who they are, where they come from, or how much they are earning. As different as cultures may be, decency is decency and I like to believe people would not bargain away decency just to save a dollar or two.

【Notes】*tuk-tuk　三輪タクシー

(1)　Choose an answer from the three alternative below to complete【　i　】～【　iii　】. (Each answer can only be used once.)

A.　$100　　B.　$1　　C.　$3

(2)　Choose the best answer for ①(　　) from the four alternatives below.

A.　What an invidious distinction it is!　　B.　What's wrong with that?

C.　That is a little out of the way.　　D.　Something is wrong.

(3)　Choose the one that best completes ②(　　) from the four alternatives below.

A. worth　　B. best　　C. most　　D. least

(4) Choose the one that is NOT close in meaning to the underlined words ③ from the four alternatives below.

A. The logic that tourists from developed countries should pay a higher price than locals in developing countries is not unfair.

B. The author doesn't want to use people in developing countries for their labor just because there are wage disparities between developed and developing countries.

C. It is affordable for tourists from developed countries to buy anything in developing countries because the prices of commodities are low.

D. Even in developing countries, people living there should not be exploited by tourists who want to satisfy themselves by bargaining over a small amount of money.

(5) Put the words from the underlined part ④[　　] in the text in the correct order.

(6) According to the text, which of the following is true?

A. Many travelers who are from developed countries have to be careful not to be overcharged in developing countries. In spite of the same service, tourists have to pay a higher price than locals.

B. The author was disgusted at the attitudes of the tourists from developed countries toward a local shopkeeper because they seemed to bargain away their decency to save a dollar or two.

C. Local people in developing countries should treat tourists especially well. Despite cultural differences, they don't pay a higher price than locals when appropriate.

D. It is logical for people from developed countries to haggle over the price of things in developing countries because locals pay lower prices than tourists do for goods and services.

(☆☆☆◎◎◎◎)

【2】*The following English passage is about how to develop American English accent by Scott Perry. Read the following passage and answer the questions below.*

Why do Japanese native speakers struggle with English pronunciation? Let's begin by dispelling two misconceptions about American English pronunciation.

Myth #1 *Japanese people need to eliminate their Japanese English pronunciation.*

Reality There is no need to eliminate or reduce the Japanese accent. Japanese English is a recognized dialect of English, just like American, British and Australian English. It is not wrong, and you do not have a problem with pronunciation when speaking Japanese (*katakana*) English. It is your accent. To eliminate your natural style of English, you would have to unlearn how to say many words that you have learned as a part of Japanese, such as *teburu*, *koppu* and *konpyuta*. It is not possible to unlearn these things once you know them. Also, you need *katakana* English to communicate to other Japanese people.

The problem is that only 40 percent of Japanese English is understood by American people. If you wish to effectively communicate using American English, then instead of trying to change or delete your existing English accent, you need to learn a new accent.

Myth #2 *Living in an English speaking country will improve your pronunciation.*

Reality Living in an English speaking country can improve your overall English skill, but it won't improve your pronunciation much. If you begin living in America as an adult, on average, your pronunciation will not improve more than 10 to 20 percent from the level it was when you started living there, even if you live there for 15 years or more. Many Japanese who've lived abroad for as much as 20 years still come to my training sessions because they still struggle with American pronunciation.

So, now let's consider some ways to improve. American English pronunciation training requires a physical adjustment in order to master the American sound. Here are a few key points that must be understood before you begin.

The first concerns muscle development. The speaking muscles that you have are designed for speaking perfect Japanese and Japanese English. To speak American English, you mostly need to develop the muscles in the corners of your lips as well as below your nose. This will help you raise your upper lip and show your teeth. Exposing your teeth with a smiling shape allows you to create many of the higher-frequency sounds used in American English. I have developed lip and tongue exercises that strengthen the muscles needed to speak American English correctly. For example, repeating the sound "See you" 25 times, alternating between opening your mouth and smiling as wide as you can and closing your lips slowly, will develop the muscles in the corners of your mouth.

The second key point concerns mouth shape. Every English sound has a specific mouth shape and tongue position. When those are incorrect, it is almost impossible to generate the desired sound. There are four major mouth shapes needed for English sounds: a smiling shape, a round-lip shape, an *F* shape (or raised-lip shape) and a closed-mouth shape. Japanese English does not require the same shapes, so I have created a mouth-exercise training system for Japanese speakers that has helped my students speak with confidence.

The third key point is breathing. American people breathe with a different rhythmic frequency than Japanese speakers do. American English is a 【 i 】-breathing, long-stretching style of speech, while Japanese English is a shallow-breathing, quick, 【 ii 】 style. You need 【 i 】 breaths and long, stretching sounds in order to speak American English properly. The development of your *diaphragm is also required to master this.

The fourth key point is avoiding common mistakes. Most Japanese speakers think the *R* and *L* sounds are difficult to make. That is true when you are using the wrong lip shapes and tongue positions, but with proper positioning, the *R* and *L* sounds are quite simple.

The *R* sound requires a rounded lip shape with your teeth only 5 millimeters apart. Do not curl your tongue; rather, pull it straight back, allow the back of your tongue to push up to the top back of your teeth, let the air out from your throat and try to make a deeper, lower sound. Imagine that the inside of your mouth is in the shape of a tube.

The *L* sound, on the other hand, presents a completely different problem. Basically, the problem is that Japanese speakers move their lips in a round shape when making the *L* sound. Actually, your lips should be in the smiling position, and your tongue should be touching where your top teeth and *gum meet. In that position, you will maintain a smile as you say the *L* sound. For example, the words *lake*, *lady* and *list* should be pronounced with a complete smile shape without movement.

I also want to say a word about coding, which I see as the future of improving American English pronunciation for Japanese speakers. For native Japanese speakers, reading English letters can actually create more problems than it solves. This is because native Japanese speakers have been taught to associate every English syllable and letter with a *katakana* sound. American English speakers associate those same syllables and letters with completely different sounds. So when Japanese speakers look at English letters, they are actually "seeing" *katakana*, not the American English sounds they need. Some letters create more problems than others—the English letters *I*, *R*, *L*, *O*, *U*, *V*, *F* and *TH*, to name a few.

My method of phonetic coding allows you to grasp proper sounds and repeat them over and over. Repetition is the key to *muscle memory for English sounds. My coding system allows students to rewrite English letters based on sound, not spelling. Take the word *California* for example. If you make sounds based on this spelling, your pronunciation will not be correct. You actually need to say *Cal-lah-forn-nya* to sound native. My coding system gives you hints that show you exactly which sound to make and when. It is like a new set of phonetic symbols for Japanese speakers. The results are amazing, and it has reduced the learning time from around 10 months to just three or four months.

People generally group all parts of English learning together, but actually, pronunciation needs to be separated. Pronunciation is physical, and every other part of English learning is mental memorization. The reason English instructors fail to get positive results in the area of pronunciation is that they fail to address the physical aspect of speaking English. It is no different than exercising. In order to master English pronunciation, you need to exercise your speaking muscles, understand the proper tongue positions, connect your words, and breathe deeply while speaking. With the help of coding, Japanese speakers can avoid the common mistakes caused by years of associating English sounds with Japanese sounds. Everyone can master American English pronunciation. It's just a matter of proper exercise, muscle development and knowing the exact sound.

【Notes】*diaphragm　横隔膜　　*gum　歯茎　　*muscle memory (繰り返しによって作られる)神経と筋肉の記憶

(1)　Complete the following sentences ①－⑥ by choosing the best answers.

①　The principal answer to the Myth #1 is that Japanese native speakers should ________.

A.　add new ways to pronounce words to their existing English accent

B.　correct monotonous tones of *katakana* English

C.　eliminate the problem of speaking *katakana* English

D. inquire about the necessity of American pronunciation

② Probably the first key point to improve American English pronunciation is ________.

A. to develop lip and tongue exercises that strengthen muscles to speak American English correctly

B. to train the speaking muscles in the coner of your lips to speak perfect American English

C. to make many of the higher-frequency sounds used in American English to expose your teeth

D. to repeat the sound "See you" 25 times to develop the speaking muscles designed for speaking Japanese and Japanese English

③ According to the passage, to make the *R* or *L* sounds properly, ______.

A. your tongue should be curled in a round shape when you make the *L* sound

B. your lips should be in the smiling position, and your tongue curled when you make the *R* sound

C. your tongue should not touch where your top teeth and gum meet when you make the *L* sound

D. your lips should be in a round shape with your teeth 5 millimeters apart when you make the *R* sound

④ The method of phonetic coding Scott Perry devised ________.

A. helps Japanese native speakers create more problems when they read English letters

B. makes Japanese native speakers associate every English syllable and letter with a *katakana* sound

C. leads Japanese native speakers to understand and use proper sounds, not the *katakana* sounds they have been taught

D. teaches us how Japanese native speakers associate English syllables and letters with completely different sounds

⑤ According to Scott Perry, pronunciation needs to be separated from other parts of English learning ________.

A. to master specific sounds of Japanese English

B. to address the physical aspect of speaking English

C. to get positive results in the area of mental memorization

D. to avoid misconceptions about American English pronunciation

⑥ This article mainly ________.

A. answers the questions that Scott Perry had for a long time

B. illustrates Scott Perry's methods how to eliminate the Japanese accent

C. provides an explanation for a mistaken belief among Japanese people

D. allows Japanese people to understand some ways to improve their American English pronunciation

(2) Choose the best answer for 【 i 】【 ii 】 from the four alternatives below.

A. i deep ii smooth　　B. i strong ii smooth

C. i strong ii choppy　　D. i deep ii choppy

(☆☆☆☆◎◎◎)

【3】 Read the following passage and answer the questions below.

Bees are so socially advanced that they even vote on critical issues such as relocating the hive. Each spring about half the bees depart with the queen to begin a new colony elsewhere, leaving a number of other potential queens to vie for control of the existing nest amongst themselves. But where should the emigrants locate their new nest? Getting this right is crucial for their future well-being. It must be not too exposed to (　　) such as birds, not too far from good sources of food, nor liable to be flooded or blown away by the wind.

Usually bees will identify as many as twenty possible locations within a one-hundred-square-kilometre area, and about 90 per cent of the time they appear to choose what seems to be the best place. The system for their decision-making is remarkably effective. Each bee has the chance to vote, giving the colony the best chance of making the right decision for its future survival. About 5 per cent of the bees scout out to find the prospective sites, reporting the location of each back to the rest of the community using their various dances. Other bees then check out these sites, returning to the nest and dancing longer and harder in the direction of the site they think is best. After about two weeks the site with the strongest, most vigorous dance is the winner. Having voted with their feet, the bees then swarm.

Ants belong to the same family as honeybees: the oldest ant fossil yet discovered is a specimen trapped in amber, estimated at more than eighty million years old. Their civilizations include the earth's first schools, what look like the beginnings of slavery, and even a bizarre attempt at behaving like an early type of computer. There are many similarities between ants' nests and honeybees' hives, but ants do not dance. Instead, they communicate through chemicals called pheromones that other ants can smell. When an ant finds food it will leave a trail of scent along the ground all the way home, to lead others to its source. It then finds the way back by remembering certain landmarks often using the position of the sun as its guide. As other ants follow the first trail each one leaves more scent, until the food source is completely exhausted. Once the ants no longer leave a scent the smell evaporates, and the trail is lost for ever.

Ants' smells say other things, too. For example, if an ant gets squashed, its dying gift is a smell that triggers an alarm to all the other ants nearby, sending them into a mad panic as they run around in a rush trying to avoid the same fate. Ants mix pheromones with their food so they can pass on messages to each other about health and nutrition. They can even identify themselves through smells as belonging to different groups of castes within the nest, each of which is responsible for certain activities in the civilization. The queen produces a certain pheromone without which the workers would start to raise a new queen. It acts as a safety device in case the queen dies.

(1) Choose the one that best completes the (　　) from the four alternatives below.

A. negotiators　B. predators　C. casualties　D. victims

(2) Explain in English how bees make the decision to move their nest for future survival in 10 words or less.

(3) What is NOT true about ants?

A. With the help of pheromones, they pass on messages to each other about health and nutrition.

B. Through pheromones, they leave a trail of scent to lead others to a food source.

C. Because of pheromones, ants are drawn to dangerous situations like being squashed.

D. As long as the queen produces a certain pheromone, the workers will not start to raise a new queen.

(☆☆☆◎◎◎)

【４】Translate the underlined sentences into English.

(1) 中1といえば大人の入り口。<u>何事にも背伸びをするのは成長の証でもあろう</u>。

(2) 多様な栄養素をまんべんなく摂取しないと，からだに障る。脳も同じらしい。<u>色々なことをバランスよく経験すると，若々しさが保たれるという</u>。

(☆☆☆◎◎◎)

【５】In 2020, English is going to be a subject at elementary schools. Considering this situation, what should English lessons at junior high schools be like? Write your answer with concrete reasons in approximately 100 words.

(☆☆☆◎◎◎◎)

【高等学校】

【１】Read the following passage and answer the questions below.

We agree that all children need to succeed; but do we mean the same thing? My own feeling is that success should not be [①] or easy, and should not come all the time. Success implies [②] an obstacle, including, perhaps, the thought in our minds that we might not succeed. It is turning "I can't" into "I can, and I did."

We ought also to learn, beginning early, that we don't always succeed. A good batting average in baseball is 300; a good batting average in life is a great deal lower than that. Life holds many more defeats than [③] for all of us. Shouldn't we get used to this early? We should learn, too, to aim higher than we think we can hit. "A man's reach should [④] his grasp, or what's a Heaven for?" What we fail to do today, we, or someone, may do tomorrow. Our failure may pave the way for someone else's [⑤].

Of course we should protect a child, if we can, from a diet of unbroken failure. More to the point, perhaps, we should see that failure is honorable and [⑥], rather than [⑦]. Perhaps we need a semantic distinction here, between nonsuccess and failure.

It is tempting to think that we can [⑧] the work of unsuccessful students so that they think they are succeeding most of the time. But how can we keep secret from a child what other children of his own age, in his own or other schools, are doing? ⑨<u>What some of these kids need is the experience of doing something really well—so well that they know themselves, without having to be told, that they have done it well.</u> Maybe this means that someone must supply them, from outside, with the concentration and resolution they lack.

(1) Choose the best word for [①]-[⑧] from the four choices below.

① A. difficult B. quick C. slow

D. temporary

② A. creating B. inspecting C. moving
D. overcoming

③ A. advantages B. conflicts C. fights
D. victories

④ A. exceed B. equal C. overestimate
D. undergo

⑤ A. contribution B. failure C. sacrifice
D. success

⑥ A. accusable B. constructive C. laborious
D. superfluous

⑦ A. admirable B. controversial C. humiliating
D. praiseworthy

⑧ A. arrange B. criticize C. ignore
D. recite

(2) Translate the underlined sentence ⑨, explaining what "these kids" refers to, into Japanese.

(☆☆◎◎◎)

【2】The following passage is written by Donald Keene, an American-born Japanese scholar, historian, teacher, writer and translator of Japanese literature. Read the passage and answer the questions below.

The two years I spent in Kyoto were extremely happy in almost every [①]. While in England I had convinced myself that the scholar's life, bounded by the library and the college buildings, was exactly what I wanted for myself, and even after I arrived in Japan I did not intend to change this. I enrolled at Kyoto University and planned to attend lectures regularly. But, as I soon discovered, the attitude towards lectures was a good deal more casual at Kyoto than at Cambridge. Often I would go all the way to the university only to discover the lecture had been cancelled. Besides, I no longer felt like a student, and it was difficult to concentrate my attention on a single document of Tokugawa literature when I was surrounded by so much of Japanese history and literature in the monuments of Kyoto.

But the greatest distraction from my studies of Basho was the increasing interest I felt in modern Japan. This was due largely to the conversations almost every night at dinner with Nagai Michio. After having been away from Japan for five years in America, he was rediscovering his country, even as I was discovering it for the first time. I may have influenced him by passing on some of my enthusiasm for traditional Japan, but his concern with contemporary Japan totally changed my outlook. Several years later, when I wrote the book *Living Japan*, which included many sections borrowed from his conversations, I expressed my thanks in the introduction, saying that "②I might have remained buried in my studies of old literature had it not been for Japanese friends who first enabled me to understand how fortunate I was to be in Japan, now of all times."

Not all my experiences in Kyoto were agreeable, however, and sometimes Nagai-san was obliged to cheer me up when I felt a particularly ③chagrined. My broblem was that I had become so enamoured of Kyoto that I wanted ④(a peculiar *gaijin* / as / as / be accepted / but / merely / not / someone / to / who belonged) in the city. There was nothing I could do about changing my face to look more like a Japanese, but I tried speaking with a Kyoto accent, and I spent many hours roaming the city, learning what each quarter was like. I attended every festival, and I paid my [⑤]s at the graves of a hundred famous writers. I joined several groups of intellectuals and faithfully attended meetings. But ⑥no sooner did I begin to feel that I was accepted, than someone was sure to ask what I, as a *gaijin*, thought of a painting, a play or a restaurant. I became the representative of all the *gaijin* of the world. Nobody seemed interested in my personal opinions, and if I offered them the usual response was, "*Naruhodo*, that is exactly what a *gaijin* would think."

The contradiction between my own conception of myself as a participant in the intellectual life of Kyoto, and the other people's conception of me as a *gaijin* who imparted an international flavor to their gatherings, on some occasions irritated me so much I decided not to attend any more meetings. Although several professors at Kyoto University, notably Noma Koshin and Yoshikawa Kojiro, generously gave me their time when I had problems in my work, on the whole, I had little contact with the professors, and even the students, with a few exceptions, ignored me.

When I think back on their behavior, it now seems absolutely normal. Considering the difficulties I experienced in America and in England in finding people who understood my feelings, why should I have expected there would be no problems in Kyoto? The difference was that essentially I didn't care whether or not people liked me in America or England, but in Kyoto I was desperately eager to be accepted. Nagai-san always managed, with his eminently humane and commonsensical explanations, to make me see ⑦the illogicality in my own feelings.

But, as I gradually realized, Nagai-san was also an outsider. Although a graduate of Kyoto University, his earlier education had been in Tokyo, and this made him an outsider in the eyes of some of his colleagues (though others, of course were kindly disposed towards him). If he happenedd to have lunch with another professor who was also from Tokyo, it did not take long for whispers to circulate that these outsiders were planning something together.

The atmosphere in the intellectual world sometimes made Kyoto a difficult place, both for Nagai-san and me. But the city offered many compensations. I can never forget our long walks together back to Imakumano after seeing some play at Shijo together—for example, *Wakodo yo yomigaere* by Mishima Yukio. As we walked through the dimly-lit streets, talking about the play, we would often hear music or catch a glimpse of a geisha on her way back from a party. But even a completely deserted street, where our footfalls resounded, seemed every step of the way to be Kyoto, and only Kyoto.

(1) Write one word that best fits both [①] and [⑤].

(2) Translate the underlined sentence ② into Japanese.

(3) Substitute the underlined word ③ with the best alternative from the four choices below.

A. angry and violent B. annoyed and disappointed

C. pleased and satisfied D. worried and restless

(4) Put the words from the underlined part ④ in the correct order.

(5) Translate the underlined sentence ⑥ into Japanese.

(6) Explain the meaning of the underlined phrase ⑦ <u>within 80 Japanese letters</u>.

(7) According to the text, which of the following is NOT true?

A. The author became more and more interested in modern Japan while he was studying in Kyoto, so he was not able to concentrate as much on his studies about Japanese literature as before.

B. While the author was away from Japan and staying in America for five years, his friend, Nagai Michio, was realizing new and attractive aspects of his country, Japan.

C. The author participated in the intellectual life of Kyoto as an individual, but others treated him as if he were a representative of all foreigners, which made him feel uncomfortable.

D. The author thought Kyoto was a difficult place for him to feel accepted because he was not native; however, he still felt attracted by experiences and sights that were unique to the city.

(☆☆☆◎◎◎◎)

【3】Read the following passage and answer the questions below.

Which is more important: to communicate in a second language or to test well? Often in language education, skirmishes break out among parents, teachers—and even the students themselves—over this thorny question. Of course, being able to do both is the ideal, but how can we as learners and teachers ensure we keep a healthy balance between social and academic language acquisition?

Linguist Jim Cummins believes that these two types of learning and the skills they involve are separable: On one side of the fence are social language skills, which are needed to communicate within society; on the other are academic language skills—those needed to succeed in a classroom or on an exam. Social language skills do not require any specialized vocabulary, Cummins argues, and often comprehension is aided by the context of the social situation. For example, a child in a playground or a university exchange student at a party would rely on various nonverbal social clues when seeking to understand and respond appropriately to a specific situation.

Standardized tests attempt to measure academic language skills, or what Cummins calls cognitive academic language proficiency (CALP). These skills take much longer to acquire. Various cognitive skills such as synthesizing, evaluating, comparing or ①inferring become necessary, not to mention a high level of communicative skill, both verbal and written. Another major difference is the issue of [②]: Formal, professional or academic settings demand an exactness of language not mastered in classes focusing on social communication skills.

For most language learners, both types of learning are important. The company executive who can pass any English grammar test but [③] is at a clear disadvantage; verbally gifted students proficient in the latest slang but who [④] similarly limit their own future options.

English proficiency as an educational goal in Japan remains firmly tied to exam scores, starting with the Eiken test for school-age children. From high school onward, the Test of English as a Foreign Language (TOEFL) or the Test of English for International Communication (TOEIC) are regarded as the standard gauges of English ability. Japanese companies set pass rates of these tests as incentives for bonuses; frequently the tests are also required for admission to overseas study programs at foreign universities, where students could gain valuable immersive experience to improve their communicative skills.

With such an emphasis on teaching to test in Japan, it can be hard to shoehorn more communicative exercises into lessons. To address this imbalance, Bern Mulvey, a professor of humanities and science at Iwate University with over 20 years experience as a language teacher, professor and university administrator, suggests teachers need to get creative.

"It is very possible to teach to these tests in a communicative fashion," Mulvey says. "I have done so, and I've seen others do so too. Conversely, I've been struck by how even many supposedly communicative classes in this country feature no communication at all."

Mulvey argues that the problem is not the exams per se, but the predominant teaching traditions in this country: the twin emphases on line-by-line translation and rote memorization—traditions that predate the exams in question. He believes that the low level of English ability among Japanese students in comparison to many of their peers in other non-English-speaking countries is the direct result of this approach.

"I wish more of my students had acquired even the meager skill set seemingly demanded by, say, the Center exam," Mulvey says, referring to the unified Japanese university entrance test. "Too often, they lack even basic grammar knowledge, ostensibly a strength of the current system."

As most language teachers are well aware, balance is the key. To reach a high level of fluency in any foreign language, memorization of more sophisticated vocabulary, higher-level thinking skills in the target language and comfort in both academic and social situations are essential.

Furthermore, Mulvey feels that classes need to become less teacher-centered, with students allowed to take more individual responsibility for their own learning. "Teaching to the exams solely via lectures and repeated drills produces passive, unmotivated students who often do poorly on the exams as a result," he says.

Research supports the idea that a communicative approach to teaching cognitive academic literacy helps the student acquire both thinking and language skills. Good practice starts with "affirming the students' identity and scaffolding new learning to previous understandings which may be in the mother tongue," accorging to Carol Inugai-Dixon, language and learning director for the International Baccalaureate in The Hague. When Inugai-Dixon first started as an English language teacher in Japan over 30 years ago, it was the norm to "forbid discussion in the mother tongue and to teach skills in isolation by drill and repetition." Part of Inugai-Dixon's life's work has involved trying to change such attitudes and to provide practical skills for language teachers in the classroom.

"Learning language is also about acquiring an identity in that language, so it is important to validate that identity by activating knowledge already available in the native language," she explains. "It is also important to make sure the students cover the entire spectrum of communicative skills within each class, from speaking, interacting and listening to reading and writing. This framework applies to any subject taught, as second-language learners are constantly learning language, regardless of the discipline."

Increasingly, in our rapidly globalizing world, students will require communicative skills in more than one language so they can think clearly and articulate complex thoughts with others around the world. Similarly, the ability to listen for understanding and meaning to other perspectives is already an important skill for any type of communication.

The sharing of ideas in dialogue with others is full of potential for creativity. That creativity should start in the classroom, whether the immediate goal involves improved conversation or review for an exam. At some level, every teacher is a language teacher, using words to communicate higher-level ideas in a shared mother tongue or in a second or third language for students.

As Mulvey concludes: "No perfectly valid and reliable diagnostic exam exists, which in a sense mirrors real life—how the language preparation in our classrooms never completely covers all the contingencies involved with communication outside the classroom. Still, preparing for even imperfect exams can be a healthy challenge, forcing students to learn new skills and constantly reevaluate their own level of L2 (second language) understanding. ⑤Particularly given the lack of exposure most Japanese have to English outside of class, tests can serve as an additional motivational tool, with a place even in a communicative classroom."

(1) Choose the most appropriate answer to explain the meaning of the underlined word ①.

A. to conclude something from evidence and reasoning rather than from explicit statements

B. to fasten something securely in a particular place or position

C. to reconsider and alter something in the light of further evidence

D. to persuade someone to do or continue to do something by giving support and advice

(2) Choose the best word for [②] from the four choices below.

A. correctness B. interest C. readiness D. validity

(3) Choose one phrase for each of [③] and [④] from the four choices below.

A. does not have any difficulty in communicating with others

B. is familiar with methods or styles of formal documents

C. cannot communicate easily with potential clients

D. lack knowledge of formal conventions

(4) According to the text, there are four things that are needed to reach a high level of fluency in a foreign language. Find these four necessary things and write them down.

(5) Translate the underlined sentence ⑤ into Japanese.

(6) Considering what is written in the passage, what skills do you want your

students to learn and why? How are you going to teach these skills in high school English classes? Express your own ideas in English, <u>using approximately 150 words</u> and <u>providing some examples in your answer</u>.

(☆☆☆☆◎◎◎◎)

【４】Read the following passage and answer the questions below.

Two men meet on a plane from Tokyo to Hong Kong. Chu Hon-fai is a Hong Kong exporter who is returning from a business trip to Japan. Andrew Richardson is an American buyer on his first business trip to Hong Kong. It is a convenient meeting for them because Mr. Chu's company sells some of the products Mr. Richardson has come to Hong Kong to buy. After a bit of conversation they introduce themselves to each other.

Mr. Richardson : By the way, I'm Andrew Richardson. My friends calls me Andy. This is my business card.

Mr. Chu : I'm David Chu. Pleased to meet you, Mr. Richardson. This is my card.

Mr. Richardson : No, no. Call me Andy. I think we'll be doing a lot of business together.

Mr. Chu : Yes, I hope so.

Mr. Richardson (reading Mr. Chu's card) : "Chu, Hon-fai." Hon-fai, I'll give you a call tomorrow as soon as I get settled at my hotel.

Mr. Chu (smiling) : Yes. I'll expect your call.

When these two men separate, they leave each other with very different impressions of the situation. Mr. Richardson is very pleased to have made the acquaintance of Mr. Chu and feels they have gotten off to a very good start. They have established their relationship on a first-name basis and Mr. Chu's smile seemed to indicate that he will be friendly and easy to do business with. Mr. Richardson is particularly pleased that he had treated Mr. Chu with respect for his Chinese background by calling him Hon-fai rather than using his western name, David, which seemed to him an unnecessary imposition of western culture.

In contrast, Mr. Chu feels quite uncomfortable with Mr. Richardson. He feels it will be difficult to work with him, and that Mr. Richardson might be rather insensitive to cultural differences. He is particularly bothered with the fact that Mr. Richardson used his given name, Hon-fai, instead of either David or Mr. Chu. It was this embarrassment which caused him to smile.

This short dialogue is, unfortunately, not so unusual in meetings between members of different cultures. There is a tendency in American business circles to prefer close, friendly, egalitarian relationships in business engagements. This system of symmetrical solidarity, which has its source in the Utilitarian discourse system, is often expressed in the use of given (or "first") names in business encounters. Mr. Richardson feels most comfortable in being called Andy, and he would also like to call Mr. Chu by his first name. At the same time, he wished to show consideration of the cultural differences between them by avoiding Mr. Chu's western name, David. His solution to this cultural difference is to address Mr. Chu by the given name he sees on the business card, Hon-fai.

Mr. Chu, on the other hand, prefers an initial business relationship of symmetrical deference. He would feel more comfortable if they called each other Mr. Chu and Mr. Richardson. Nevertheless, when he was away at school in North America he learned that Americans feel awkward in a stable relationship of symmetrical deference. In other words, he found that they feel uncomfortable calling people Mr. for any extended period of time. His solution was to adopt a western name. He chose David for use in such situations.

When Mr. Richardson insists on using Mr. Chu's Chinese given name, Hon-fai, Mr. Chu feels uncomfortable. That name is rarely used by anyone, in fact. What Mr. Richardson does not know is that Chinese have a rather complex structure of names which depends upon situations and relationships. This includes school names, intimate and family baby names, and even western names, each of which is used just by the people with whom a person has a certain relationship. Isolating just his given name, Hon-fai, is relatively unusual and to hear himself called this by a stranger makes Mr. Chu feel quite uncomfortable. His reaction, which is also culturally conditioned, is to smile.

In this case there are two issues of intercultural communication: one is the basic question of cultural differences, and the second is the problems which arise when people try to deal with cultural differences, but, like Mr. Richardson, actually make matters worse in their attempts at cultural sensitivity.

(1) Summarize this story within 80 Japanese letters.

(2) What lessons about foreign language education can you draw from this story? Express your own ideas in English, using approximately 80 words.

(☆☆☆◎◎◎)

解答・解説

【中高共通】

【1】(1) C　(2) A　(3) B　(4) B　(5) D　(6) C
(7) B　(8) A　(9) B　(10) D　(11) C　(12) C
(13) C　(14) B　(15) C　(16) D　(17) C　(18) D
(19) B　(20) B

〈解説〉(1) 空欄以下に「あなたの安全と，ほかの運転者の安全のための交通ルール」とあるので，C「遵守する」が適切。 (2) 英文の大意は「多くの芸術家が参加したので音楽フェスティバルは大成功だった」なので，A「参加した」が適切。take part inは前置詞で終わるので，後ろにinの目的語が必要となる。 (3) 英文前半は「医者は鎮痛剤の～を書いた」という意味なので，B「処方箋」が適切。 (4) confide in＋人で「人に打ち明ける」という意味。 (5) for signs of wear and damage「摩耗や損傷のあとを求めて」とあるので，D「入念に調べられる」と考える。 (6) 私が運転するのではなく，夫に車を運転してもらい仕事に行くとあるので，「私の免許証が切れた」からだと考える。「(免許証などが)期限が切れて無効になる」はexpire。 (7) 前半に「確かにSarahが料理に手を貸そうとしていた」とあり，butで後半の文を続けているので，料理に手を貸そうとした→しかし邪魔だった，と考え，B「妨害。障害」とする。 (8) 空欄の直前にwas accused of「～で告発された」とあるので，悪いことをして告発されたと考える。後にof millions of dollars「何百万ドルも」とあるので，defraud ～ of …「～から…をだまし取る」にする。intersect「～と交差する」，reclaim「返還を要求する」，provide「提供する」。 (9) expectancy単独では「期待。待望」という意味になるが，life expectancyで「平均余命」という意味。composure「平静」，expectation「期待」，guarantee「保証」。(10) leading「一流の」。 (11) insist on ～で「～を主張する」。動名詞の主語に代名詞を使う場合所有格にする。 (12) the ～(比較級), the …(比較級)で「～すればするほど，ますます…」という意味。I am more impressed by ～のmore impressedが倒置されて前に出てきている。(13) recommendに続くthat節の中はS＋(should)＋V(動詞の原形)～となり，shouldが省略されて動詞の原形だけが残る。「passwordsは人によって変えられる」と考え，受け身にする。 (14) for以下は「この町の農村地域に引っ越すことを考えている人たち」という意味。thoseはpeopleの意味で使われることがある。 (15) when I was a child「子どもだった頃」と過去の1時点の話なので，完了時制は使えない。

(16) should＋have＋動詞の過去分詞形で「～すべきだったのに」と過去の後悔を表す。 (17) 原級を用いて比較をする場合，形容詞＋単数形の名詞の場合，as＋形容詞＋a/an＋単数形の名詞＋asの語順にする。(18) haveは使役動詞。have＋～＋…(過去分詞)で，「(誰かに)～を…してもらう」という使役動詞。「(誰かに)血圧を定期的にチェックしてもらう」となる。 (19) the house which my brother lived inの文尾のinが関係代名詞whichの前に来た形。 (20) the dayはforgetの目的語なので，目的格の関係代名詞にする。

【中学校】

【１】(1) i B ii C iii A (2) B (3) D (4) C
(5) it would be for the shopkeeper in front of me (6) B

〈解説〉(1) i，iiについて，第4段落3文目に「まったく同じサービスに対し，地元の人たちは旅行者よりも安い値段を享受している」とあり，その具体例として述べられているので，地元民のほうが外国人観光客よりも三輪タクシーの値段は安くなる。また，iiiはカンボジアの首都プノンペンにおける平均月収の金額を推定する。 (2) 空欄の直後の第6段落冒頭に，「シンガポールで同様のサービスに対してもっと多くの額を支払ったことを考えると，私には値段は妥当だった」とある。筆者は旅行者が地元民よりも多く払うことに問題を感じていないので，B「それの何が問題なのか」が正解。 (3) 第8段落2文目の空欄②を含む文は「それは素晴らしいサービスに対して，感謝の気持ちを示すために私ができた～だった」という意味。その次の文にalso「～もまた」があり「それはまた，先進国と発展途上国の間にある所得の不均衡を減らそうと哀れな試みをするために私ができる最小限のこと」と，同じ最小限のことだとあるので，空欄にも「最小限」を意味する語が入る。bare minimum「最小限」。 (4) Cの「発展途上国では日用品の値段が安いから，先進国から来た旅行者がそこで買い物をする値段は妥当である」という記述は本文にはない。なお，Aは第6段落3文目，Bは第6段落2文目，Dは第9段落2文目の内容と一致する。
(5) 第9段落2文目の「私(アメリカ人ライター)が買い物体験に勝利したような気持ちになりたいために，彼女(店主)に値段を下げさせることは1ドルの価値もない」とあるので，先進国から来た自分が値引くことは簡単だろうがそんなことをする価値がないという流れだと考える。「(豊かな先進国から来た)私がそのドルを替える(貧しさにつけ込んで安い値段に替える(下げる))ことは，私の目の前にいる(貧しい発展途上国に住む)店主が(生活のために商品を売りたくて，無理な値引きの要求に対ししぶしぶ)値段を下げるよりはるかに簡単であろう」と続く。　(6)　本文最後の1文に「文化はそれぞれ違うかもしれないが，品位は品位で，1，2ドルを値引くためだけに，品位を安売りはしないと信じたい」とあり，B「著者は，1，2ドルを値引くために，品位を安売りするように見えるので，先進国から来た旅行者が地元の店主に示す態度にうんざりした」と一致する。Aの「先進国からの旅行者たちは不当に高い値段に気をつけるべき」という記述，Cの「発展途上国の人々は旅行客を特別に良く扱うべき」という記述は本文にはない。Dの「地元民が品物やサービスに対し安い値段を払っているので，先進国から来た人たちが値切るのは理に適っている」という内容は本文の主旨と反対のことである。

【2】(1)　①　A　②　B　③　D　④　C　⑤　B　⑥　D　(2)　D

〈解説〉(1)　①　問題文は「Myth #1(神話1)に対する主要な答えは，日本語を母語とする話者は～すべきである」。Myth #1のRealityの2段落目の2文目に「アメリカ英語を使って効果的にコミュニケーションをとりたいなら，現在使っている英語のアクセントを変えようとしたり，取り除こうとするのではなく，新しいアクセントを習得する必要がある」とあり，Aと一致する。　②　問題文は「おそらくアメリカ英語の発音を改善するための最初の重要な点は～である」。Myth #2のRealityの3段落目冒頭に「最初(の重要な点)は筋肉の発達と関係がある。話すときに使う今ある筋肉は，完全な日本語と日本人風の英語を話すために作られている。アメリカ英語を話すために，鼻の下と唇の端の筋肉を発達させる必要がある」とあり，Bと一致する。　③　問題文は「本文によると，R音かL音を正しく作るために～」。下から5段落目の1文目に「R音は上の歯と下の歯を5mmだけ離して，唇を丸くする必要がある」とあり，Dと一致する。　④　問題文は「Scott Perryが開発した音声コーディングメソッドは～」。下から2段落1文目に「私の音声コーディングメソッドを使うと正しい発音を理解し，何度も何度も繰り返し発話することを可能にする」とあり，8文目に「それ(私のコーディングシステム)は日本人の話し手のための新しい発音記号である」とあり，Cと一致する。　⑤　問題文は「Scott Perryによると，～するために，発音は英語学習のほかの面とは切り離す必要がある」。最後の段落の1～2文目に「一般的に英語学習のすべての面をひとまとめにして取り組むが，実際，発音は切り離す必要がある。発音は身体と関係し，英語学習のほかの面はすべて精神的な暗記である」とあり，Bと一致する。　⑥　本文のテーマを問う問題。最後の段落6～8文目に「コーディングを活用すると，日本人話者が何年もの間，英語の音を日本語の音と関連付けていたことによって生じるよくある間違いを避けることができる。みんながアメリカ英語の発音をマスターできる。それは正しい練習であり，筋肉の発達であり，正確な音を知ることである」とあり，Dと一致する。　(2)　空欄iを含む文の前半は「アメリカ英語は～な呼吸で，長く伸びる発話スタイルである」と述べられ，そのあとwhile「しかし一方」が使われ，対照的な内容が後に続く。「日本人風の英語は浅い呼吸で，早く，～である」とあるので，「浅い呼吸」に対して「深い呼吸」となり，「長く伸びる発話スタイル」に対して「途切れ途切れ(の発話スタイル)」と考える。

【3】(1)　B　　(2)　Bees(They) vote for where to relocate their hive(nest) by dancing.　(10 words)　　(3)　C

〈解説〉(1)　第1段落はハチが巣を移動させるときの話で，空欄を含む文は「それ(新しい巣)は鳥のような～にさらされ過ぎてはいけない」とあり，ハチにとって鳥がどういう存在か考える。A「交渉者」，B「捕食者」，C「死傷者」，D「犠牲者」。　(2)　第2段落4～5文目を要約すると「巣に住むハチの5％が次の候補となる場所を探しに出かけ，様々なダンスをして，それぞれの場所の位置を伝える。残りのハチがこれらの場所に出かけ，巣にもどって一番よいと思う場所の方向を向いて，長く激しいダンスをする」となる。この内容を10語以内でまとめる。　(3)　第4段落2文目に「もしアリが踏みつぶされたら，その死に際に残す贈り物は，近くにいるほかのアリに警告を発するにおいである。そのにおいを嗅ぐとアリは同じ運命(踏みつぶされること)を避けようと急いで走り回り，パニックになる」とあり，Cの「フェロモン(＝におい)のため，アリは踏みつぶされるような危険な状況に引き寄せられる」とは一致しない。なお，Aは第4段落3文目，Bは第3段落5文目，Dは第4段落5文目と一致する。

【4】(1)　Children attempt to act older than they are, but that itself is proof of their growth.　(2)　Exposure to diverse experiences in a balanced manner is said to keep the brain “young”.

〈解説〉　(1)「(子どもは)何事にも背伸びをする」→「子どもは彼らが今の状態よりも年上として行動しようとする」と，英語にしやすいように考えるといい。「成長の証し」はそのままproof of their growthで表される。　(2)「色々なことをバランスよく経験すると，若々しさが保たれるという」→「バランスのとれた方法で様々な経験にさらされることが脳を若く保つと言われている」と，解釈しなおすと，英語に訳しやすい。「～にさらされること」と無生物を主語にする英語らしい表現がすぐに思いつけば難しくはないだろう。

【5】In 2020, in English class at an elementary school, children are expected to develop basic communicative abilities in English.

Considering this situation, English lessons in junior high schools should be more focused on communication in English. English teachers should only use English in class in order to encourage students to speak English, and create a lot more opportunities that allow students to communicate with each other in English.

In addition, English teachers at elementary school and junior high school should share their English teaching plans and set the consistent goals for students' English proficiency.　(94 words)

〈解説〉現行の小学校学習指導要領における外国語活動では，音声面を中心としてコミュニケーション能力の素地を養っており，中学校の外国語科ではこの養ったコミュニケーション能力を踏まえ，一貫性をもって，「聞くこと」，「話すこと」，「読むこと」，「書くこと」の4技能をバランスよく育成することがねらいとなる。このことを骨組みにして具体的に書いていけばよいだろう。文法的な誤りやスペルミスがないように注意し，「先生は授業中は英語を話す」や「小学校と中学校の先生が協力し合う」など，できるだけ具体的な内容にすること。

【高等学校】

【1】(1)　①　B　②　D　③　D　④　A　⑤　D　⑥　B　⑦　C　⑧　A　(2)　学習がうまくいかない生徒の一部に必要なことは，何かを本当にうまくやりとげる経験であり，それも，それをうまくやったと他人に言われるまでもなく自分自身でわかるほどに，何かを申し分なくやりとげる経験である。

〈解説〉(1)　①　第1段落冒頭に「子どもはみんな成功する必要がある」とあるが，2文目で筆者は「～に簡単に成功すべきではなく，いつでも成功がくる(成功する)べきではない」と，少し条件を付けて述べていることから判断する。　②　第1段落の最後の文に「成功とは，できないことをできることに変え，実際に行った結果である」とあるので，心にある成功しないかもしれないという考えを含む障害(できないと考えること)に「打ち勝つこと」を成功は含んでいると考える。
③　第2段落は人生を勝負事である野球にたとえているので，すべての人にとって，人生は「勝利」よりも敗北を抱えているとする。
④　空欄を含むフレーズは「人の手の届く範囲は，しっかり握ることを超える」→「人は手の届かない(しっかり握ることのできない)ところを目指すべきだ。そうでなければ天は何のためにあるのか」という決まった表現。　⑤　第2段落7文目に「私たちが今日失敗したことは，

誰かが明日成功するかもしれない」とあり，8文目にだから私たちの失敗は誰かの「成功」に道を拓くかもしれないと考える。
⑥・⑦　第2段落の後半で失敗は誰かの役に立つと述べられていて，第3段落の2文目に「もっと的確に言うと，失敗は～というよりはむしろ称賛に値し，～であるとみるべきだ」と続くので，失敗は悪いことではなく，良いことであるいう文脈で考える。したがって，⑥には「建設的」，⑦には「恥ずかしい」という意味の英語が入る。　⑧　第4段落2文目に，「どうやって同年代の他の子どもたちが，同じ学校や他の学校でしていることを秘密にすることができるだろうか。(いやできない)」とあるので，成功しない(学習がうまくいかない)生徒の課題を成功させるように「お膳立てをして」も，それを隠し通すことができないと考える。　(2)「これらの子どもたちの一部に必要なことは，本当にうまくやり遂げる経験であり～」とあるので，お膳立てをしてもらってうまくいくのではなく自分の実力でやり遂げると考え，お膳立てをしてもらうunsuccessful studentsがthese kidsにあたる。

【2】(1)　respect　　(2)　いつの時代にもまして現在，私が日本にいられることがいかに幸運であるかということを，初めて私に理解させてくれた日本の友人たちの存在がもしなかったならば，私は古い文学の研究の中にいまだ埋もれたままであったであろう。　　(3)　B
(4)　to be accepted not merely as a peculiar *gaijin* but as someone who belonged　(・to be accepted not as a peculiar *gaijin* but merely as someone who belonged　　・not to be accepted merely as a peculiar *gaijin* but as someone who belonged　　・not to be accepted as a peculiar *gaijin* but merely as someone who belonged)　　(5)　自分が(京都に)受け入れられたと感じるやいなや，誰かが必ず，ある絵画や演劇やレストランのことを，ひとりの「外人」としてどう思うか尋ねてくるのだった。
(6)　外国で理解者を得るのは困難だと経験上当然予測でき，米国や英国では他者の自身に対する態度に頓着しなかったのに京都では受容されたいと強く望む筆者の感情の非論理性。(79字)　　(7)　B

〈解説〉(1)　①は「私が京都で過ごした2年はほとんどすべての～で，とても幸せでした」で，⑤は「私はすべての祭りに参加し，100人の著名な作家の墓で～を払った」とあるので，「点」と「敬意」の両方の意味を持つrespectにする。「～の墓で敬意を払う」とは「墓参りをする」という意味。　(2)　had it not been forはif it had not been for「もし～がなかったならば」のifを省いて，it hadをhad itにした倒置の文。大まかに「日本の友だちがいなかったならば，研究に埋もれていたかもしれない(実際にはいたので埋もれていなかった)」と，過去の事実に反したことを仮定する仮定法過去完了の文。now of all timesは直訳すると「すべての時の中で今」となり，「いつの時代にもまして現在」などとする。　(3)　著者の気持ちは，「京都に魅了されていたので，風変わりな外人としてだけでなく，京都に帰属している人としても受け入れてもらいたかった」のにそうしてもらえないことが問題で，それに対しイライラや失望感を表す語を選ぶ。　(4)　asにはいろいろな意味があるが，この場合be acceptedと結びつき，「～として(受け入れられる)」という前置詞としてとる。またnot merely ～ but (also) …で「～だけでなく…もまた」となる。大まかに「私は～としてだけでなく…としてもまた受け入れられたかった」と考える。　(5)　no sooner ～ than …は「～するや否や…」，be sure to doは「必ず～する」という意味。askは大きく「頼む」と「尋ねる」という意味がある。この場合は目的語に疑問詞のwhatがあるので，私が何を思っているか尋ねるとする。
(6)　illogicalityは「非論理性」という意味。第5段落2文目以降に，著者がアメリカやイギリスでは自分の感情をわかってくれる人(わかってくれて自分のことを好きになってくれる人)を探すことは困難だったので，自分は好かれようが好かれまいが気にしなかったとあり，論理的である。京都では，第4段落にあるように自分の意見よりもすべての外人の代表者として扱われ，教授たちとの連絡もなくなり，生徒たちも著者のことを無視するようになったので，自分は受け入れられなくてもいいと考えるのが論理的だが，第5段落3文目に「京都では是が非でも受け入れられたいと思った」とあり，論理的ではないことがわかる。 (7) 第2段落3文目に「日本から離れてアメリカで5年間いた後に，彼(ナガイミチオ)は，私(著者)が初めてそれ(日本)の良さを理解しかけているときに，彼の国(日本)を再発見していた」とあり，日本を離れてアメリカに5年いたのは著者ではなく，ナガイミチオなのでBは一致しない。

【3】(1) A (2) A (3) ③ C ④ D

(4) ・memorization of more sophisticated vocabulary ・higher-level thinking skills in the target language ・comfort in both academic and social situations ・classes that are less teacher-centered (5) 特に，大半の日本人が授業以外で英語に触れる機会を十分に得られないという状況を考慮に入れると，コミュニケーションの授業内であっても，試験を実施することは生徒のやる気を出させる補助的な手段となりうる。

(6) I want my students to learn the skills to communicate in English as well as a fundamental knowledge about English words and grammar. As the author mentioned, one of the reasons for the low level of English ability among Japanese students is the lack of experience in expressing their opinions and sharing their ideas with others in English. I think teachers should provide students with more chances to talk in English with others, helping them to improve their communication skills. Students will need these skills for thier futures in the global world.

To do so, I would set individual interview tests at the end of each school term. I would inform them of the topic in advance and give them some time in class to talk about the topic with their classmates to prepare for the test. I think by including such tasks in my classrooms, I will encourage and motivate my students to communicate in English. (157 words)

〈解説〉(1) 様々な認識能力の1つ。inferは「推測する」という意味なので，A「明確に述べられたものよりも証拠や推理から物事の結論を出す」と一致する。B「特定の場所や位置にものをしっかり留める」，C「さらなる証拠と照らし合わせて物事を再考し変えること」，D「支援や忠告をしながら，行動するよう，あるいはし続けるように説き伏せる」。　(2)　語学教育で習得する能力には大きく，社会の中でコミュニケーションをするときに必要とするsocial language skills「社会言語能力」と，教室やテストで成功するために必要なacademic language skills「学習言語能力」があり，それに関して話が展開されている。第3段落は学習言語能力に関する記述で，空欄を含む文の直後の文に「フォーマルな，あるいは専門的，学術的な状況では社会言語能力に焦点を当てた授業では習得されない言語の正確さが求められる」と詳しく述べられていることから，もう1つ社会言語能力と大きく異なる点は「正確さ」の問題だと判断する。　(3)　第4段落では社会言語能力と学習言語能力の2つとも重要だとある。空欄③はその具体例として，2文目に「どんな英文法のテストでも受かるのに～な会社の重役は明らかに不利である」とあり，テストでいい点を取る学習言語能力は優れているのに，社会言語能力が劣っているので不利だと考える。空欄④はもう1つの具体例で，言葉で表現する能力に優れ，最近の俗語に詳しいが，～な学生は将来の選択肢が限られている」とあり，社会言語能力は優れているのに，学習言語能力が劣っていて選択肢が限られていると考える。　(4)　質問文は「文章によると，高いレベルで外国語に堪能になるときに必要な4つのことがある」という意味。第10段落2文目に「高いレベルで外国語に堪能になるためには」とあり，具体的に3つ述べられている。加えて，第11段落冒頭にFurthermore「さらに」とあり，もう1つ述べられていて合計4つになる。
(5)　givenは前置詞的に用いて「～を考慮すると」という意味。exposure toは「～にさらされること」，have the lack ofは「～の不足をもっている」→「～が不足している」という意味。exposureとto Englishで「英語にさらされること」，the lack と(which/that) most Japanese haveで「ほとんどの日本人がもっている(英語にさらされることの)不足」となる。serve asは「～として役立つ」。　(6)「文章に書かれていることを考慮して」とあるので，著者の意見に言及して書くとよい。著者は語学教育にはコミュニケーション能力が身につく「社会言語能力」と「学習言語能力」があり，日本は「学習言語能力が身につくよう，逐語訳と丸暗記の授業をして，テストでいい点を取ることを目標として動機づけている。ところが本来，語学学習としてはどちらもバランスよくつくのがよいので，コミュニケーション能力が身につくやり方として，英検，TOEFLやTOEICなどのテスト対策を行い，同時にコミュニケーション能力を身につけて，相手のことを理解し，複雑な考えを説明，共有できるようにしてグローバル社会に適合できるようにするとしている。著者の主張はどうやってコミュニケーション能力をつけていくか，その方法論を述べているので，コミュニケーション能力を取り上げ，なぜ生徒が学ぶ必要があるのか第1段落で説明する。そのあとで，高校の授業でどうやってコミュニケーション能力を身につける授業を展開するのか，具体例もあげて第2段落で説明する。最初に問題の意図に沿って大まかな段落分けをして，その後，それぞれの段落の細部を詰めていくのがいいだろう。

【4】(1)　異文化交流の際には文化の違いという根本的な問題とその問題解決の際に生じる別の問題があり，異文化への理解や配慮が不十分なために良い関係を築けないことがよくある。(79字)　(2)　I learned that understanding other cultures is as important as studying languages. If we are to understand each other well in inter-cultural communication, we need to understand the cultural backgrounds of each other as well as the common language to convey our ideas and feelings. Without knowing the thoughts or customs of people talking with us, we cannot fully understand how they will feel or what they might think of our suggestions. We have to study both language and culture for a better inter-cultural communication.　(85 words)

〈解説〉(1)　最後の段落に「この場合，文化間のコミュニケーションに2つの問題がある。1つは文化の相違に対する基本的な問題で，2番目は文化の相違に対応しようとするときに生じる新たな問題」とあるので，文化の相違から生じる問題とその問題を解決しようとするときに生じる別の問題のことを80字以内にまとめる。　(2)　この話はMr.

RichardsonとMr. Chuが香港行きの飛行機で偶然知り合ったことから始まる。Mr. Richardは仕事でよい人間関係を築くために自分のことをAndyと呼ばせ，Mr. Chuのことは西洋文化を押し付けてはいけないと洋風の名前のDavidと呼ばず，親しみを込めてHon-faiとfirst nameで呼ぶことを選択した。一方Mr. ChuはHon-faiとfirst nameで呼ばれることを，相手に対して敬意がないと不快に思い，仕事をしていくのは難しいと判断する。単語や文法を覚えて使えるようにするだけでなく，この文化の相違とそこから生じる問題を解決するように授業を展開することを考える。

2016年度　実施問題

【中学校】

【1】Choose the one that best completes the sentence from the four alternatives.

(1) "I have a table (　　) for two tonight."
"May I have your name, please?"
A. reserving　B. reserved　C. to reserve　D. reserve

(2) I asked two people the way to the airport, but (　　) knew the area.
A. none　B. either of them　C. neither of them　D. either

(3) Rick went out with his friends and didn't come home until after midnight (　　) made his parents worry.
A. , that　B. that　C. , which　D. which

(4) She (　　) the book I lent her, but she hasn't finished it yet. I think it's very difficult for her.
A. hasn't read　B. has been reading　C. hadn't read
D. has read

(5) His Spanish isn't good—(　　) after three years in Mexico as a special correspondent.
A. even　B. even if　C. even though　D. if

(6) We are not able to schedule a meeting (　　) she purchases a flight ticket to Japan.
A. and　B. during　C. instead　D. until

(7) The company is seeking someone who has (　　) experience and expertise to the current technicians.
A. comparably　B. comparable　C. compared
D. compare

(8) Jenny said that she was going away for a few days and (　　) me when she got back.

A.　will call　　B.　called　　C.　would call　　D.　had called

(9)　One purpose of distributing a phone chain to employees is to keep them in touch with (　　).

A.　each other　　B.　the other　　C.　other　　D.　another

(10)　According to the Domestic Research Center's survey, (　　) young men tend to do housework.

A.　each　　B.　almost　　C.　much　　D.　many

(☆☆☆◎◎◎)

【２】Choose the one that best completes the sentence from the four alternatives.

(1)　Boston Investment Group manages funds (　　) a local charity.

A.　in honor of　　B.　in search of　　C.　on behalf of

D.　in accordance with

(2)　There were some advertisements in the paper that I wanted to keep, so I (　　) them out.

A.　cut　　B.　set　　C.　let　　D.　put

(3)　TKM Stores never take its shoppers (　　) as its staff always offers helpful and friendly service.

A.　into account　　B.　in mind　　C.　for granted　　D.　seriously

(4)　Instead of using off-the-shelf concepts, K&J Architects always designs structures (　　).

A.　as is　　B.　from scratch　　C.　either way　　D.　in brief

(5)　The chief researcher, Kate Taylor, (　　) up her keynote speech by noting the many advances being made in development of specific medicines against cancer.

A.　drew　　B.　hung　　C.　showed　　D.　wrapped

(6)　Local (　　) predict light rain in the morning, clearing by noon to make way for sunny skies for the remainder of the day.

A.　spectators　　B.　prosecutors　　C.　meteorologists

D.　physicians

(7) The western (　　) of our city contains a world heritage site, alongside traditional houses and small shops.

A. district　B. state　C. system　D. treat

(8) The major (　　) to developing new drugs is the high cost of research.

A. device　B. solution　C. substitute　D. obstacle

(9) Professor Stephanie Harrison had her students (　　) their graduation theses several times.

A. merge　B. modify　C. prescribe　D. imply

(10) Crescent Logistics Co. (　　) all employees have an opportunity to take 20 paid vacation days per year.

A. ensures　B. wonders　C. matters　D. restores

(11) My brother works at JIR Printing Co., which has a (　　) international workforce of over 10,000 employees.

A. urgent　B. imminent　C. diverse　D. rigid

(12) Practicing *karate* is a favorite (　　) of Dawn Croft, who has enjoyed it since she met a great teacher in Japan.

A. article　B. preview　C. athlete　D. pastime

(13) Bill has had better career (　　) since he obtained his computer programming certificate.

A. prospects　B. duties　C. concerns　D. tendencies

(14) My daughter and son work in the Tokyo and Fukuoka office branches (　　).

A. thoroughly　B. respectively　C. certainly　D. quarterly

(15) Dara hadn't been to her hometown in over ten years, so she was surprised that it remained (　　) unchanged. Everything looked the same as she remembered it.

A. specifically　B. randomly　C. virtually　D. rapidly

(☆☆◎◎◎)

【3】Read the following passage and answer the questions below.

Luxury cars, big yachts, bigger homes—it's *fast times for the superrich. Even during five years of economic shock, the superrich got richer, widening the gap with the very poor. The charity *Oxfam is calling for action to ①address the ever-widening wealth gap, which it says is creating serious economic instability and ②(　　).

A major new report from Oxfam, entitled *Even It Up*, includes these claims: The total wealth of today's billionaires increased by 124 percent in the last four years, to around $5.4 trillion. The number of billionaires has doubled since the economic crisis began, to 1,645 people. A tax of just 1.5 percent on the world's billionaires ③[in / that / save / by / healthcare / 23 million lives / money / investing / could].

Last year, we had $159 billion sitting in tax havens that could've been spent on poverty reduction. That money is more than every single dollar that was spent by every single donor globally on ④(　　) around the world.

Of course, some billionaires already agree with paying more tax, including Bill Gates and Warren Buffett, while Pope Francis has stated that "inequality is the root of social evil."

But reports like *Even It Up* often come out and sink without trace. This time, Oxfam says, with everyone from President Obama to the pope to some of the richest people on earth talking about wealth and poverty, there may just he a ⑤consensus growing to tackle to the extremes.

【Notes】*fast time　悦楽のひととき
*Oxfam＝Oxford Committee for Famine Relief

(1) Choose the most appropriate word from the text to replace the underlined word ① to make a comprehensible sentence.

(2) From the context, choose the best answer for ②(　　) from the four alternatives below.

A. tax revenue

B. terrible social injustices

C. raising minimum wage

D. thriving economy

(3) Put the words from ③[ ] in the text in the correct order.

(4) Choose the best answer for ④( ) from the four alternatives below.

A. fighting poverty and humanitarian crises

B. widening gap between the rich and the poor

C. causing economic instability and poverty

D. sustaining inequality and economic crises

(5) Choose the word that is closest in meaning to underlined word ⑤ from the four alternatives below.

A. criterion B. statement C. initiative D. agreement

(6) Choose the most appropriate title for this article from the four alternatives below.

A. Increased Billionaires

B. Wealth Reduction

C. Widening Inequality

D. Political Instability

(☆☆☆◎◎◎)

【4】Read the following passage and answer the questions below.

HANNIBAL, Mo.—The Mississippi River, which flows from north to south in the United States, became an important commercial artery in the 19th century, with many steamboats sailing on it. Many small towns were built at ports along the river. Hannibal, Missouri, in the Midwestern United States, is one such town.

Samuel Clemens, who would later become a famous American novelist under the pen name of Mark Twain, moved here with his family when he was 4. They lived in a two-story house about a five-minute walk from the river.

①( ) no TV in those days, children played outdoors in nature. One favorite play spot was a cave at the edge of the town.

The cave, which stretches in many directions and has a total length of about five kilometers, is still there. In summer, 600 to 700 fans of the writer visit the cave from all over tire world every day. Inside the cave, ②(　　) done by children over the years remains. 【 A 】 The scenes are very similar to those described in the climax of Twain's novel, "The Adventures of Tom Sawyer," published in 1876. "Mark Twain played here as a child and that's where he got a lot of ideas for his stories," Sam Lucas, a 24-year-old guide in the town, said proudly. Local people say Twain watched steamboats arrive at the riverside. Watching people and goods coming and going, a young Twain must have felt an increasing desire to find out about the outside world.

At age 17, Twain left the town and gained experience working at many jobs, including as a printer, newspaper reporter and a pilot for steamships, moving around the United States. In the 1860s, Twain began traveling to Europe and the Middle East and also began writing novels and travel articles.

【 B 】 Black slaves working at his home and in his relatives' houses were servants but also playmates of Twain. However, Twain learned during his wanderings in later years that there was a part of the world without slaves.

Henry Sweets, 65, the executive director of the Mark Twain Boyhood Home & Museum, explained that exposure to new cultures changed Twain's views about slaves that were accepted as a matter of course. 【 C 】

Another of Twain's major books, "Adventures of Huckleberry Finn," was published in 1885, nine years after "The Adventures of Tom Sawyer." It is an adventure in which the title character tries to help Jim, a black slave who is gentle and honest, escape from his owner. The text includes bad language used by children in those days, as well as terms of racial disparagement. Twain did not refrain from using the discriminatory terms so that images of black people forced to live by obeying white people and other social realities of those years could be reproduced without understatement. 【 D 】

What did Twain want to convey through the story? Faye Dant, 65, who runs a museum of African-American history in Hannibal, said that even if the terms are regarded as discriminatory by today's standards, ④(　　) Dant also said that Twain squarely faced the system of slavery and was one of the first white writers who gave ⑤(　　) to black characters in novels.

(1) Choose the one that best completes the ①(　　) from the four alternatives below.

A. For　B. In　C. About　D. With

(2) Choose the most appropriate word for ②(　　) to make a comprehensible sentence.

A. virtue　B. stroke　C. graffiti　D. hatch

(3) Choose the most appropriate place, from 【 A 】～【 D 】, to put the sentence below. During Twain's childhood days, Hannibal was a typical rural town where there was still slavery.

(4) Choose the one that best completes the ④(　　) from the four alternatives below.

A. using them was necessary to convey the realities of those days

B. it was inevitable that they used such language in those days

C. they were used as a matter of course among children of those days

D. they were deemed to be terms of racial disparagement to black people in those days

(5) Choose the best answer for ⑤(　　) from the four alternatives below.

A. prejudices　B. personalities　C. offences

D. disparagements

(6) According to the passage, which of the following is NOT true about Mark Twain?

A. In the climax of "The Adventures of Tom Sawyer,"" he described the scenes that were similar to those seen in the cave where he had played as a child.

B. During his travels around the world, he went to parts of the world without slavery, leading him to openly challenge the system of slavery in his book.

C. He accepted black slaves working in his home as a matter of course, while he helped Jim, a black slave who was his playmate, escape from his owner.

D. It's probable that watching a constant flow of people and goods coming and going an steamboats got him interested in seeing the world beyond his town.

(☆☆☆◎◎◎)

【５】The following English passage is taken from Rachel Carson's *A Fable for Tomorrow* in *Silent Spring*. Published in 1962, this book brought attention to the dangers of pesticides on the environment. Read the following passage and answer the questions below.

There was once a town in the heart of America where all life seemed to live in harmony with its surroundings. The town lay in the midst of a checkerboard of prosperous farms, with fields of grain and hillsides of orchards where, in spring, white clouds of bloom drifted above the green fields. In autumn, oak and maple and birch set up a blaze of color that flamed and flickered across a backdrop of pines. Then foxes barked in the hills and deer silently crossed the fields, half hidden in the mists of the autumn mornings.

Along the roads, *laurel, *viburnum and *alder, great *ferns and wildflowers delighted the traveler's eye through much of the year. Ever in winter the roadsides were places of beauty, where countless birds came to feed on the berries and on the seed heads of the dried weeds rising above the snow. The countryside was, in fact, famous for the abundance and variety of its bird life, and when the flood of migrants was pouring through in spring and autumn people traveled from great distances to observe them. Others *came to fish the streams, which flowed clear and cold out of the hills and contained shady pools where trout lay. So it had been from the days many years ago when the first settlers raised their houses, sank their wells, and built their barns.

Then a strange *blight crept over the area and everything began to change. Some evil spell had settled on the community: mysterious maladies swept the flocks of chickens; the cattle and sheep sickened and died. Everywhere was a shadow of death. The tarmers spoke of much illness among their families. In the town the doctors had become more and more puzzled by new kinds of sickness appearing among their patients. There had been several sudden and unexplained deaths, not only among adults but even among children, who would be stricken suddenly while at play and die within a few hours.

There was a strange stillness. The birds, for example—where had they gone? Many people spoke of them, puzzled and disturbed. The feeding stations in the backyards were deserted. The few birds seen anywhere were moribund; they trembled violently and could not fly. It was a spring without voices. On the mornings that had once throbbed with the dawn chorus of robins, *catbirds, doves, *jays, *wrens, and scores of other bird voices there was now no sound; only silence lay over the fields and woods and marsh.

On the farms the hens brooded, but no chicks hatched. The farmers complained that they were unable to raise any pigs—the litters were small and the young survived only a few days. The apple trees were coming into bloom but no bees droned among the blossoms, so there was no pollination and there would be no fruit.

The roadsides, once so attractive, were now lined with browned and withered vegetation as though swept by fire. These, too, were silent, deserted by all living things. Even the streams were now lifeless. Anglers no longer visited them, for all the fish had died.

In the gutters under the eaves and between the shingles of the roofs, a white granular powder still showed a few patches; some weeks before it had fallen like snow upon the roofs and the lawns, the fields and streams.

No witchcraft, no enemy action had silenced the rebirth of new life in this stricken world. The people had done it themselves.

This town does not actually exist, but it might easily have a thousand counterparts in America or elsewhere in the world. I know of no community that has experienced all the misfortunes I describe. Yet every one of these disasters has actually happened somewhere, and many real communities have already suffered a substantial number of them. A grim specter has crept upon us almost unnoticed, and this imagined tragedy may easily become a stark reality we all shall know.

What has already silenced the voices of spring in countless towns in America? This book is an attempt to explain.

【Notes】 *laurel　月桂樹　　*viburnum　ガマズミ
*alder　カワラハンノキ　　*ferns　シダ
*migrants＝migrating birds
*come to fish the stream＝come to fish in the stream
*blight　胴枯れ病　　*catbirds　ネコマネドリ
*jay　カケス　　*wren　ミソサザイ

(1) There was once a town where ________.

A. in autumn, multiple fires burned through the pine forests
B. the face of the countryside was flooded through spring and autumn
C. in winter, people came to fish the trout where the first settlers raised their houses and barns
D. from autumn to spring, migrations of birds fascinated many people who traveled from long distances to see them

(2) There was no sound in the town which was once in harmony with its surroundings, for ________.

A. children weren't allowed to go outside so as not to be stricken suddenly and die
B. the berries and the seed heads of dried weeds were withered up, and there were no voices anywhere
C. the spread of mysterious maladies in the flocks of chickens and all domestic animals were unexplained

D. a strange disease crept upon the town and every creature, such as cattle, sheep, birds, and even human beings, died

(3) ________ by their own actions.

A. Many birds trembled violently and could not fly

B. People brought death to a once attractive town

C. A beautiful town deserted by all people had silenced the voice of spring

D. The doctors became more and more puzzled by new kinds of sicknesses

(4) The story makes the point that ________.

A. many real communities may suffer from the same type of disasters described in her imaginary world

B. people have already caused millions of sudden unexplained deaths in thousands of towns in the world

C. a grim specter crept upon us and many real communities suffered a substantial number of disasters

D. the author knows all the misfortunes have become a stark reality in countless towns in America

(☆☆☆◎◎◎)

【6】Translate the underlined sentences into English.

(1) 修学旅行は，生徒が視野を広げ，学習した知識を実際の社会経験と結び付けるまたとない機会である。最近では修学旅行で海外に行く学校も増えている。

(2) 寛容という言葉は，他者を受け入れること，意見の違いを認めること，と辞書にある。そうありたいと願うが，人はしばしば排他的になる。ここに1つの疑問が生まれる。不寛容に対しても人は寛容であるべきなのか。

(☆☆☆◎◎◎)

【7】Write the benefits of Active Learning using concrete examples to support your reasoning in approximately 100 words.

(☆☆☆◎◎◎)

【高等学校】

【1】Choose the answer that best completes the sentence from the four alternatives.

(1) The news of his marriage (　　) a lot of people, for no one expected it.

A. anticipated　B. addressed　C. astonished　D. ascended

(2) The professor was a passionate (　　) of environmental protection and spent much of her free time giving lectures on the subject.

A. advocate　B. hypocrite　C. monarch　D. applicant

(3) Many people are worried about what will happen when all the earth's oil reserves have been (　　) and there's nothing left to exploit.

A. occupied　B. decreased　C. exhausted　D. moderated

(4) The admissions officer said, "Proficiency in a second language is (　　) for all students entering our graduate program."

A. supplementary　B. compulsory　C. redundant

D. plausible

(5) After looking carefully at the ransom note, the handwriting expert was able to (　　) that it had been written by the suspect.

A. abstain　B. duplicate　C. extort　D. verify

(6) The politician got upset to find her view had been (　　) by the journalist's misleading article.

A. adored　B. distorted　C. implied　D. proclaimed

(7) The police suspected the woman because she (　　) her earlier statements about where she had been on the night of the crime.

A. embraced　B. acclaimed　C. interrogated

D. contradicted

(8) Traffic has been seriously ( ) in Thailand because of the typhoon.

A. disrupted B. dissolved C. discarded D. disengaged

(9) The car crash wasn't an accident; it was a ( ) attempt to kill the lawyer.

A. declarative B. defeatist C. deliberate D. dejected

(10) ( ) have I seen such a beautiful sunset.

A. Accidentally B. Formerly C. Frequently D. Rarely

(☆☆☆◎◎◎)

【2】Choose the answer that best completes the sentence from the four alternatives.

(1) I suggested to Tom ( ) with me to the new restaurant around the school, but he said he was too busy.

A. come B. that he come C. that he had come

D. to have

(2) We ( ) playing soccer for about half an hour when it started to rain heavily.

A. had been B. would be C. should be D. have been

(3) I was surprised to find that Robert was much easier ( ) than I had thought.

A. for talking B. talking to C. to talk D. to talk to

(4) Butter, eaten all over the world, ( ) made from the same liquid as cheese.

A. that B. has C. is D. which

(5) I was made ( ) for an hour until my friend came to the station.

A. wait B. waiting C. waited D. to wait

(6) I'll introduce you to a man ( ) I hope will help you find a job in this town.

A. which B. who C. to whom D. whom

(7) ( ) her for a long time, I couldn't recognize her at first sight.

A. Having never seen　B. Not had seen　C. Not having seen
D. Had not seen

(8) You ( ) sick now if you had gone out in such bad weather.

A. would be　B. were　C. had been　D. would have been

(9) America's wealth gap between middle-income and upper-income families is ( ) on record.

A. most wide　B. widest　C. the wider　D. the most wide

(10) Ms. Brown did not choose any of the three jackets because she found ( ) satisfactory.

A. both of them　B. either of them　C. neither of them
D. none of them

(☆☆◎◎◎)

【3】Read the following passage and answer the questions below.

Teachers are designers. An essential act of our profession is the crafting of curriculum and learning experiences to meet specified purposes. We are also designers of assessments to diagnose student needs to guide our teaching and to enable us, our students, and others (parents and administrators) to determine whether we have achieved our goals.

[①] people in other design professions, such as architecture, engineering, or graphic arts, designers in education must be mindful of their audiences. Professionals in these fields are strongly [②]. The effectiveness of their designs corresponds to whether they have accomplished explicit goals for specific end-users. Clearly, students are our primary clients, given that the effectiveness of curriculum, assessment, and instructional designs is ultimately determined by their achievement of desired learnings. We can think of our designs, then, as [③]. Our courseware is designed to make learning more effective, just as computer software is intended to make its users more productive.

As in all the design professions, standards inform and shape our work. The software developer works to maximize user-friendliness and to reduce bugs that impede results. The architect is guided by building codes, customer budget, and neighborhood aesthetics. The teacher as designer is similarly [④]. We are not free to teach any topic we choose by any means. Rather, we are guided by national, state, district, or institutional standards that specify what students should know and be able to do. These standards provide a useful framework to help us [⑤] teaching and learning priorities and guide our design of curriculum and assessments. In addition to [⑥] standards, we must also factor in the needs of our many and varied students when designing learning experiences. For example, diverse student interests, developmental levels, large classes, and previous achievements must always shape our thinking about the learning activities, assignments, and assessments.

Yet, as the old adage reminds us, in the best designs form follows function. In other words, all the methods and materials we use are shaped by a clear conception of the vision of desired results. That means that we must be able to state with clarity what the student should understand and be able to do as a result of any plan and irrespective of any constraints we face.

You probably know the saying, "If you don't know exactly where you are headed, then any road will get you there." The point is a serious one in education. We are quick to say what things *we* like to teach, what activities *we* will do, and what kinds of resources *we* will use; but without clarifying the desired results of our teaching, how will we ever know whether our designs are appropriate or arbitrary? How will we distinguish merely [⑦] learning from *effective* learning? More pointedly, how will we ever meet content standards or arrive at hard-won student understandings [⑧] we think through what those goals imply for the learner's activities and achievements?

⑨Good design, then, is not so much【 A 】as it is【 B 】【 C 】?

(1) Choose the best word or phrase for [①]−[⑧] among from the

four alternatives for each blank.

① A. Except for　　B. For example
　C. In addition to　　D. Like

② A. client-centered　　B. designer-centered
　C. student-oriented　　D. work-oriented

③ A. income　　B. hardware
　C. outcome　　D. software

④ A. condemned　　B. constrained
　C. conserved　　D. compromised

⑤ A. acknowledge　　B. disregard
　C. identify　　D. ignore

⑥ A. external　　B. fluid
　C. individual　　D. private

⑦ A. interesting　　B. practical
　C. sensible　　D. useful

⑧ A. because　　B. though
　C. unless　　D. while

(2) in the underlined sentence ⑨, arrange [1]～[3] below in the most appropriate order within 【 A 】～【 C 】.

[1] about learning to be more thoughtful and specific

[2] about our purposes and what they imply

[3] about gaining a few new technical skills

(☆☆☆◎◎◎)

【４】Read the following passage and answer the questions below.

How are understanding and knowledge related? The standard still leaves the relationship murky in the phrase "As a basis for understanding this concept ..." Is understanding simply a more complex form of knowledge, or is it something separate from but related to content knowledge?

Making matters worse is our tendency to use the terms *know, know how,* and *understand* interchangeably in everyday speech. Many of us would say that we "know" that Newton's Laws predict the motion of objects. And we may say we "know how" to fix our car and "understand" how to fix our car as if the two statements expressed the same idea. Our usage has a developmental aspect, too: What we once struggled to "understand" we say we now "know." ①<u>The implication is that something that once required a chain of reasoning to grasp hold of no longer does: We just "see it."</u>

Mindful of our tendency to use the words *understand* and *know* interchangeably, what worthy conceptual distinctions should we safeguard in talking about the difference between knowledge and understanding? Figure 1 presents some useful distinctions between the terms.

John Dewey (1933) summarized the idea most clearly in *How We Think*. [②]:

Figure 1

Knowledge Versus Understanding

Knowledge	Understanding
・The facts ・A body of coherent facts ・I know something to be true [ ]	・The meaning of the facts ・The "theory" that provides coherence and meaning to those facts ・I understand why it is, what makes it knowledge [ ]

To grasp the meaning of a thing, an event, or a situation is to see it in its relations to other things: to see how it operates or functions, what consequences follow from it, what causes it, what uses it can be put to. In contrast, what we have called the brute thing, the thing without meaning to us, is something whose relations are not grasped.... The relation of means-consequence *is the center and heart of all understanding.*

(1) Translate the underlined sentence ① into Japanese.

(2) Choose the best sentence for [②] from the alternatives below.

A. Understanding is becoming able to see how things are interconnected

B. Understanding is being able to contrast it with other related things

C. Understanding is to know what does not have any meaning to us

D. Understanding is to grasp meanings of consequences of one's own actions

(3) Classify ③〜⑧ into two groups in Figure 1's columns, Knowledge and Understanding, in accordance with the content of the text. Write "K" for "Knowledge" and Write "U" for "Understanding."

③ I can describe the subject in nuanced, sophisticated detail

④ I judge when to and when not to use what I know

⑤ I can say the answers automatically

⑥ Correct or not correct

⑦ Fallible, in-process theories

⑧ Verifiable claims

(☆☆☆◎◎◎)

【5】Read the following passage and answer the questions below.

As I edge towards middle age, I've noticed many of my parents' generation think social networking is something that, due to some ①<u>ineffable</u> generational divide, they are simply incapable of understanding. That attitude comes with a lingering fear that, should they try, they will somehow get it wrong. They will say the wrong thing, do the wrong thing or behave in a way that will cause the mass rolling of eyes and the loud groaning of "Dad!" But here's the first secret of social media: everybody feels this way.

Yet the generational divides we employ to dictate how we use technology are actually not generational at all. I recently found myself at a dinner with a young actor who was muttering darkly that her work as a producer demands that she join Twitter, but she consistently feels like she doesn't have anything witty to say. 【 A 】 It's the same resistance I hear from boomers, with the significant exception that my parents' *cohorts have somehow convinced themselves that age is the barrier, rather than the vagaries of individual taste.

Here's the second secret of social media: everybody uses it for more or less the same reasons. 【　B　】 We talk about this kind of contact like it's some old-fogey activity, but it is exactly why younger people use social media. The truth is most people use social media to gently keep tabs on one another, to see how those they care about are doing without needing to ring them up on the phone every night. It's true that the communications of 15-year-olds often end up being more dramatic than those of 30-year-olds, 50-year-olds or 75-year-olds. ②The more seniors that join, the more relevant the conversations taking place on these sites will become for their contemporaries.

And this is the last secret of social media: everyone gets to use it their own way. 【　C　】 Turns out, there isn't. Even inveterate users ③take to some online activities over others. Personally, I talk a lot on Twitter but shun Facebook. Plenty of people use both. Many younger users are moving to Instagram. And some people post nothing but are avid consumers of social media as readers. Social media companies seldom promote the idea of mere readership, since they'd rather see people pumping their networks full of pictures and posts, but there's no rule against ④being a fly on the wall. It's a fine way to engage.

We're quick to forget that the web wasn't invented by 13-year-olds; it was created by today's seniors. I'd never try foisting social networks on those with no interest or with an inherent aversion to frivolous twittering (hi, Dad). But ⑤don't (divides / let / of age / off / put / the talk / you). There's nothing to stop boomers from reclaiming the network their own generation created.

*cohort　同年代に生まれた人たち

(1) Substitute the underlined word ① with the best choice from the four alternatives below.

A. exceptional　　B. indescribable　　C. sacred

D. marvelous

(2) Translate the underlined sentence ② in the text into Japanese.

(3) Choose the most appropriate place, from 【　A　】～【　C　】, to put each of the sentences [1]～[3] below.

[1] Newcomers—younger and older—who worry about "getting it right" are assuming there's a right way to get it.

[2] I am also surrounded by peers who find Facebook insufferable and use it only when they need to look someone up or answer a message.

[3] Older generations often sign up to stay in touch with children, nieces, nephews and grandchildren.

(4) Substitute the underlined phrase ③ with the best choice from the four alternatives below.

A. avoid　　B. prefer　　C. recommend　　D. manipulate

(5) Choose the most appropriate answer to explain the meaning of the underlined phrase ④.

A. to behave as if you are much more important than anyone else in the room

B. to like to meet and talk to new people and make friends with anyone

C. to be able to watch what happens without other people knowing that you are there

D. to wish that you had someone else's possessions, abilities, qualities that you don't have

(6) Put the words from the underlined part ⑤ in the text in the correct order.

(7) According to the text, which of the following is true?

A. Many people in the author's parents' generation think they should try social networking, but they fear that they might make a serious mistake in using the technology.

B. The author says that older people feet like they don't have anything to post because they don't have anything witty to say, unlike younger people.

C. In a certain way, the communication styles of younger people are different from those of older people, but people of both generations use social media for the same reasons.

D. It's not absurd for younger people to become the dominant users of the social media networks because the networks were created by people of their own generations.

(☆☆☆☆◎◎◎)

【6】Read the following passage and answer the questions below.

American language expert Robert Kaplan studied different cultural thought patterns in the mid 1960s. He helped English language teachers understand the differences between English rhetoric and that of Arabic, Chinese, Japanese, Spanish, and Russian.

English speakers prefer a 'linear' style, which has one main idea. The speaker supports that idea with details or arguments, and then closes the talk by restating the idea. In other cultures, however, speakers may bring in other ideas before returning to the main point.

Charles LeBeau says some of his students prepare a speech without thinking of the main idea.

"Sometimes the bigger problem is the point that they want to make is not clear. They are not thinking clearly about "What is the key point in my presentation? And how do I want to say that, where do I want to say it?"

For presentations in English, the best time to make that point is at the beginning. Speakers should make a plan to present their ideas in the order that is common in English rhetoric. When we write our ideas down without such a plan, they are not clear and our presentation will not be well organized.

"I think they prepare the presentation kind of as a stream of consciousness activity, then finally at the end of this process they figure out, oh, what do I want to say, what is the key point in this? And it ends up being at the end of the presentation."

Professor LeBeau says he often sees the engineers he works with give a lot of technical information in their speeches. They want to tell everything they know. But, the audience may have trouble understanding which information is related to the speaker's main point. We can tell the story with facts and numbers, if they help, and then repeat the point.

"In an English language presentation, what we try and do is make it more linear. And by that, I mean, it's more of a story—we use data, and we use evidence, we use numbers, but only to help us tell the story more clearly."

Five tips for preparing your presentation

Preparing the story message helps speakers give a successful presentation. Professor LeBeau gives these five tips for academic presentations, such as those given at professional conferences.

1. Understand the difference between a title and a topic. A topic is general, but a title is more specific. Make sure the title explains the benefit of your subject.
2. Provide an image for those who are not experts in your subject. Explain how your research relates to other fields.
3. Work on transitions (linking words or phrases) as you go from image to image. These should make the connections between your ideas clear. Professor LeBeau says transitions serve as bridges to each new image.
4. [①] What questions might they have about each image? Prepare an extra image that would help explain the most difficult question you expect.
5. [②] At most conferences, there is a time limit. It is disrespectful to take more than your share of the time. Cut your presentation to fit the time you are permitted.

Professor LeBeau understands the difficulty many students of public speaking face.

"Learning a new culture for presentation is really tough for many people, as it is with all language learning. Presentation, of course, is a part of language learning. There's culture in everything we do in English, as well as in presentation."

Using these tips for improving your presentations in English should help make the process easier.

(1) What is a "linear style" presentation like? Explain it <u>within 50 Japanese letters</u>.

(2) According to the text, what kinds of presentations in English are thought to be failures? Explain them <u>within 50 Japanese letters</u>.

(3) Add <u>one sentence in English</u> in each of the blanks ([①] and [②]) to complete the fourth and fifth tips.

(☆☆☆◎◎◎)

【7】Read the following passage and answer the questions below.

I am trained to be a critic. The summer after I graduated, I had a temporary job teaching. I lectured my writing students on the power of words: "Beware the thoughtless adjective, the vague pronoun."

I drew *X*'s over entire paragraphs. I pointed at their pages and said, "Imagine you're the editor who pulled this from the slush pile. Is there a glaring typo in the first paragraph? Bam! Rejected."

A motley collection of high school students stared back at me blankly. They enjoyed writing and saw no need for histrionics.

One week, I rescheduled my classes to attend a friend's wedding in Hawaii. After a three-hour bus ride, I had tangled hair but no brush, so I ran my fingers through the worst of the knots and walked into the ceremony.

The groom's brother, James, was single and attractive and didn't care that my hair was a mess. We spun around on the lawn, and afterward he held my hand on a bench overlooking the bay and told me I was beautiful.

We stayed up all night, talking and kissing. In the morning, James began his journey to the Big Island, though he would soon be returning home to North Carolina. I caught a flight to New York. *just a wedding-night fling*, I thought.

Then the postcards arrived.

"I can't stop thinking about you, Aloha!" James wrote, but the handwriting was scrawled, and the spelling was terrible. *He cares*, I thought, *but not enough to proofread.*

To an aspiring writer proofreading is the hallmark of caring. I cannot write an email without subjecting my words to tedious revision. The day before my 30th birthday, I received an email from James. I opened it to see a photo he had taken of a flower bouquet on a black lava beach. He had written "Love and beauty, To: Jessy From. James"

The picture was lovely. The text, however, had irregular punctuation. Not to mention he had misspelled my name.

Despite these mistakes, I wrote him back immediately. The man had sent me flowers! I told him the next day was my birthday. He responded "Happy birthday! Hauoli maka hiki hAu."

I'm no expert on the Hawaiian language, but I'm pretty sure they don't insert random capitalization into the middle of words.

His next email disarmed me: "Aloha, Jessie I cried on plane, I had to leavy seat. I love Hawaii."

OK, so *leavy* isn't a word, but he had got my name right. And he wanted to see me again.

"As you must feel from my letters," he wrote, "I adore u bc of your smiles while we danced, your songs, voice, body, and beauty. Let's meet in between Southport and Brooklyn, someplace, there must be a sweet place?"

So romantic, right? If only I could get over that syntax.

I read a few of the messages to my friends and asked them to tell me the truth: was my new suitor sincere?

Give it a try, they said.

Still, I couldn't silence my inner critic. How could a man I hardly knew be so into me? Men in New York could spout a few good pick-up lines, but only James could write a messed-up sentence that got my heart pounding: "To nite

I can not sleep so I will play songs for Jessie, about Jessie, my inspiration."

I flew to North Carolina. For three days, we shucked oysters, played the guitar, and surfed. When I got a nosebleed, he held me in his arms and raised me above the waves.

A few months later, James and I moved to Hawaii. We were married on the Big Island in 2008.

I have a job teaching English at a local school, where I argue for the importance of proofreading and revision. But whenever I get a text from James, my heart starts to pound, and it's hard to remember the rules.

(1) Summarize this story within 50 Japanese letters.

(2) What lessons about foreign language education do you draw from this story? Express your own ideas <u>in approximately 150 words in English.</u>

(☆☆☆◎◎◎)

解答・解説

【中学校】

【1】(1) B (2) C (3) C (4) B (5) A (6) D (7) B (8) C (9) A (10) D

〈解説〉(1) have＋目的語＋過去分詞で「～してもらう」という使役の意味になる。進行形，原形，不定詞はあてはまらない。have a table reserved for＋人／何人で「(～人)の食事の席を予約している」。
(2) 「2人の人に聞いた」とあるので，「彼らのどちらも～ない」のneither of themがあてはまる。多人数に聞いた，という場合であれば，Aのnoneになる。接続詞butで逆接となるので，肯定の意味のBとDは不適。 (3) Rickが夜中すぎまで帰らなかったことの結果として両親が心配したのであるから，「そのことで両親は心配した」という非制限用法になりCが正答。関係詞that，what，why，howでは，非制限用法を用いることはできない。　(4)　but she hasn't finished it yet「しかしまだ読み終わっていない」とあるので，A「読んでいない，読んだことがない」，C「(貸す前に)読んではいなかった」，D「読んでしまった」は不適。　(5)　空欄直後のafter以下は副詞句なので，副詞のevenのみあてはまる。他の選択肢はいずれも接続詞なので，後にくるのは節(主語＋動詞)でなければならない。　(6)　Aのandは前後の文脈によっては不可能ではないが，この1文だけで意味のわかる文としては苦しい。Bのduringは前置詞なので後に名詞あるいは名詞句がくるが，問題文では節がきているので不適。Cのinsteadは副詞なので，and，butなどの接続詞を伴わないと，2文が互いの関係を明示しないまま並んでしまい不適。正解はDで，問題文は「彼女が日本向けの航空券を購入するまでは会合のスケジュールを立てられない」という意味になる。

(7)　(be) comparable to ～「～に匹敵する。～相当の」で，someone以下は「現在いる技術者に匹敵する経験と専門的知識を持つ誰か」となる。Aのcomparablyは副詞でtoを伴う形にはならない。Cのcomparedだとhas comparedで動詞の現在完了となり「経験を比較した人」という意味となるが，and以下が意味を成さなくなる。Dでは動詞hasとcompareが併存し，文法的に不可解。　(8)　she以下の節の動詞が主節の動詞saidにより時制の一致を受けて過去形になって，be going awayはwas going awayに，will call meは，would call meになる。

(9)　phone chainには「携帯ストラップ」の意味もあるが，ここでは「電話連絡網」。with each other で「互いに」。Bでは「別のもう一方と」，Dでは「他のもう1人と」という意味になり，「社員相互で」という文意と一致しない。Cはotherに冠詞がなく複数でもなく，with otherというかたちは文法的に不可。　(10)　eachは単数名詞を修飾するので，each menとなるAは不適。副詞almostが名詞menを修飾するかたちのBも不適。menは可算名詞なので，Cのmuchで修飾するのは不適。

【2】(1) C　(2) A　(3) C　(4) B　(5) D　(6) C
(7) A　(8) D　(9) B　(10) A　(11) C　(12) D
(13) A　(14) B　(15) C

〈解説〉(1) on behalf ofで「～のために」の意味で，manages以下は「地域のチャリティ活動のために資金を供給する」となる。A「～に敬意を表して」，B「～を探し求めて」，D「～と一致して。～に従って」。
(2) cut out「切り抜く」，set out「出発する」，let out「表に出す」，put out「明かりを消す」。英文は「取っておきたい広告があったので除外した」という意味。 (3) take ～ into account「～を考慮に入れる」，take ～ for granted「～を当然と思う」，take ～ seriously「～を真摯に受け止める」。英文は「TKMストアは買い物客の来店を当然とは考えず，店のスタッフは常に親切な対応をしてくれる」という意味。
(4) from scratch「一から，最初から」。英文は「K&J建築事務所では標準的量産品のコンセプトを使用せず，常に一から構造デザインを行う」という意味。 (5) draw up「文書等を作成する」，hang up「中断する。電話を切る」，show up「姿を見せる。現れる」，wrap up「包む。要約する」。「基調演説を要約した」でD。(2)，(3)，(5)に出題されているような句動詞はすべて，非常によく使われるものであり，ここに示した語義も一例で，他にいろいろな意味があるので，記憶があやふやな場合はよく復習しておいてほしい。 (6) 「地域の(　　)は午前中の小雨を予報した」という文脈なので，C「気象学者」が適当。A「見物人」，B「検察官」，D「医師」。 (7) 「街の西の区域」でAのdistrictが適当。 (8) developing new drugs「新薬の開発」とhigh cost of research「リサーチに要する高いコスト」から，D「障害」が適当。A「装置。意匠」，B「解答」，C「代理人。代用品」。 (9) her students以下は「学生に卒業論文を数回修正させた」の意味なのでB「修正する。変更する」が適当。A「混合する。合併する」，C「規定する。(薬を)処方する」，D「ほのめかす」。 (10) have以下は「20日の有給休暇をとる機会を保証している」の意味になる。 (11) Cを入れて「多様な国際的従業員」とするのが適当。A「緊急の」，B「切迫した」，D「厳正な」。

(12)　who以下の文脈から，Dを入れて「一番好きな趣味」とするのが適当。A「記事。品物」，B「試写。下見」，C「運動選手」。

(13)　career prospects「職業上の成功」。B「責務」，C「関心事」，D「傾向」。　(14)「娘と息子は」なのでB「それぞれ」を入れる。A「すっかり。徹底的に」，C「確かに」，D「季刊で。年4期に分けて」。

(15)　Cを入れてvirtually unchanged「事実上変化がない」として，that以下は「故郷が事実上まったく変化がないことに驚いた」という意味になる。

【3】(1)　tackle　(2)　B　(3)　could save 23 million lives by investing that money in healthcare　(4)　A　(5)　D　(6)　C

〈解説〉(1)　address「取り組む」の同義語には他に，cope (with)，manage，maneuver，treatなどがある。tackleは最後の段落に登場している。

(2)「深刻な経済的不安定とひどい社会的不公正」でB。A「歳入」，C「最低賃金の引き上げ」，D「経済の繁栄」。　(3)　③の直前までの「世界の富豪にかけられる税のたった1.5%」が名詞句で主語。続いて述部could saveがくるとまず推測し，「救う」の目的語として23 million livesを続ける。investing that moneyのかたまりと，その目的語となるin healthcareのかたまりを推定し，前後をbyで結ぶ。　(4)　④を含む英文は「その金は，世界中の貧困および人道的危機と闘うために世界中の寄贈者一人一人から寄せられた1ドル1ドルの総額より多いのである」となる。B「貧富の差の拡大をはかる」，C「経済的不安定と貧困の原因となる」，D「不平等と経済危機を持続させる」。　(5)　consensusは「総意」。A「判断基準。尺度」，B「提言。発言」，C「主導権。独創力」，D「意見の一致。同意」。　(6)　A「億万長者の増加」，B「富の減少」，C「広がる不平等性」，D「政情不安定」で，本問のテーマとしてはCが適切。

【4】(1)　D　(2)　C　(3)　B　(4)　A　(5)　B　(6)　C

〈解説〉(1)　with no ～はwithout ～と同義で，「～なしに」。Aのforは理由

を表す接続詞なので，後に文がこなければならない。For there was no TV in those days, ～であれば可。　(2)「洞穴の内側には，何年もの間に子供たちによって描かれた(　　)」という文脈なので，C「落書き」が適当。A「徳。善行」，B「打撃。(鳥の)羽ばたき」，D「孵化。昇降口」。　(3) 英文は「Twainの幼少時代には，Hannibalはまだ奴隷制の残る典型的な田舎町であった」の意味。したがって，奴隷制や黒人の存在に最初に触れている箇所の前後に入ると推測し，「彼の家や親類の家で働く黒人奴隷は…」という文の続くBが適当。　(4)「たとえその言葉が今日の標準では差別的であるとみなされたとしても」に続く箇所なので，「当時の現実を伝えるために，それら(の言葉)を使用することが必要だった」とするAが適当。　(5) A「偏見」，B「人格」，C「攻撃」，D「不一致」。本文最後の1文のone of以下は「小説の中で，黒人の登場人物に(　　)を与えた最初の白人作家のひとり」という文脈なのでBが適当。　(6) Aは第4段落に同内容の言及がある。Bは第6段落の後半と，Dは第4段落最後の部分と内容が一致する。Cは第8段落の内容と一致しない。

【5】(1) D　(2) D　(3) B　(4) A

〈解説〉(1) 第2段落のThe countryside was …以下に「渡り鳥で有名な土地で，春から秋には渡り鳥を見に観光客がはるばるやってくる」との記述があり，Dと一致する。　(2) 第3段落に，原因不明の病気が鶏や牛，羊の群れに，そして住民の間で蔓延する様子が書かれており，Dと内容が一致する。　(3) 最後から3番目の段落に，「何らかの魔法や敵の攻撃がこの打ちひしがれた世界での生命の再生を沈黙させたわけではない。人々が自らの行動によって，それを引き起こしたのである」とあり，Bと一致する。　(4) B，C，Dいずれも本文に描かれた内容が実世界でも起こる，という点についての文だが，現在完了あるいは過去形で「既成事実」として書いている点で，最後から2番目の段落の「私(筆者)は，ここに描いた不幸をすでに経験した，という地域を知っているわけではない」という記述と矛盾する。「彼女(筆者)の想像上の世界での厄災と同じタイプの被害を，実際の社会の多くが経験するかもしれない」とするAが適切。

【６】(1)　A school trip (A pre-graduation study tour も可) gives students a good chance (opportunity も可) to broaden their view and connect their knowledge (what they learned at school も可) with real-world(life) experience.

(2)　Even though most people wish to be tolerant, people have difficulty in accepting differences.

〈解説〉(1)　英作文問題の訳語や表現は唯一のものではないので，知っている表現の中で自信をもって使用できるものを使えばよい。日本語の文を英語に置き換える場合最も重要なのは主語と述部の抜き出しと，文型の決定であり，元の文の述語を正しく把握することが残りの部分の表現や形も決定する。英語の文章を多く読み，英語の自然なリズムを身に付けることが大事である。　(2)「そうありたい」で始まる文の英訳なので，パラグラフの一部を抜き出して訳す問題であるということを念頭に，「そう」の部分が何を意味するかをきちんと表現して書くことが，この問題のポイントとなっている。「そう」は「寛容で，他者を受け入れる態度」を指しているので，generousやbroad-mindedでもよいだろう。「排他的」はexclusiveという語もあるが，本問の場合「グループから異分子を排除する」といった意味合いよりも「自分と他者といった人間関係」について述べているので，解答例では下線部直前の「意見の違いを認めること」が困難になる，という表現を用いている。

【７】Active Learning differs from Lecture－Style classroom activities in many ways. In the case of Active Learning, teachers support heuristic learning, problem resolution in group discussions, and group work to help students advance their learning autonomously. Through these methods, students are expected to cultivate logical thinking skills and abilities to seek solutions to problems. In addition, learners are expected to use their experience, based on fundamental knowledge, to expand their thinking. Using linguistic activities, students exchange their opinions and learn deeply. Active Learning enhances students' motivation to keep learning throughout their lives.　(92 words)

〈解説〉教育用語についての解説や実例，それについての考えを英語で書く問題は，例年出題されている。今回は教育法というくくりの中でも比較的大きな概念を扱っているが，「ディベート」「シャドーイング」などのより具体的な指導法・勉強法について，あるいはT-Tなどの制度上の方法論について問われる場合もある。具体的かつ理解しやすい表現で説明できるよう，教室での活動をイメージして自分なりの考えをまとめておく必要がある。なお，文部科学省ではアクティブ・ラーニングを「課題の発見と解決に向けて主体的·協働的に学ぶ学習」と定義しているので確認しておこう。

【高等学校】

【1】(1)　C　(2)　A　(3)　C　(4)　B　(5)　D　(6)　B　(7)　D　(8)　A　(9)　C　(10)　D

〈解説〉(1)　for no one expected it「というのも，誰もそれを予測していなかったから」とあるので，「驚かせた」のCが適切。A「予想した」，B「話しかけた」，D「上がった。向上した」。　(2)「熱心な提唱者」でA。B「偽善者」，C「君主」，D「出願者」。　(3)　whatから空欄部分までの大意は「地球上の石油が(　　)しまった時何が起きるか」でC「枯渇した」が適当。A「占領された」，B「減少した」，D「やわらいだ」。(4)　発言の大意は「第二言語能力は，当大学院に入学する全学生にとっての(　　)である」でB「必須事項」を入れる。A「補助の」，C「余分の」，D「もっともらしい。口のうまい」。　(5)　the handwriting expert以下は「筆跡鑑定者はそれ(身代金要求のメモ)が被疑者によって書かれたと(　　)ことができた」でD「実証する」を入れる。A「慎む。控える」，B「複写する」，C「強要する。金銭を取り上げる」。
(6)　had been以下は「その記者の，誤解を招くような記事によって

(　　)られた」でB「歪める」を入れる。A「崇拝する」，C「ほのめかす」，D「宣言する」。　(7)　she (　　) her earlier statements「彼女は前の証言と(　　)」なのでD「食い違ったことを言った」を入れる。A「抱きしめた」，B「称賛した」，C「尋問した」。　(8)　空欄部分までの意味は「交通はひどく(　　)」でA「混乱した」を入れる。B「溶けた」，C「捨てられた」，D「解放された」。　(9)　セミコロン以下は「その弁護士を殺害しようとの(　　)企て」でC「意図的な」を入れる。A「叙述の」，B「敗北主義者の」，D「元気のない」。　(10)　英文の大意は「こんなに美しい夕日は滅多に見たことがない」。正答の副詞rarelyを強調するために前に出し，SVが倒置している点に注意。強調がなければI have rarely seen such a ～となる。A「偶然」，B「昔は」，C「頻繁に」。

【2】(1)　B　　(2)　A　　(3)　D　　(4)　C　　(5)　D　　(6)　B
(7)　C　　(8)　A　　(9)　B　　(10)　D

〈解説〉(1)　suggest thatに続く節の動詞は，原則として原形になる。現在形ではなく原形なので，三人称単数現在形につくべき「s」はつかず，Bが正答。　(2)「雨が降り出した」という過去の一時点まで，その時点よりさらに前の30分間について述べているので「過去完了」で表現する。現在完了は「今まで」の継続的時間内に起きた事について述べる表現なので，「雨が降ってきたその時まで」とする本問にはあてはまらない。　(3)　誰かについて，「話しやすい人。親しみやすい人」と言う場合，その人に「対して」話すわけなので easy to talk to (someone)と，toが必要。　(4)　Butterが主語なので「作る」ではなく，「作られる」と受動態にしなくてはならないため，唯一のbe動詞であるCが適当。　(5)　be made to ～で「～させられる」の意味。使役動詞でも受動態になると，原形ではなく不定詞がくるので注意。

(6)　I hope以下の節はa manを修飾するものなので，人を表す先行詞に続き主格を表す関係代名詞whoを入れるのが適当。　(7)「一目では，彼女だと気づかなかった」を導く「長い事会っていなかったので」の部分を選択する問題。選択肢のどれにも主語がないので分詞構文と考える。分詞構文の否定形は，Not ～ing, …であるからCが正答。
(8)　if節が仮定法過去完了なのでDにしたいところだが，nowとあるので「あの時出かけていたなら，今頃は病気をしているところだ」で，Aのwould be sickとなる。「寒い中出かけていたら，あの時病に倒れていたかもしれない」と今考えている，という場合であれば，もちろんwould have been sickとなる。　(9)　最上級＋on recordで「記録に残る中で最高の」という意味になる。wideは2音節なので，最上級はmost wideではなくwidestとなる。　(10)　both，either，neitherいずれも2者のなかでの比較であり，問題文はany of the three jacketsなので，noneしかあてはまらない。

【3】(1)　①　D　②　A　③　D　④　B　⑤　C　⑥　A　⑦　A　⑧　C　(2)　A　3　B　1　C　2

〈解説〉(1)　①　文冒頭で「教師はデザイナーである」と言っており，教師の仕事をデザイナーになぞらえて書いているので，「他のデザイン分野のデザイナー同様に」と考えてDを入れる。　②　直前の1文に「教職におけるデザイナーは観客に留意しなければならない」とあるので，「顧客を中心においた」のAが適当。　③　教育は内面を育てるデザインと考えられるので，softwareのDを入れるのが適当。A「収入」，C「支出」はここの文脈とは無関係。　④　続く文に「私たちは教える主題の選択や指導方法について自由ではない」とあるので，「束縛されている」のBが適当。　⑤　空欄を含む一文の前半は「これらの基準は教え，学ぶ際の優先順位を(　　)のに役立つ」でC「明確にする」を入れるのが適当　⑥　ここまでで「国家，地域，地区，組織によって規定される基準」について述べてきたので，それを受けた「外的基準」のA。　⑦　merelyとあるので，直前のappropriateとarbitraryの対比に対応するものを選択する。appropriateは*effective* learningに対応するので，arbitraryと対応する語としてmerely interesting「単に面白いだけのもの」とするA。　⑧「学習者の目標を考えることをしないで，どうやって私たちは基準を満たすことができるだろうか？」(学習者の最終目標を意識して教えない限り，必要な基準を満足に満たすことはできないだろう)と考え，Cを入れる。　(2)　not so much X as Yで「Xというよりは Yだ」。「いくつかの専門的技術を得ることというより」で，Aには3が，「私達の目的と，それが暗示するものについて，より思慮深く具体的であることを学ぶことである。」となるように，Bに1，Cに2となる。

【４】(1)　ここで含意されているのは，かつては手がかりを得るために一連の推論を必要としていた何かが，もはやそうではなく，ただ「それとわかる」ということである。　(2)　A　(3)　③　U　④　U　⑤　K　⑥　K　⑦　U　⑧　K

〈解説〉(1)　that once ～ hold ofの節はsomethingを修飾する形容詞句で，これを脇において下線部①を見ると，The implication is that something no longer does「ここで含意されているのは，何かが，もはやそうはしない，ということだ」，という比較的シンプルなSVC構造だということがわかる。doesは小さなthat節の中のrequiredが助動詞で置き換えられたものなので「もはや必要とされない」と訳してもよいが，解答例のようにそのまま「もはやそうではない」と訳しても十分意味が通る。(2)　B「他の関連事項」，C「私たちに何の意味もないこと」，D「人自身の行動の結果」はともに，「知る事と理解する事」の議論にはあまり関係がない。正解はA「理解(する事)とはいかに物事が相互に連結しているかがわかるようになることである」。　(3)　Understandingのグループには，③I can describe in detail，④I judge when to and when not to use，⑦in-process theoriesといった，「推論による内容把握」を表現しているキーフレーズがある。

【５】(1)　B　(2)　利用する年配の人が多ければ多いほど，これらのサイトで行われる会話の内容は彼らの同世代の人たちにとって，より関わりが深いものになるだろう。　(3)　A　2　B　3　C　1

(4)　B　　(5)　C　　(6)　let the talk of age divides put you off
(7)　C

〈解説〉(1)　ineffableは「言葉では言い表せない」の意。Bが同義。A「例外的な」，C「聖なる」，D「素晴らしい」。　(2)　contemporariesは名詞でここでは「同世代の人々」の意味。the more ～, the more …の構文で「～すればするほど…だ」。後の節の主語がthe conversations taking place on these sitesと長いが，形容詞句を脇におくと，The more seniors that join, the more relevant the conversation will become for them「年配者がより多く利用するほど，会話は彼らにとってより関係の深いものになるだろう」という基本構造がつかみやすいだろう。まず構文をきちんと把握することが日本語訳のポイントである。　(3)　A　空欄直前の「一緒に食事をした若い人がTwitterで洒落たことが言えない，と冴えない表情で嘆いていた」に関連して，「Facebookには我慢できないと感じ，他の人にコメントするくらいしか利用しない人がまわりにたくさんいる」とする2が適当。　B　空欄に続く文に「私たちはこういう交流を時代遅れな行動，と言うが」とあり，「年配者が子どもや孫とコンタクトを取るためにソーシャルメディアを利用する」とする3についての文とわかる。　C　空欄直前のto use it their own wayと1のthere's a right wayが呼応している。「始めるときは，何か正当な使い方があると思って始めるが実はそうではなく，決まった使い方もないし，みなそれぞれのやり方で使っている」という一連の説明の一部。
(4)　take toは「(人・場所・考えなど)を好きになる」で，同義となるのはB。A「避ける」，C「推奨する」，D「操る」。　(5)　a fly on the wallは「人に気付かれずに観察する人」の意味の成句なので，説明文としてはCが適当。　(6)　語群の直前がdon'tなので，続いて動詞原形がくると予測できるが，let，putの2つがあるので，まずは選択肢の中でかたまりを作る。dividesはここでは名詞で「分割。分裂。意見の相違」で，文脈からage divides「いろんな世代的相違」と考える。putはoffがあるのでput you offというかたまりを考える。残りのletを文の動詞と置くと，Don't let … put you off「…があなたに躊躇させるのを許すな」というおおまかな形が決まる。あとはthe talk of age divides「年齢の相違についての話」というかたまりがつかめれば構文ができる。

(7)　Aのusing the technologyは文中に言及がない。B のthey don't have anything witty to sayは年配者ではなく，第2段落2文目に若い俳優の言葉として引用されているものである。Dのnetworks were created by people of their own generationsは，最後の段落の1文目it was created by today's seniorsと不一致。「コミュニケーションのスタイルは世代により異なるが，ソーシャルメディアを活用する理由はどちらの世代でも同じだ」とするCが第3段落の内容と一致する。

【６】(1)　明確な主題を冒頭に述べ，補足情報や論拠でその主題を立証し，発表の最後に再び主題を述べる形式の発表。(49字)　(2)　思いつくまま言葉を述べるせいで主張が明確に伝わらない発表や，情報が多すぎて焦点が伝わりにくい発表。(49字)　(3)　①　Look at each image from the audience's point of view.　②　Rehearse your presentation with a timing device.

〈解説〉(1)　第2段落に"linear style"について最初の言及があるので，その概要を適切な字数に要約した日本語訳とする。　(2)　第5段落に，英語によるプレゼンテーションのよくない例が引かれているので，そこをまとめる。　(3)　Five tips for preparing your presentation「プレゼンテーションを準備する際の5つのヒント」の4つ目は，空欄①に次いで「質問に備える」と言っているので，「聴衆の反応や質問に備えるにはどのような準備あるいは心構えが必要か」についての文が書かれていればよい。5つ目は空欄②の後にthere is a time limitと言っており，また「許された時間を超えそうなら短縮すべきだ」とも言っているので，「時間内に収まるよう練習する」，「時間内に収まるよう編集する」といった主旨で書かれていればよい。

【７】(1)　文書は校正をして誤りを無くす事が重要だが，想いが通じれば問題にならない事もあると感じた英語教師の話。(50字)

(2)　Teaching grammar and vocabulary is very important in language education, for if you speak with inappropriate words, ignoring grammar, you will not be able to make yourself understood at all. But grammar and vocabulary are not the only factors which are important to communicate with others. Grammar and vocabulary are only "tools" for communication. If, in a classroom, a teacher points out a student's grammatical mistakes too rigidly, what would happen? The student might lose his confidence and become afraid of making mistakes, which might make him a quiet student with no more motivations to learn. But if a teacher listens to the student and tries to understand him, he would keep trying to express himself. The teacher can point out the student's mistakes later, without spoiling his speech interrupting him in the middle of it. The most important thing is to motivate the students to communicate in the first place. (151 words)

〈解説〉(1)「文章は校正を重ねて正しいかたちに完成させるべき」および「正しい文でなくても感動を呼び起こすことがあり，それも重要なことである」という2点を盛り込めばよい。筆者の具体的な経験については言及せず，経験から得られた知見をまとめること。要約の問題はおおむね，主要テーマを抜き出し，まとめ，文字数が多すぎれば重要度の低いものから削る，という作業となる。　(2)　設問は「この物語から，外国語教育についてのどんな教訓を引き出したか，自分の考えを述べよ」。問題文は「誤りのない文章は大事だが，それが問題とならないような，より大切なものがある」という主旨なので，これを無視した「やはり英語教育では誤りのない文章を書き，誤りのない発言を目指すべき」といった内容は避けるべきだろう。なお，「おおよそ150語」とある語数制限について，公開された採点基準では，128～170語を想定しており，部分点が与えられる最低ラインを83語としている。この他，「多面的な視点を備え且つ独自性のある，首尾一貫した主張がある」「主張を効果的に伝える論理的段落構成がある」などの採点基準も示されている。

2015年度　実施問題

【中高共通】

【１】Substitute the underlined phrase with the best alternative from the four choices.

(1) Why should we <u>put up with</u> such terrible noise?

A. accept gladly　B. make unwillingly　C. change suddenly

D. bear without complaining

(2) The two items are <u>much the same</u>.

A. far from equivalent　B. closely involved　C. very similar

D. almost indifferent

(3) They are <u>taking on</u> a new assistant at that company.

A. employing　B. expanding　C. sharing　D. expecting

(4) I can't <u>figure out</u> the math problem.

A. examine　B. solve　C. express　D. share

(☆☆☆◎◎◎)

【２】Choose the one that best completes the sentence from the four alternatives.

(1) For the past few years, the T&J Hotel has offered a morning buffet, (　　) provide its customers with more variety.

A. due to　B. in order to　C. according to　D. owing to

(2) The school cafeteria is not large enough to (　　) all the students at the same time.

A. integrate　B. compromise　C. customize　D. accommodate

(3) Since Michael has a good (　　) of Spanish, many people think he is from Spain.

A. command　B. order　C. skillful　D. speech

(4) The new system allows companies to carry out medical background checks to inquire into the health of their (　　) employees.

A. predicting B. dormant C. foreseeing D. prospective

(5) At a conference today, environment ministers from 25 nations failed to reach a ( ) on how to stop the exploitation in the Antarctic. Environmental groups called it a "dark day" for the Antarctic.

A. consensus B. consistency C. presumption D. proposition

(6) Opinions on the committee are so diverse that ( ) decisions are rarely achieved.

A. anonymous B. continuous C. momentary D. unanimous

(☆☆☆◎◎◎)

【3】Choose the one that best completes the sentence from the four alternatives.

(1) Under the new curriculum, first-year junior high school students ( ) more than 900 hours studying English in class by the time they graduate from high school.

A. spend B. spent C. have spent D. will have spent

(2) I received a letter ( ) an electricity supplier claims they can lower my electric bill if I switch from my current electricity supplier to them.

A. which B. that C. in which D. in that

(3) I had a brother ( ) shopping with.

A. gone B. went C. to go D. going

(4) My wife and I saved ( ) we could to buy an environmentally friendly car.

A. as a lot of money as B. as much money as C. money as a lot as
D. money as much as

(5) To all the audiences' surprise, the quiet girl spoke as if she ( ) much older than her actual age.

A. were B. be C. would be D. has been

(6) No one is allowed to enter that room ( ) they have an ID approved by the police department.

A. however B. whatever C. otherwise D. unless

(7)　(　　) the heavy rain the boat racing event received a lot of support and attracted a great crowd.

A. because　　B. despite　　C. instead of　　D. though

(8)　Daniel (　　) and lost all his money.

A. had been stolen his bag　　B. had stolen his bag

C. had his bag stolen　　D. was stolen his bag

(9)　Of my five friends, one wanted to go shopping, three wanted to go to the theater, and (　　) wanted to bake some cakes.

A. another　　B. other　　C. the another　　D. the other

(10)　Many people criticized him, but he did what (　　).

A. he thought he was right　　B. he thought it was right

C. he thought was right　　D. he was thought right

(☆☆☆◎◎◎)

【４】Read the following passage and answer the questions below.

One sunny September day, Pen-chan, a stuffed penguin from Ishikawa Prefecture, went on an excursion with a stuffed sheep named Hiroshi from Kyoto Prefecture and three other companions. They weren't told where they were going, as the trip was to be a mystery tour.

Ultimately, they enjoyed a bike ride in Yoyogi Park in Tokyo, where they took in the 1964 Tokyo Olympic monument and had pancakes for lunch. In the afternoon, they visited the observatory of the Tokyo Metropolitan Government Office in Shinjuku Ward. Altogether, the tour cost ¥2,000 per animal.

Yes, you read that correctly—①(　　) were traveling, not their owners.

For the last three years, Sonoe Azuma, 38, of Unagi Travel has organized tours targeting stuffed animals. She sometimes posts travelogues and snapshots on Facebook, allowing their owners to experience the trip vicariously.

Azuma got the idea for Unagi Travel by taking her handmade stuffed eel on trips and putting up its travelogue on her blog. The idea was received well among her friends, which eventually led her to launch the travel agency.

She started small, as participants came to her through word of mouth. Lately, the tours have become popular, however, and she organizes a maximum of 10 trips a month.

Destinations include Izumo, Shimane Prefecture; Kamakura, Kanagawa Prefecture; Yokohama and even the United States.

"So far, more than 200 stuffed animals have participated in the trips, and some of them ②(　　) regularly. I would say 40 percent of my business is repeat customers," Azuma said.

Owners send their stuffed animals out on trips for various reasons.

"I want to see and walk around the sights that I viewed through my stuffed animal's journeys someday," said a 51-year-old woman from Saga Prefecture who became reclusive after it became difficult for her to walk due to illness. She said she has changed after having her stuffed animal travel on Azuma's tours, working to rehabilitate her legs, which she was reluctant to do before. She even went shopping all the way to the next prefecture for the first time in several years.

"Seeing my stuffed animal traveling encouraged me. I began to think that I should do what I can do, instead of ③(　　) things that I can't," the woman said.

A severely impaired woman in the Kanto region who uses a wheelchair is a regular participant in Azuma's tours. The woman has seen her stuffed animal walk along narrow roads and stairs, and support other animals in a group photo.

According to Azuma, the woman was so impressed with the animal "④(　　)" that she visited Azuma, although she usually doesn't like to go out.

Azuma said she has received such feedback as: "My family was despondent over losing my father, but the stuffed animal's trip cheered us up, and we now have more conversations at home" and "It was a good opportunity for my son in primary school, who couldn't let his stuffed animal go, to become independent."

Another person said, "I'm worried about changing jobs, but I enjoy interacting with strangers whom I met through my stuffed animal."

According to Ochanomizu University Prof. Nario Ihara, such stuffed animals may fulfill the role of an "imaginary companion."

⑤Imaginary companions are a psychological phenomenon seen often among children. People in this psychological state regard imaginary beings, such as animals and fairies, as friends in their own fantasy world, and talk or play with them to compensate for loneliness. The phenomenon usually disappears as they grow up.

Imaginary companions seem to serve as an intermediary for people to take a next step.

"Making their *alter ego travel acts as a bridge until the owners can actually go into the outer world and interact with others. Stuffed animal tours may serve as a rehearsal for their mental stability," Ihara said.

Azuma ⑥(hopes / for / will / begin / to / a good opportunity / owners / be / her tours / warm communication), rather than just be satisfied with letting their alter egos travel.

"I'm happy if my activities encourage those who can't be positive to take a step forward," Azuma said.

【Notes】 *alter ego　分身

(1)　Choose the most appropriate words from the text for ①(　　) to make a comprehensible sentence.

(2)　What made Ms. Azuma start Unagi travel? Choose the answer from the four alternatives below.

A. She found the stuffed animals' tours would enable owners to experience the trip vicariously.

B. She organized tours targeting stuffed animals and the tours have become popular through word of mouth.

C. She posted travelogue of trips with her stuffed eel on her blog, which gained a good reputation among her friends.

D. She hoped that stuffed animals would be able to encourage their owners to go back into society.

(3) Choose the best answer for ②( ) from the four alternatives below.

A. sign up B. sign over C. sign off D. sign out

(4) Choose the best answer for ③( ) from the four alternatives below.

A. ripping off B. lamenting over C. pulling through

D. indulging in

(5) Choose the best answer for ④( ) from the four alternatives below.

A. to launch a new business

B. being reluctant to go

C. to cheer her up

D. doing what she can't

(6) Translate the underlined sentences ⑤ into Japanese.

(7) Put the words from ⑥( ) in the correct order.

(8) According to the text, which of the following is true?

A. An excursion with stuffed animals inspires their owners to be reclusive.

B. The stuffed animals satisfy their owners by letting them travel.

C. Imaginary companions cause children to become despondent.

D. The stuffed animals' journeys seem to help their owners to be positive.

(☆☆☆◎◎◎)

【中学校】

【1】The following English passage is a part of the speech that Malala Yousafzai delivered at the United Nations Headquarters in 2013. Read the following passage and answer the questions below.

Today, it is an honor for me to be speaking again after a long time. Being here with such honorable people is a great moment in my life.

I don't know where to begin in my speech. I don't know what people will be expecting me to say. But first of all, thank you to God, for whom we all are equal. And thank you to every person who has prayed for my fast recovery and new life. I cannot believe how much love people have shown me. I have received thousands of good-wish cards and gifts from all over the world. Thank you to all of them. Thank you to the children whose innocent words encouraged me. Thank you to my elders whose prayers strengthened me.

Dear brothers and sisters, do remember one thing: Malala Day is not my day. Today is the day of every woman, every boy and every girl who have raised their voice for their rights.

Dear friends, on the 9th of October 2012, the *Taliban shot me on the left side of my forehead. They shot my friends too. They thought that the bullets would silence us. But they failed. And out of that silence came thousands of voices. The terrorists thought that they would change my aims and stop my ambitions, but ①(　　) changed in my life except this: weakness, fear and hopeless died; strength, power and courage was born. I am the same Malala. My ambitions are the same. My hopes are the same. And my dreams are the same.

Dear sisters and brothers, I'm not against anyone. ②(　　) am I here to speak in terms of personal revenge against the Taliban or any other terrorist group. I'm here to speak up for the right of education of every child. I want education for the sons and daughters of the Taliban and all the terrorists and extremists. I do not even hate the Talib who shot me. Even if there is a gun in my hand and he was standing in front of me, I would not shoot him.

Dear sisters and brothers, now it's time to speak up. So today, we call upon the world leaders to change their strategic policies ③(　　) peace and prosperity. We call upon the world leaders that all the peace deals must (　a　) women's and children's rights. A deal that goes against the rights of women is unacceptable.

We call upon all governments to (　b　) free compulsory education all over the world for every child. We call upon all the governments to fight against terrorism and violence, to (a) children from brutality and harm.

We call upon the developed nations to support the expansion of education opportunities for girls in the developing world.

We call upon all the communities to be tolerant; to reject prejudice based on caste, creed, sect, color, religion or gender; to (b) freedom and equality for women so that they can flourish. ④<u>We cannot all succeed when half of us are held back</u>.

We call upon our sisters around the world to (c); to embrace the strength within themselves and realize their full potential.

Dear brothers and sisters, we must not forget that millions of people are suffering from poverty, injustice and ignorance. We must not forget that millions of children are out of school. We must not forget that our sisters and brothers are waiting for a bright, peaceful future.

So let us wage a global struggle against illiteracy, poverty and terrorism. Let us pick up our books and our pens. They are our most powerful weapons. One child, one teacher, one book and one pen can change the world. Education is the only solution. Education first. Thank you.

【Notes】*Taliban　イスラム系武装組織。パシュトー語で「神学生」を意味するTalibの複数形

(1) Answer with the most appropriate word for ①(　　) to make a comprehensible sentence.

(2) Choose the one that best completes ②(　　) from the four alternatives below.

A. In spite of　　B. Either　　C. Neither　　D. Nevertheless

(3) Choose the one that best completes ③(　　) from the four alternatives below.

A. antagonistic to　　B. likely to　　C. regardless of　　D. in favor of

(4) Choose the most appropriate answer for (a)～(c) from the words below. (Each word can only be used once.)

[be brave / prompt / commend / prevent / ensure / be pamper
flatter / corrupt / be courteous / relinquish / be sly / protect]

(5) Translate the underlined sentence ④ into Japanese.

(6) What is the thing that she wants to assert the most in her speech? Explain in 1-2 English sentences.

(☆☆☆◎◎◎)

【２】Translate the underlined sentences into English.

(1) 親離れと子離れ，どちらが難しいだろう。作家の森崎和江さんが「母性とは，抱く強さと同じ強さで放つもの」と書いていたのを思い出す。抱くことだけに一途では駄目らしい。

(2) 言った側は忘れても言われた人の傷は深い。感情を止める堤防が低くなって，たちまち洪水を起こしてしまう。喜怒哀楽の「怒」は大切な感情だが「キレる」のとは違う。

(☆☆☆◎◎◎)

【３】Regarding the selection of teaching materials to comprehensively cultivate communication abilities such as listening, speaking, reading, and writing, what should you take into consideration as an English teacher? Write two points and support your opinions with concrete reasons in approximately 120 words in English.

(☆☆☆◎◎◎)

【高等学校】

【１】Read the following passage and answer the questions below.

When we communicate, we use the language to accomplish some function, such as arguing, persuading, or promising. [①], we carry out these functions within a social context. A speaker will choose a particular way to express his argument not only based upon his intent and his level of emotion, but also on whom he is addressing and ②[his / is / person / relationship / that

/ what / with]. For example, he may be more direct in arguing with his friend than with his employer.

Furthermore, since communication is a process, it is insufficient for students to simply have knowledge of target language forms, meanings, and functions. Students must be able to apply this knowledge in negotiating meaning. ③It is through the interaction between speaker and listener (or reader and writer) that meaning becomes clear. The listener gives the speaker feedback as to whether or not he understands what the speaker has said. In this way, the speaker can revise what he has said and try to communicate his intended meaning again, if necessary.

The most obvious characteristic of the Communicative Approach is that almost everything that is done is done with a communicative intent. Students use the language a great deal through communicative activities such as games, role-plays, and problem-solving tasks.

Activities that are truly communicative, according to Morrow (in Johnson and Morrow 1981), have three features: information gap, choice, and feedback.

An information gap exists when one person in an exchange knows something [④]. If we both know today is Tuesday and I ask you, "What is today?" and you answer, "Tuesday," our exchange isn't really communicative.

In communication, the speaker has a choice of what she will say and how she will say it. If the exercise is tightly controlled so that students can only say something in one way, the speaker has no choice and the exchange, therefore, is not communicative. In a chain drill, [⑤], if a student must reply to her neighbor's question in the same way as her neighbor replied to someone else's question, then she has no choice of form and content, and real communication does not occur.

True communication is purposeful. A speaker can [⑥] evaluate whether or not her purpose has been achieved based upon the information she receives from her listener. If the listener does not have an opportunity to provide the speaker with such feedback, then the exchange is not really communicative. Forming questions through a transformation drill may be a worthwhile activity, but it is not communicative [⑦] a speaker will receive no response from a listener. She is thus unable to assess whether her question has been understood or not.

Another characteristic of the Communicative Approach is the use of ⑧<u>authentic materials</u>. It is considered desirable to give students an opportunity to develop strategies for understanding language as it is actually used by native speakers.

(1) Choose the best answer for [①], [⑤], [⑥], and [⑦] from the alternatives below.

A. for example　B. however　C. moreover　D. since　E. thus

(2) Put the words from ②[ ] in the correct order.

(3) Translate the underlined sentences ③ into Japanese.

(4) Choose the best phrase for [④] from the four alternatives below.

A. that the other person doesn't

B. that the person thinks is important

C. that the other person knows, too

D. that the person wants to share

(5) Explain the meaning of the underlined words ⑧ in Japanese with a concrete example.

(6) According to the text, which of the following is true?

A. Pattern practice is one of the techniques of the Communicative Approach.

B. If students acquire the knowledge of a target language, they can communicate with native speakers.

C. In the Communicative Approach, almost all activities are done in order to communicate with someone else.

D. Teachers need to strictly control what students say in the class when they teach the language.

(☆☆☆☆◎◎◎◎◎)

【２】Translate the underlined part into English.

(1)　富士山は麗峰にして霊峰である。日本人には特別なその山が，ユネスコの世界遺産に登録された。それぞれの思いを背負って，年に約30万人もの人が登る山である。さすがの霊峰も重いことだろう。届いた朗報を喜びながら，いたわり，守る決意をあらたにしたいものだ。

(2)　心理学の研究によれば，目標を達成するのに必要な性質，たとえばねばり強さ，自制心，勇気などを体現している「お手本となる人」のことを思い浮かべると，活力と自制心が高まるということです。「お手本となる人」がいることがどれだけ有益になりうるかを認識すれば，意志の力を高める別の方法も見つかるかもしれません。つまり，自分が誰かの「お手本となる人」になるのです。研究者によると，意志の力は感染するそうです。自分の努力や自制心が，友達や家族，同僚に移ることがあるのです。やる気を見出す必要がある時には，問いかけてみましょう，自分は誰に刺激を与えられる存在になりうるかを。自分の努力が他人に与えうるプラスの影響を思い出すようにしましょう。

(☆☆☆☆◎◎◎◎◎)

【３】Read the following passage and answer the questions below.

Globalization brings about unprecedented necessity of English in universities and enterprises; on the other hand, it is pointed out that students have few opportunities to feel the necessity of English.

According to a survey on curriculum implementation held in 2003, third-year junior high school students who believed that they could not follow English classes amounted to about 30 percent, ①the proportion being high as compared to other subjects. In addition, more than 60 percent of students liked English learning in the first year of junior high school but this proportion decreased over time dropping below 50% in the third year; again, this decrease was high as compared to other subjects. Therefore, it is important to reduce the number of students who believe that they do not understand English, or who do not like English, while enhancing the skill of those who possess advanced English skills.

In order to stimulate students' motivation for English learning, it is most important to use educational materials based on actual English usage, to actively introduce debates and discussions, and to resort to other means for improvement of lesson quality.

Besides, students should be shown concretely how mastering English would expand their opportunities in future, and how English can be used in any profession and position. ②This is required to provide the children with a 'global perspective', and to enhance their motivation for English learning. In the past, there were attempts to engage corporate employees experienced in overseas operations and other people from the private sector in terms of international education; however, motivation for English learning is promoted by providing opportunities to see how people actually use English in their work, and to imagine how the students will use English in their future activities.

(1)　Explain the word "the proportion" in this context and translate the underlined part ① into Japanese.

(2)　Explain what the underlined word ② indicates in this context in Japanese.

(3)　According to the passage, students have few opportunities to feel the necessity of English in Japan.

Answer the questions 1) and 2) below.

1)　What does the author think is most important to motivate students to learn English? Explain the three important actions from the text in Japanese.

2) What would you do as an English teacher to stimulate students' motivation for English learning? Based on the author's ideas, express your own ideas in approximately 120 words in English.

(☆☆☆☆◎◎◎◎)

解答・解説

【中高共通】

【1】(1) D (2) C (3) A (4) B

〈解説〉 (1) put up withは「耐える，我慢する」(endure, stand)という意味である。Aは全く正反対の意味になるので注意すること。
(2) much the sameは「非常に似た」(exactly the same)という意味である。Aは全く正反対の意味になるので注意すること。 (3) take onは「雇う」という意味である。 (4) figure outは「解決する，算出する」という意味である。ここでは口語的な表現で使われている。

【2】(1) B (2) D (3) A (4) D (5) A (6) D

〈解説〉(1) ここでのprovideは動詞であり，B以外はtoの後が名詞表現となっている。 (2) accommodateは「収容する」という意味である。
(3) commandは「(言語などを)使いこなす力」という意味であり，ofが続く。この部分はMichael is good at Spanishでも同じ意味である。
(4) prospectiveは「将来性のある，見込みのある」(potential) という意味である。 (5) consensusは「同意，一致」(an opinion that all members of a group agree with) という意味である。 (6) unanimousは「満場一致の」という意味である。。

【3】(1) D (2) C (3) C (4) B (5) A (6) D
(7) B (8) C (9) D (10) C

〈解説〉(1)　接続詞by the timeは，「…までには」の意味であり，その時点では未来完了形となる。なお，副詞節の中では，未来形の代わりに現在形を用いる点にも注意する。ここでは，will graduateではなくて，graduateである。　(2)　an electricity supplier以下の内容が「その手紙の中に」書かれていたので，前置詞が必要である。関係代名詞のthatは，特殊な用法以外では前置詞の直後には用いない。　(3)　不定詞の形容詞用法で，「(私が)一緒に行く」という意味である。　(4)　as … as ～は「～と同じぐらいの…」の意味である。　(5)　仮定法過去の用法で「まるで…かのように」の意味であり，as if以下が主節の示すときと同時の事柄を表すときは仮定法過去を使う。ここではspokeだが，speaksでもas if以下はかわらない点に注意すること。　(6)「IDが無ければ入室できない」といった意味であり，unless = if notと考える。

(7)　AとDは接続詞，Cは「…の代わりに」という意味なので誤りである。　(8)　have＋目的語＋過去分詞で「(目的語が)…される」の意味で，経験受動態と呼ばれることがある。「ダニエルはバッグを盗まれた」の意味である。なお，Dのように記述すると，ダニエルが盗まれたことになってしまうので注意すること。　(9)　最初に5人と限定している点に注意。最初の1人がoneならば，この時点で残り4人はthe othersである。この中の3人を除けば，最後の1人はthe otherである。なお，another = an otherなので，the anotherはあり得ない。　(10)　複合関係代名詞のwhatである。that whichの意味なのでCが適切。Cのhe thoughtは挿入部分である。

【4】(1)　stuffed animals　(2)　C　(3)　A　(4)　B　(5)　D

(6)　想像上の仲間とは，主に子どもに見られる心理現象で，この心理状態にある人々は架空の人や動物や妖精などの想像上の生き物を自分の空想の世界の中で友人だとみなし，一緒に話したり遊んだりして，孤独を補う。この現象は，成長するにつれ見られなくなる。

(7)　hopes her tours will be a good opportunity for owners to begin warm communication　(8)　D

〈解説〉(1) stuffedは「(詰め物をした)縫いぐるみ」の意味であり，第1パラグラフの最初の文で縫いぐるみ2体と同行者3人でtheyとなる。だが，第3パラグラフではnot their ownersとあるので，この後のstuffed animalsが適切である。 (2) 第5パラグラフの2文目にあるThe idea以下がヒントである。was received wellはgained a good reputationと同義である。 (3) 第8パラグラフのparticipateがヒントである。参加のためには契約が必要なので，Aが適切である。 (4) ③の意味は「できないことを(　　　)代わりに，できることをすべき」となるので，文脈から判断すること。なお，Aは「切り取る」，Cは「切り抜けさせる」，Dは「惜しまずに与える」という意味である。 (5) 第12パラグラフ2文目のThe woman以下がヒントになる。この女性は車椅子を使用している。 (6) 下線部2文目のregard imaginary … as friendsの表現に注意すること。「想像上の存在を友人として認める」の意味である。このbeingsをsuch asで補足説明をしている。 (7) まず，rather than以下の「分身に旅をさせるよりはむしろ」という意味がヒントになる。さらに，ここまでの文脈を踏まえれば，彼女が主催する旅行がどういう意味を持つのかを考えるのがポイントになる。「縫いぐるみの所有者が互いに関係をもつ」と考えることが重要。 (8) Aの「縫いぐるみの旅は，持ち主を世捨て人のようにする」は不適。Bも持ち主は旅に同行しないので不適とわかる。Cも第18パラグラフのImaginary companions seem …の主旨とあわないため不適である。Dは「縫いぐるみの旅は持ち主が前向きになるのを助けるようだ」といった意味になる。

【中学校】

【1】(1) nothing (2) C (3) D (4) a protect
b ensure c be brave (5) 私たちの半数を(占める女性が)おさえつけられていたら，男性も女性も成功を収めることはできません。
(6) She asserts equality of educational opportunity for every children and women.

〈解説〉(1)　第4パラグラフ第6文目のexcept this以下と第7，8文が決め手となる。「これらを除いては何も変化しなかった」という論旨である。

(2)　②の直前の文の後半は，I'm against no oneと同義である。これを受けて，「…もまた～でない」となるので，Cが適切である。なお，否定が強調されているので，倒置されている点にも注意すること。

(3)　第6パラグラフ第2文のcall upon … policiesとpeace and prosperityの部分を考えれば，D(…に賛成して)が適切である。　(4)　aは直後の部分と次の文，さらに7文目の最後を考えれば，「守る」という意味になる。bは第7と第9パラグラフに該当箇所がある。前者はfree compulsory education，後者はfreedom and equality for womenがそれぞれ直後にきている。これらに共通する単語は「保障する」である。cは，直後の部分の意味がほぼ言い換えられていると考えればよい。　(5)　短い文だが，ポイントはnot allで部分否定であること，whenという接続詞がここではifの意味で使われていることがあげられる。　(6)　演説の中のeducation firstが重要である。これを中心に考えればよい。次の英文を参考にするとよいだろう。

What she wants to assert the most is equality of education, and she is to fight against illiteracy, poverty and terrorism. In order to solve the problem, she speaks up for the right of education.

【2】(1)　Motherhood is about letting go /(of a child) with the same strength /as holding it.　(2)　A person may get deeply hurt by someone's words, whereas the person who inflicted the pain may quickly forget it.

〈解説〉(1)　日本文の意味をよく考えなければならない。日本文の最後に「抱くことだけに一途では駄目」とあるので，「抱く」ことと「突き放す」ことが同じ強さであると考える必要がある。したがって，「母性とは，抱くことと突き放すことが同じ強さのものである」と考えればよい。次の英文を参考にするとよいだろう。

Motherhood is of the thing that accepting her child is much the same as letting go her child in strength.

(2) 日本文の意味をよく考えること。「ある人が怒りに任せて発言し，その内容を忘れても，言われた人は深く傷つく」と考えればよい。たとえば，次の英文を参考にするとよいだろう。

Though a person will speak to the other angrily and is to forget his or her saying, the other person will be deeply shocked with it.

【3】First, teaching materials should take into consideration authentic language-use situations and functions in order to develop interactive communication abilities. Examples of language-use situations are greetings, self-introduction, telephone calls, shopping, home life, local events, etc. Examples of language functions are facilitating communications, expressing feelings, conveying information, conveying thoughts and intentions, and asking for action. Second, the topics should relate to the everyday life, manners, and customs, tales, geography, history, traditional culture, natural science, and other topics of Japanese people and English speakers around the world. The topics should be varied to suit the students' stages of development, interest, and concerns. Teachers should choose the topics which would help students to understand various viewpoints and my way of thinking, and to cultivate fair judgment and broad-mindedness.

〈解説〉生徒にコミュニケーション能力の4技能を育成するための教材選択に関して，英語教師としての配慮事項は何か，2点を挙げてそれぞれの根拠を示して120語前後の英語でまとめよ，という設問である。次の英文や文部科学省の資料なども参考にするとよいだろう。

I take the following two points into consideration. One is to understand various viewpoints and ways of thinking, and to cultivate fair judgment and rich sensibility. The other is to broaden and deepen their horizons, their international understanding as Japanese world citizens who foster international cooperation and harmony. Teaching materials should take into consideration authentic language-use situations and functions for the purpose of developing integrative communication abilities in listening, speaking, reading and writing. Topics should relate to the everyday life, manners and customs, tales, geography, history, traditional culture, natural science and so on, of people around the world, especially of people using English, and of Japanese people. These topics should be varied to suit the students' stages of development, interest and concerns.

【高等学校】

【1】(1) ① C　⑤ A　⑥ E　⑦ D　(2) what his relationship with that person is / what his relationship is with that person　(3) 話し手と聞き手(あるいは書き手と読み手)の相互作用を通してこそ意味が明らかになるのだ。聞き手は話し手が言ったことを理解したかどうかについて話し手にフィードバックを与える。このようにして，話し手は自分が述べたことを修正して，必要であれば意図した意味をもう一度伝えようとすることができるのだ。　(4) A　(5) ある言語を(母語として)話す人々の生活において，実際に用いられている(英語を理解するため手立てを発達させる機会を与えるのに望ましい)言語材料のこと。例えば，アメリカで発行されている新聞やイギリス国営放送のニュース番組など。　(6) C

〈解説〉(1) ① 第1パラグラフの第1～2文の関係を考える。3つの機能を記述した後で，さらに発展的な内容の記述があることがポイントである。　⑤ 第6パラグラフ第2と第3文で，コミュニカティブではない例を記述している点がポイントとなる。　⑥ 第7パラグラフ冒頭で「コミュニケーションには目的がある」と記述し，それを受ける形で「したがって」という論理展開になっている。　⑦ 「活動としては価値があるが，コミュニカティブではない。なぜならば」という論理展開である。　(2) 「彼とその人物との関係がどのようなものであるか」といった意味になる。　(3) ポイントは，第1文のIt is … that ～の強調構文をきちんと訳すことであろう。　(4) Information gap について述べているので，両者の関係を記述している選択肢を探せばよい。　(5) 下線部の内容を次の文It is 以下が説明している。いわゆる標準的な英語が使われている言語材料のことであり，イギリスではBBC，アメリカではCBS等のニュース，活字媒体ではフィナンシャルタイムズなどの新聞があげられる。 (6) Aはpattern practiceが誤り，Bは第2パラグラフの最初，Dは第6パラグラフ第2文に誤りの理由が述べられている。

【2】(1) It's a mountain that attracts as many as 300,000 climbers a year, and each of them has his or her own thoughts. Even for a sacred mountain, it must be quite a burden. While we celebrate its new status as a World Heritage site [the good news], we should also renew our determination to care about and protect Mount Fuji. [think seriously about good ways to care about and protect Mount Fuji once again]. (2) Your own hard work and self-control can encourage your friends, family, and coworkers. When you need to find your own motivation [need to encourage yourself], ask yourself who you might be an inspiration to [who you might be able to inspire/ cheer on / encourage].

〈解説〉(1) 英作文では，まず文法的に誤りのない英文を書くことが重要である。そのためには，直訳をせずに，日本文の意味をよく考えることが必要である。おおよそ次のような日本文にすればよい。「富士山は年に約30万人もの人がそれぞれの思いを背負って登る山である。富士山もその重さを感じているだろう。私たちは，世界遺産登録という朗報を喜びながら，富士山をいたわり，守る決意をあらたにしたいものだ」。次の英文を参考にするとよいだろう。

Mt. Fuji is the mountain that about 300,000 people climb every year with each emotion and thoughts. The mountain may be feeling so heavy with the weight of such huge number of people and the registration of the big name, World Heritage. We should have a firm recognition newly to cherish and maintain Mt. Fuji, with accepting the good news.

(2) この問題も日本文の意味をよく考える必要がある。「移る」は感染する・転移する，「やる気を見出す」は集中する，「問いかける」は自問する，「与えられる存在になりうるか」は与えられるかと考えればよい。次の英文を参考にするとよいだろう。

Your efforts and self-control sometimes tend to transfer to your friends, your family members and your colleagues. If you need to be concentrated, ask yourself whether or not whom you can stimulate his or her motivation.

【3】(1)　(2003年に行われた教育課程実施状況調査において約30パーセントにものぼった)英語の授業がわからないと考える中学3年生の生徒の割合は，その他の教科と比較してみると高かった。

(2)　英語が使えるようになると将来どのように活躍の場が広がるかということや，これからはどのような職業や立場であっても英語を使う可能性があるということを，生徒たちに具体的に示すこと。

(3)　1)　・実際の英語の使用場面に即した題材を扱うこと。　・ディベートやディスカッションなどを積極的にとりいれること。　・授業の質を向上するために他の方法にも頼ること。　・英語が使えると将来どのように活躍の場が広がるのかということや，これからはどのような職種や立場であっても英語を使う可能性があるということを，生徒達に具体的に示すこと。　2)　As the author says, in order to stimulate students' motivation for English learning, we should provide them with opportunities to see how people actually use English. To give these chances while attracting students' interest, for all learning activities I would choose authentic materials whose topics have a lot to do with real lives of the students. For example, I will introduce news articles written by native English speakers about Japan. Through reading the articles they will be able to get valuable information about their own country and also broaden their mind by knowing how foreign people think and feel about what is happening in Japan. This experience will surely motivate them to learn English as a communication tool. Thus, I will encourage students to learn English with these attractive materials.

〈解説〉(1)　下線部の構造に注意すること。分詞構文であり，the

proportion was high as compared to other subjectsの同じ意味である。
(2)　直前のhowで始まる2つの英文のことであり，1つ目はhowからin futureまで，もう1つは，howからpositionまでである。　(3)　1)　第3パラグラフの後半にあるit is most important以下をまとめればよい。
2)「筆者の考えを基にして」とあるので，これらを参考にして考えればよい。筆者は「実際に使われている英語の教材，ディベートや討論，授業改善のための様々な手段」と述べている。したがって，これら4技能を適宜組み合わせて記述することになる。

●書籍内容の訂正等について

弊社では教員採用試験対策シリーズ（参考書，過去問，全国まるごと過去問題集），公務員試験対策シリーズ，公立幼稚園・保育士試験対策シリーズ，会社別就職試験対策シリーズについて，正誤表をホームページ（https://www.kyodo-s.jp）に掲載いたします。内容に訂正等，疑問点がございましたら，まずホームページをご確認ください。もし，正誤表に掲載されていない訂正等，疑問点がございましたら，下記項目をご記入の上，以下の送付先までお送りいただくようお願いいたします。

① **書籍名，都道府県（学校）名，年度**
（例：教員採用試験過去問シリーズ　小学校教諭 過去問　2025 年度版）
② **ページ数**（書籍に記載されているページ数をご記入ください。）
③ **訂正等，疑問点**（内容は具体的にご記入ください。）
（例:問題文では“ア〜オの中から選べ”とあるが,選択肢はエまでしかない）

〔ご注意〕
○ 電話での質問や相談等につきましては，受付けておりません。ご注意ください。
○ 正誤表の更新は適宜行います。
○ いただいた疑問点につきましては，当社編集制作部で検討の上，正誤表への反映を決定させていただきます（個別回答は，原則行いませんのであしからずご了承ください）。

●情報提供のお願い

協同教育研究会では，これから教員採用試験を受験される方々に，より正確な問題を，より多くご提供できるよう情報の収集を行っております。つきましては，教員採用試験に関する次の項目の情報を，以下の送付先までお送りいただけますと幸いでございます。お送りいただきました方には謝礼を差し上げます。
（情報量があまりに少ない場合は，謝礼をご用意できかねる場合があります）。

◆あなたの受験された面接試験，論作文試験の実施方法や質問内容
◆教員採用試験の受験体験記

送付先
○電子メール：edit@kyodo-s.jp
○FAX：03-3233-1233（協同出版株式会社　編集制作部 行）
○郵送：〒101-0054　東京都千代田区神田錦町2-5
協同出版株式会社　編集制作部 行
○HP：https://kyodo-s.jp/provision（右記のQRコードからもアクセスできます）

※謝礼をお送りする関係から，いずれの方法でお送りいただく際にも，「お名前」「ご住所」は，必ず明記いただきますよう，よろしくお願い申し上げます。

教員採用試験「過去問」シリーズ

京都府の
英語科 過去問

編　集	© 協同教育研究会
発　行	令和5年12月25日
発行者	小貫　輝雄
発行所	協同出版株式会社
	〒101-0054　東京都千代田区神田錦町2－5
	電話　03－3295－1341
	振替　東京00190－4－94061
印刷所	協同出版・POD工場

落丁・乱丁はお取り替えいたします。